PHILOSOPHIES
of
CRIME FICTION

PHILOSOPHIES

of

CRIME FICTION

JOSEF HOFFMANN

TRANSLATED FROM THE GERMAN BY
CAROLYN KELLY, NADIA MAJID,
JOHANNA DA ROCHA ABREU

NO EXIT PRESS

First published in 2013 by No Exit Press,
an imprint of Oldcastle Books Ltd,
PO Box 394,
Harpenden, Herts,
AL5 1XJ
www.noexit.co.uk
Edited by Steven Mair

A CIP catalogue record for this book is available from the British Library.

ISBN
978–1–84344–139–7 (print)
978–1–84344–140–3 (epub)
978–1–84344–141–0 (kindle)
978–1–84344–142–7 (pdf)

2 4 6 8 10 9 7 5 3 1

Typeset by Avocet Typeset, Somerton, Somerset
in 11.5pt Minion
Printed in Great Britain by 4edge Ltd, Hockley, Essex.

For more information about Crime Fiction go to @crimetimeuk

There is no escape from philosophy. The question is only whether [a philosophy] is good or bad, muddled or clear.

Karl Jaspers, *Way to Wisdom: An Introduction to Philosophy.*

And since I wanted you to feel as pleasurable the one thing that frightens us – namely, the metaphysical shudder – I had only to choose (from among the model plots) the most metaphysical and philosophical: the detective novel.

Umberto Eco, postscript to *The Name of the Rose.*

Table of Contents

Contents

Preface

This book does not claim to analyse the topic of the philosophies of crime fiction in an academic manner. Rather, it is a selection of related essays that refer to aspects of academic research in crime fiction and philosophy. The text is aimed at readers of crime fiction who would like to know more about their favourite literature and I would be delighted if there were one or two philosophers or readers of philosophy among the readers of this book.

For critical reading, references and suggestions, I am grateful to Peter Philipp, Hilde Ganßmüller, Jutta Wilkesmann and above all my wife Gabriele Kern.

1
Crime Fiction and Philosophy: Introduction and Overview

Crime fiction and philosophy – how might they be related? Firstly, we can analyse the influence of philosophy on writers of crime fiction and their oeuvre. Secondly, crime fiction may have influenced philosophers and their writings. There is a third possibility, the philosophy-thriller, composed of philosophical texts and narrative strategies commonly found in crime fiction. I am thinking here of books such as Markus Thiele's *HirnStröme* and Tibor Fischer's *The Thought Gang*. However, I shall not address such hybrids here since they appear to me to be of little significance and even less appeal. This leaves only the first two possibilities. The mutual influence of philosophy and crime fiction is manifold and can be made explicit by way of a quotation or implied more subtly in the structure of the text. Further, it may include ways of thinking or argumentation, themes, narrative styles or aesthetic reflections regarding the literary form. However, when we examine the interrelationship between crime fiction and philosophy, we encounter a fundamental problem. Globally, the sheer volume of crime fiction is so large that no one can claim to have read even just a tenth of it. The number of philosophical texts is equally overwhelming, which makes it necessary to confine oneself to selected texts.

I have restricted myself, firstly, to works and writers of the western tradition and, secondly, to the so-called classics. Even this would normally be too large an area to cover, which is why the third restriction is a completely subjective one. I include crime writers whom I have enjoyed reading during at least some stage of my life. A further restriction results from the choice of topics: crime fiction rather than philosophy is of primary interest here. An expert in philosophy will hardly come across anything new here, while I hope that readers of crime fiction will gain deeper insight into their favourite books.

a) The philosophical thoughts of crime writers and crime fiction

The title of this book deliberately reads *Philosophies of Crime Fiction* instead of *The Philosophy of Crime Fiction*. In view of historical changes and the diversity of crime fiction and philosophical writings, one must resist the temptation to model *the* philosophy of *the* crime narrative. Umberto Eco – the crime writer, philosopher, cultural theorist and more, whose historical detective novel *The Name of the Rose* is enriched with philosophical and theological allusions, ideas and explanations, – already succumbed to this temptation. In his postscript to *The Name of the Rose* he adds a chapter entitled 'The Metaphysics of the Crime and Detective Story (*romanzo poliziesco*)'. In it, Eco explains that the pleasure of reading crime fiction is due neither to a fascination for murder and manslaughter nor to the re-establishment of order after the crime, but rather to the fact that the crime novel represents the purest form of conjecture. The reader is attracted by the adventure of speculating and testing those speculations step by step. The investigating detective seeks to answer the same questions as a metaphysician does. 'Ultimately, the fundamental question of all philosophies is the same basic question asked by the detective novel: who is to blame? To know the answer, one must assume that all facts underlie a formal logic, the logic that the culprit has put upon them.' According to Eco, a story substantiated in such a manner leads to an abstract model of conjecture, to the labyrinth. Eco adopts the labyrinth metaphor from the introduction to the Encyclopaedia by the philosophers of the French Enlightenment, and it represents the manifold connections between the production, collection and localisation of knowledge. The detective – like the reader – finds himself confronted by a tangle of traces, clues and statements. He must find his way through this labyrinth, this time and space, by arranging particles and sequences of knowledge. At the centre of the labyrinth is the monster, the crime (or the criminal), which the detective must conquer. The detective is the hero in a narrative about a journey to the centre and back, the archetypal hero on a quest. In crime fiction, however, the detective – as opposed to the mythical hero Theseus – does not have Ariadne's thread at his disposal to bring him back to safety once he has accomplished his quest in the social labyrinth in which the criminal is to be found and punished. The detective must patch together his own Ariadne's thread bit by bit with the help of observation, interrogation, discussions, violent acts and collaborators so as not to lose himself in this criminal labyrinth, but instead to reach the exit. In this regard he is a true *philosophos* in the ancient Greek sense of the word. Accordingly, a philosopher is not someone who loves wisdom, but rather someone who appropriates knowledge, who actively pursues it. Socrates saw himself as the progeny of the genius inventor Daidalos, who devised both the labyrinth and Ariadne's thread, a magical ball of yarn. The thoughts and conversations in Socrates' dialogues reflect a search within the labyrinth of imagination, opinion and concepts of truth, whereby 'logos', reasonable consideration, is meant to guide us as a kind of Ariadne's thread that, nonetheless, does not guarantee certain knowledge. Rationality, or reason, is also an important tool in a detective's work, though by no means the only one.

Those who are even slightly familiar with crime fiction and philosophy will consider Eco's bold claim regarding the connection between the two subjects to be a highly subjective opinion without general validity. Frederic Jameson believes even a typical detective story to be a literary form without explicit political, social or philosophical meaning, though this does not exclude a subtle, hidden meaning. In crime fiction, the fundamental question regarding the perpetrator is reserved solely for the classic whodunit. Other subgenres of crime fiction, such as the psycho thriller, the gangster thriller and the police procedural, often make do without the search for the perpetrator because he or she is presented to the reader from the outset. This is even the case in some detective novels. Nor does the fundamental question have a monopoly in philosophy. An alternative fundamental question might be, for example, 'What can we know?' This need not have anything to do with the action of a guilty party. The multiple approaches of philosophical thought as well as crime fiction prohibit a *single* philosophy of *the* crime fiction. All that remains is to analyse texts by various writers in both fields and create a joint discourse.

There are classic writers of crime fiction whose work includes philosophical references. And there are also several significant philosophers who regularly read crime fiction, traces of which can be found in their own work. Furthermore, some crime writers have composed philosophical texts. The primary example of this is Edgar Allan Poe's 'Eureka', a natural philosophical essay. G. K. Chesterton published several philosophical monographs and a biography of Thomas Aquinas, one of the greatest philosophers and theologians. Dashiell Hammett composed a shorter philosophical essay, published posthumously, entitled 'The Boundaries of Science and Philosophy'. On 5 March 1935 Dorothy

Sayers gave a talk in Oxford on 'Aristotle on Detective Fiction', while Jorge Luis Borges' narratives and essays overflow with philosophical thoughts. The same is true of Eco.

W. H. Auden and Umberto Eco later both referred to Aristotle's poetics to analyse the aesthetics of detective fiction. They did so without recognising or even mentioning Sayers' famous talk. At the beginning of her lecture she makes the bold claim that Aristotle, for historical reasons, sets out his poetic criteria based on Greek theatre, but that he actually desired a good detective story. To prove her assertion, she quotes several passages from Aristotle's *Poetics* and compares them to texts of detective fiction. Thus Aristotle finds that we take pleasure in the realistic illustration of things, such as dead bodies and repugnant animals, which we would only watch with unease in reality. He appreciates a myth (fable) in which the sequence of single episodes is probable and necessary and which contains the essential component of recognition, in other words a transformation from ignorance to knowledge. This can take the form of discovering whether or not someone has committed a crime. Aristotle demands of the tragedy, which Sayers considers to be the ancient Greek version of the detective story, the presentation of a serious and completed plot. Both requirements also apply to the detective story because murder is a serious plot element and the construction of a detective story should conclude with all questions answered. Like a tragedy, it should lead to catharsis, a cleansing through the stimulation of pity and fear. To accomplish this, it is important that the detective represents virtue and that the novel sublimates potential vices through emotional and intellectual beauty.

As with the tragedy, plot and characterisation are the essential elements of the detective story. The plot must have beginning, middle and ending. A detective story usually begins with a murder. The middle consists of the investigation of the crime and the resulting peripeteia, or vicissitudes of fate. The ending features the perpetrator's unmasking and execution. In order to remain in the reader's memory, the plot should be of appropriate length. This is especially important in crime fiction, where the reader must remember clues from the first to the last chapter in order to appreciate and fully enjoy the final revelation. The plot should be long enough to represent the switch from happiness to unhappiness or unhappiness to happiness. Yet the plot should not depict everything. The parts of the plot should be connected in such a manner that the whole is changed if only a small section of it is removed or rearranged. In a detective story this is especially true of those parts that contain a clue for the solution. In choosing the plot – and equally in creating the characterisation – the impossible but probable must take preference over the possible but improbable. It may well be that the criminal investigative proof is impossible according to the latest scientific knowledge, but it will not bother the uninformed reader to whom such proof seems plausible. However, the reader distrusts a protagonist with a particular character and social status if he does something that might indeed be possible, but utterly unlikely. All parts of the narrative must be comprehensible.

Plot in crime fiction contains three essential elements: pathos, peripeteia (change in the plot), discovery. *Pathos* consists of an act that leads to destruction or agony such as death, injury and the like. Pathos should be used to serve the consequences of the criminal act, and not to create a thrill or disguise a weakness in the plot. *Peripeteia* may affect a single protagonist or all of them: a rich person can be turned into a corpse by murder, or a wrongfully accused person may be saved from death row as a result of exonerating evidence. Such plot twists make for an action-filled story and evoke emotions such as fear and pity in the reader. Ideally, fateful incidents should result from a mistake by the person concerned rather than by chance. For example, a detective might himself create problems due to an erroneous observation or hastily drawn conclusions. Or an innocent suspect brings himself into a precarious situation because he has suppressed evidence, and so on. *Discoveries* lead to the solving of the crime and generally relate to the perpetrator's identity or the sequence of events. Discoveries made by the author himself are particularly questionable in detective stories and are only considered when the perpetrator is known. Often, the discovery is made based on clues. It is also common for discoveries to be made based on memories; for instance, when the detective remembers a previous technical process similar to the one used to commit this particular murder. The most common method is the discovery by conclusion, where, based on crime scene evidence and the time of the crime, only one person fitting all criteria could possibly be the murderer. Aristotle is also aware of the discovery by misconception, which Sayers interprets as a discovery by bluff. A bluffing detective may, for instance, declare a random weapon to be the murder weapon in order to lead the murderer to incriminate himself.

The entire art of the detective novel is characterised by Aristotle with the term *paralogism*, false conclusion. Thus the reader of a story with two actions easily succumbs to the false conclusion that, if one of them is true, then the second, related one must also be true, even though it never happened. A crime writer must master the art of deception. The reader must be led to believe that the criminal is innocent and an honourable character guilty; that a false alibi is true and a living person is dead, etc. The correct way to tell a detective story is to present the truth in such a way that the intelligent reader is led to create his own mesh of lies. It is unfair and therefore unacceptable for the author to lie to his readers.

Sayers also demands a certain degree of realism when it comes to characterisation. She follows Aristotle only to a certain extent in his demand that the protagonists must be noble. Sayers believes they must display a 'measure of human dignity' for the reader to take them seriously. Even the worst criminals must not be portrayed as pure monsters or caricatures of evil. According to Aristotle, characters must be reasonable, which Sayers interprets as meaning that they should act in a believable and not entirely improbable manner. According to some translators, Aristotle furthermore demands that characters are in line with their tradition. This, says Sayers, does not mean that they resemble traditional stereotypes, but that they are realistic. Thus protagonists in crime stories should resemble in language and actions the men and women we are familiar with in our own time. For this reason, the plot should not be concerned with the discovery of a monstrously evil perpetrator, but rather an honourable but flawed person. The more average-seeming the criminal, the more the reader will feel pity and fear when faced with his deed and the greater the surprise when he is revealed. Generally, the same applies to innocent suspects and the police; they should be characterised realistically. The most difficult Aristotelian rule to follow is that which deems that characters must be uniform from beginning to end. Even though the perpetrator's identity should surprise the reader, it should still be plausible. His identity must correspond to the traits and actions described beforehand. Any flaws in his characterisation would destroy the plot's plausibility and break the fair play rule.

Sayers concludes that Aristotle's *Poetics* contains fundamental truths for all forms of literary art and that it is the best guidebook for any up and coming crime writer. Every ambitious author of detective fiction should write in a way Aristotle would approve of.

In a similar vein to Sayers, Auden compares classic detective stories with Greek tragedies based on Aristotle's poetics. The detective story also includes ignorance, discovery and peripeteia. Innocents appear guilty while the guilty appear innocent until the truth is revealed. There is a double twist in such a story – on the one hand, the twist from supposed guilt to innocence and, on the other, from supposed innocence to guilt. Once wrongly localised guilt is replaced by the establishment of true guilt, this leads, according to Auden, to catharsis. Additionally, there is another similarity between Greek tragedy and classic detective story that differentiates them from modern tragedy: the protagonists remain unchanged by their actions. In Greek tragedy the reason for this is that the plot is predetermined, while in a detective story the murder, the crucial act, has already taken place. To Eco, the detective novel is Aristotle's poetics reduced to its most essential elements because the novel contains a series of events (pragmata), the threads of which are tangled or have been lost. The plot (mythos) depicts how the detective finds these threads and connects them again.

The Swiss dramatist Friedrich Dürrenmatt wrote *The Judge and His Hangman*, *The Quarry of Suspicion* and *The Pledge: Requiem for the Detective Novel*, three detective novels that critically reflect the genre. In these narratives, the detective's domineering intellect must take a back seat so that chance can take its rightful place in life, i.e. in the conflict between police and criminals. This is particularly evident in the novel *The Pledge*. Here the detective is unable to fulfil his promise, made to a murdered child's parents, to find the culprit, because before the latter can be caught, he himself is killed in a car collision. In this 'Requiem for the Detective Novel', a retired policeman criticises crime stories in a conversation with a crime writer. Such stories, he believes, create the illusion that the detective re-establishes order and justice and that criminals get their deserved punishment. Even worse, in his opinion, is the illusion of a logically constructed plot according to which police investigations proceed as logically as in a game of chess. In reality, however, chance and various disruptions interfere in the methodical investigative process. He claims that, in literature, the truth has always been abused by the rules of dramaturgy. They should be dispensed with in order to allow for chance. A series of events cannot be resolved perfectly for the simple reason that only a limited number of necessary factors are known. The rules are based merely on statistical likelihoods and are therefore only generally valid. The individual, on the other hand, remains outside such calculations.

Chance also plays a great part in Dürrenmatt's philosophical 'Monster Lecture on Justice and Law' which he held at the Johannes Gutenberg University in Mainz in 1969. He begins with a tale from *One Thousand and One Arabian Nights* in which, at the foot of a lonely hill, there is a well where a horseman lets his animal rest. Unknowingly, he loses a pouch of coins before riding on. Another horseman comes to the well, finds the money and takes it with him on his journey. Then a third horseman reaches the well and encounters the first who has returned, having realised his loss. He accuses the third horseman of stealing the money, upon which they argue and the third horseman is killed. The first horseman is surprised not to find his money on the man and rides away.

Dürrenmatt shows this incident through the eyes of several characters, such as the prophet Mohammed, Allah, a thief who steals the money, a scientist, a representative of a civil society and a representative of a socialist society, all of whom are invisible to the horsemen. Each character's perspective changes the perception of justice. While the prophet, for instance, considers the events to be unjust, the omniscient God sees actions by participants that are concealed from the human observer, meaning that each injustice suffered is seen as being justified from the higher perspective of divine providence. To accept this, however, requires a belief in divine justice. The scientist, in contrast, questions the validity of such a paradigm. He provides no definitive answer because the data pool is too specific. The representative of the civil society takes as his starting point the rules and values of his social order, which is based on the tenet that man is wolf to man, or 'homo homini lupus'. The socialist interprets these events based on the rules and values of a socialist hierarchy that officially functions according to the good shepherd game, but which in reality takes on characteristics of the wolf game. A thief will interpret events very egotistically, if he has any sense of right and wrong at all. To sum up, right and wrong are a matter of perspective; there is no such thing as one clearly defined justice. Above all, as the story of the horsemen and the well proves, chance rules everything and often decides over fortune and misfortune.

In *Criminal Convictions*, the famous crime writer Nicolas Freeling published an essay entitled 'Crime and Metaphysics'. According to Freeling, access to metaphysical truth is best found in art and literature.

A metaphysical force is in effect when a writer has the impression that a higher power guides his hand and pens the text. Such an experience is primarily emotional and less able to be explained rationally and logically. A crime is also a metaphysical phenomenon, in at least as great a measure as it is a physical act. It often comprises the destruction of the mind rather than the body. Murder, which entails the loss of life, reminds us of our fear of death. Death is irreversible but trivial compared to crimes against the mind. These can take place in childhood, leaving lingering traces of enduring ruin and suffering. Crimes are not only prevalent in crime literature, but in narrative literature as a whole.

The examples given above should suffice to prove that it is worth searching for philosophical influences in selected crime writers' works. This is the case particularly with older writers who have been educated in Greek and Latin, which entailed the reading of classical texts by the philosophers of antiquity. While philosophical assumptions form the backdrop of older crime writers' texts, this changes with Georges Simenon and Patricia Highsmith. From then on psychological and sociological observations and theories in particular are woven into the crime story, which does not exclude the presence of philosophical sprinklings in some more recent and contemporary texts of crime fiction. When postmodern theory became popular and widely accepted in the 1980s, philosophy – and not just postmodern philosophy – increasingly found its way into crime fiction. A particularly popular method seems to be to enrich a narrative with philosophical references by having the detective read a famous philosophical text and interspersing the story with quotes, making the detective ponder their significance. For example, Zoj Werstein in Jean-Bernard Pouy's *La Pêche aux Anges* reads Wittgenstein's *Tractatus*, while Ulrich Ritzel's Commissioner Hans Berndorf reads the work of a different philosopher in every novel. Wittgenstein, in particular, is a philosopher held in high esteem by crime writers. The German title of Philip Kerr's crime novel about a serial killer is *Das Wittgenstein-Programm*, the Wittgenstein programme, while its original English title *A Philosophical Investigation* imitates the title of Wittgenstein's famous second book. Jens Johler invented a serial killer who calls himself 'Kant' and murders brain specialists attempting to find proof against free will. Modelled on Kant's *Critique of Pure Reason* and *Critique of Practical Reason*, the crime novel's title reads 'Critique of Murderous Reason'. Other criminals also have philosophical preferences, such as the professional burglar and antiques dealer Bernie Rhodenbarr, who likes to read Spinoza and other philosophers in Lawrence Block's *The Burglar who Studied Spinoza*.

The historical crime novel is particularly suitable for philosophical references, since a famous philosopher of a bygone era may investigate in it. In Pablo De Santis' book *Voltaire's Calligrapher*, for instance, Voltaire has his scribe investigate the case of Jean Calas, a real case in which Voltaire intervened as counsel for the defence. In Margaret Doody's crime novel *Aristotle Detective*, Aristotle investigates in ancient Athens, though he seems not to have done so in reality. In *Roman Blood*, author Steven Saylor has Cicero defend a man accused of patricide. In order to find exonerating material, Cicero assigns Gordianus, an investigator, to the task.

Alexander McCall Smith created a popular detective series with a philosophical touch, set in the present. The first novel, entitled *The Sunday Philosophy Club*, revolves around amateur detective Miss Isabel Dalhousie, a studied philosopher, editor of a journal of applied ethics and member of a philosophical debating club. Miss Dalhousie is characterised not only by her amiability, but by the way she approaches events in the crime narrative from a philosophical point of view.

b) The philosophers' views on crime fiction

Let us move from crime writers with philosophical affiliations to philosophers who enjoyed reading crime fiction and demonstrated this fact in their texts. In this context, Sartre's comments in his autobiographical work *The Words* are probably the best known. In the book, he explains the passion with which he bought and read crime stories featuring Nick Carter and other detectives from kiosks and booksellers on the banks of the Seine as a boy. He once even stole a crime novel at the age of 32, as he had not enough money to buy it. Sartre pointed out that he still preferred crime novels to Wittgenstein's texts. As it happens, the opposite was also true. Wittgenstein, who read detective stories with a passion after his return to Cambridge, apparently never read or commented on any of Sartre's texts. Neither in Ray Monk's extensive, detailed bibliography nor in *Wittgenstein in Cambridge: Letters and Documents 1911–1951* do we find any mention of Sartre, while Wittgenstein's interest in crime stories is copiously documented.

Twentieth-century philosophers writing in German who are worth mentioning here are Walter Benjamin, Siegfried Kracauer and Ernst

Bloch. Walter Benjamin wrote about crime stories in 'One Way Street' and 'Travelling With Crime Novels' and referred to Conan Doyle, A. K. Green and Gaston Leroux, among others. According to the view expressed in *One Way Street*, the centre of terror in certain crime novels is the grandly furnished home. The arrangement of the furniture is at the same time the site plan of deadly traps, and the suite of rooms prescribes the fleeing victim's path. The bourgeois apartment tremulously awaits the nameless murderer 'like a lascivious old lady her gallant'. In his second essay, Benjamin explains the popularity of crime novels on railway journeys with the fact that they cover fears connected with travel with artificially aroused fear from the narrative. In 1925, Siegfried Kracauer composed the 'philosophical treatise' *The Detective Novel* which was only published in its full length in 1971. In 1960, Ernst Bloch composed the essay 'Philosophical Views of the Detective Novel' to which we will return towards the end of this chapter.

Apart from Sartre, there are a number of famous French philosophers of the twentieth century who are connected to crime fiction. Albert Camus referred to the American crime novel in his book *The Rebel*. The psychoanalyst with philosophical leanings, Jacques Lacan, wrote an article about Poe's detective story 'The Purloined Letter'. Jacques Derrida and Gilles Deleuze both made references to this and to Lacan's text in their own philosophical writings. Further, Deleuze published a short essay on the 'Philosophy of the Série Noire', the most renowned series of crime novels in the French language.

In this essay, he contrasts the concept of the old, classic crime novel with the philosophy of the Série Noire novels. In the former, the detective devotes himself, quite philosophically, to the search for truth as a result of the actions of the mind. The police investigation adds an 'unusual object, the crime that is to be solved' to the philosophical enquiry. The police appeal to justice to legitimise their actions. The classic French detectives use primarily deduction, based on basic intellectual intuition, which places them in the same tradition as Descartes. English detectives, in contrast, interpret primarily tactile or visible signs and pursue an inductive approach, thus following in Hobbes' tradition.

In the Série Noire novels – Deleuze names the writers Chester Himes, James Hadley Chase, Charles Williams and James Gunn – the police investigation 'has nothing to do with a metaphysical or scientific search for truth'. Any breakthroughs in the investigation are based on

21

denunciation, information from spies or even torture. The guilty person, the murderer, is often known and the main point is to devise a trap to catch him in the hope that he will commit yet another crime, possibly of a different kind such as tax evasion. The detective takes chances and risks being proved wrong, but he believes that his actions will have some kind of successful outcome. The criminal also makes mistakes, despite his in-depth preparation of the coup. In this respect, the aim of the police investigation is not to uncover the truth, but to achieve equilibrium, an 'evening-up of mistakes'. Ultimately, the aim is to 'uphold a balance that represents society as a whole *in its highest power of the false*'. Capitalist society excuses murder, child abuse or rape more readily than a bad cheque. The mutual intersection of police and criminal activity is real, and the agreement is compensatory. The power of the false is characterised by denunciation, corruption and torture. 'A society is reflected in its police and its criminals, even while it protects itself from them in equal measure through a deep-seated complicity.' For Deleuze this is the common thread, the philosophy of the Série Noire. By providing the police and criminals with only limited room for manoeuvre in relation to each other, capitalist society prevents the emergence of a police state or a criminal society and can, for the most part, go about its business undisturbed.

Deleuze's philosophy is also influenced by crime fiction. In one of his main works, *Difference and Repetition*, he claims that a philosophical book must in part be a special kind of crime novel. This means that concepts must be applied within a certain operating range in order to solve a local issue. These concepts change along with the problem. The question is: how many, how, when, which? The question is not, what is? The significant question is not about the essence, but rather the accident, the event, and multiplicity. The event that evokes the right questions (who, where, when, how, why) that help to solve an issue is the crime itself, determining the course of the investigation and its handling. This usually differentiates a crime novel from a philosophical text, even one by Deleuze.

I would like to highlight two philosophers in particular who engage intensively with literature, including crime fiction. One is the American philosopher Stanley Cavell, who, in his well-known article 'The Uncanniness of the Ordinary', refers to Poe, among others, and his 'The Purloined Letter'. He interprets the story as an allegory of the philosophy of the ordinary language and its impositions. While Freud understands the uncanny to be something that is evoked by the threat of castration, Cavell argues that, in fact, the point is the differentiation between inanimate/animate. Daily life appears uncanny to an individual if the oedipal drama of the threat of castration has not been overcome, then he is unable to recognise others as living, animate, independent beings whose speech and actions may appear strange. Poe's narrative deals with a stolen letter hidden quite openly in a card rack. When the letter is recognised, found and returned, it is perceived as something familiar, resulting from a feeling of the unfamiliar and a recurrence. Thus it also returns as something uncanny or odd. Poe's detective, Dupin, believes his abilities of detection to be a kind of mind-reading ability. As an example, he uses the childhood game 'even or odd', in which one player holds a few marbles in his closed hand while the other players try to guess whether they are even or odd in number. In this mind-reading context, the child who manages to correctly assess the opponent wins. The game is a form of communication just like reading and writing, particularly the reading of Poe's detective story. For when perusing this story, the reader tries to read the author's mind in a contest and is challenged by the text to guess whether individual events in the story are even/everyday/ordinary, or odd/remarkable/extraordinary.

The Slovenian psychoanalyst, philosopher and cultural critic Slavoj Žižek also refers to Poe's story of the purloined letter and other crime stories and films in his different works, particularly in *Looking Awry: An Introduction to Jacques Lacan through Popular Culture* from 1991. According to Žižek, there are two ways to avoid the real of desire (as defined by Lacan): the Sherlock Holmes mode and the Philip Marlowe mode. It begins with murder as the traumatic act that cannot be reconciled with one's personal history and experience. In the classic whodunit, the detective must, at the end, provide a detailed explanation of the case by relating the true sequence of events and their consequences. This explanation is structured in a chronological and linear manner, which differs from that of the detective story itself, which is built up on the crime, a mystery and the investigation. The way in which a classic detective such as Sherlock Holmes proceeds resembles in some ways the methods of psychoanalysis, but it is also quite distinctive. On relating his dream to the psychoanalyst, the patient constructs a certain superficial unity and coherence that disguises the chaos of heterogeneous elements that underlie it. Yet one paradoxical element stands out as being irrational in reality, and this is then used by the analyst as a means to interpret the dream. In a detective story, this element would be the clue or clues: obviously awkward or unusual details the detective uses to decipher the story – devised by the perpetrator with illusions much like a dream – that surrounds the crime. In the Sherlock Holmes story 'The Adventure of the Speckled Band', the dying woman's information about the speckled band is one such unusual detail. This does not, however, as the undiscerning witness may think, point to a band of gypsies camping near the crime scene, but rather the impression of a speckled deadly snake, which the murderer let into the victim's room. In order to see through the murderer's intention to deceive, the detective must first examine closely the exact sequence of events with Watson's help. Only by realising the wrong conclusion can he discover the clues and ultimately interpret them in such a way that the illusion is broken and the murderer is caught. The detective in this crime story is thus viewed as the subject who is assumed to be in the know, much like the psychoanalyst when treating a patient. What differentiates the two, however, is that by catching the murderer, the detective removes all blame from the remaining suspects who also had murderous thoughts and intentions, thereby ensuring their and 'our' innocence. This is an elementary lie, a kind of realised hallucination that requires a scapegoat in the form of the captured murderer to make up for our sins. It seems as though no one must pay a painful price for the realisation of his desire. The psychoanalyst, by contrast, confronts the patient with the price, which is the loss that accompanies the access to one's desire.

The old-school detective not only keeps a level head, but also an inner *distance* when dealing with the investigation and his clients. His fee after the completion of his duties also serves as a means to prevent any further obligations, to free both parties from any debts, and to guarantee the independence of the detective. It is a different matter, on the other hand, in the hard-boiled school, a prime example of which is Chandler's Philip Marlowe. He jumps head first into the fray that has been caused by the murder and risks becoming a victim of violence himself. Marlowe is also emotionally engaged when he uncovers the morass of the crime. His fee is of minor importance; what matters are his male pride and his professional reputation. Usually, a femme fatale forms the centre of the crime rather than a gangster and she exerts a damaging but seductive power over men. The hard-boiled detective must now prove himself to her. This femme fatale draws her fascination from a radical ethical stance: she embodies the woman who embraces her desire and gets what she wants, even if it means – sometimes literally – over someone's dead body. She accepts the death wish without reservation. The instant she is revealed as the murderer, thus breaking down and losing her seductiveness, is the moment of triumph for the hardened detective. By rejecting her ultimately in spite of her sexual allure, he regains his integrity. As long as the femme fatale embraces her fate completely, it remains only for the hero either to sacrifice his desire, reject the woman, re-establish his imaginary, narcissistic identity and play chess with himself or to identify with her and face his own ruin in this suicidal gesture. This, briefly and simply, is Žižek's theory of the classic and hard-boiled detective story in which philosophy, literary theory and psychoanalysis are seamlessly joined.

Now, at the end of this chapter, we shall focus our attention on Bloch's essay on the affinity between detective stories and philosophy since he, like Eco, claims to present the – or at least one – philosophy of the detective novel. Like Eco, Bloch restricts himself to the classic whodunit, at the core of which a detective investigates. The detective novel, or rather its philosophy, is characterised by three traits: the suspense of guessing, the uncovered revealed (of which the most important is often gained from seemingly unrelated sources), and actions or events that must first be introduced from the untold pre-story. Bloch considers the latter to be the essential trait: 'One dark aspect has as yet remained unnoticed. It is the aspect from which and towards which all following events are set in motion: a crime, usually murderous, stands at the beginning… Nor are the dark events depicted in any part of the previous plot, simply because it is not yet possible to depict them other than with the help of detection and clues that allow us to reconstruct them.' Bloch defines the detective novel's form as oedipal, which says a lot about the type of crime story he refers to and also about his understanding of philosophical methods, which consist mainly of guessing, revealing and reconstructing. Bloch finds parallels to a dark criminal original event in the works of the German philosopher Franz Baader and the later writings of Schelling. A wider philosophical spectrum comes into view if the dark refers not to a crime, but simply to the 'incognito of the beginning'. No one has as yet solved the mystery of the 'incognito of that which is', the reason why what we perceive as the world exists in the first place. Moreover, it is clear, according to Bloch, that no process would exist – be it searching, changing, possibly healing – if there were not something that should not be as it is. After all, even the reader trying to solve the mystery in the dark remains in what Bloch calls his ever-beginning, not yet visible being in the moment. The sphere of the unknown is enhanced by the situation of estrangement in which the individual finds himself. It includes both the people around us and the created environment and lends a fundamental insecurity to life, a state of being displaced or dissembled, which corresponds to general mistrust. Anything can now be expected from anyone, according to the barter economy, which can now also refer to faces, and which does not know the direction from which the blow comes, Bloch claims. That is why it is not entirely implausible for an apparently innocent character in a detective story to be revealed eventually as the murderer.

A micrological view is essential for the explanatory work of a detective. It is the only constant in a variety of detective stories. While Sherlock Holmes, for instance, proceeds scientifically and inductively and unveils the truth behind carefully arranged details, Hercule Poirot, on the other hand, intuitively gauges the entirety of the case by using his 'little grey cells'. According to Bloch, then, Bergson's philosophy or method has replaced that of John Stuart Mill in crime detection. The micrological view, nonetheless, is and remains necessary in order to look behind the camouflage of the individual and the façade of the environment.

c) *Philosophical themes and methods in crime fiction*
The examples given prove that there are references between crime fiction and philosophy, from crime writers and philosophers in both directions. Central themes are discussed and treated by each, such as truth, justice and injustice, power and violence, causality and free will, intent and coincidence, evil, fear and death. There are also similarities in argumentation and ways of thinking, and not only where logic is concerned. Therefore, it is not uncommon for a detective to use 'Ockham's razor' to solve a case. This law of economy, named after William of Ockham, requires that the simplest hypothesis is preferable to more complex ones. This would be the case, for example, if a detective focused on the spouse of a murder victim who would profit from their partner's death. Consequently, all other suspects would be exonerated on

evidence and the spouse's seemingly secure alibi would be shattered in order to prove his guilt. However, a detective may also act contrary to this approach, using instead Derrida's method. Derrida mistrusts simple explanations that derive from a cause-and-effect relationship or deed-guilt complex. He thinks it is necessary to complicate and differentiate things. In crime stories, suspicion is often cast initially on a single person who is then arrested by the police, though in fact innocent. A private detective or lawyer who believes in his client's innocence later uncovers a complex conspiracy involving several people, leading to his client's release. Our next chapter examines further the early beginnings of crime fiction in which a noticeable connection between genres and schools of thought in philosophy and fiction becomes evident.

But what, readers familiar with literary theory will ask, about the metaphysical detective story? Is it not *the* philosophical crime story par excellence? Yes and no. The term 'metaphysical detective story' is ambiguous. Other common expressions such as 'anti-detective story' and 'deconstructive mystery' are more to the point, which becomes clear when we look at an authoritative definition of the so-called 'metaphysical detective story'. Two leading experts, Patricia Merivale and Susan Elizabeth Sweeney, supply the following definition: 'A metaphysical detective story is a text that parodies or subverts traditional detective-story conventions – such as narrative closure and the detective's role as surrogate reader – with the intention, or at least the effect, of asking questions about mysteries of being and knowing which transcend the mere machinations of the mystery plot.' Such detective stories are merely metaphysical in the traditional philosophical sense as far as questions of being and knowledge are – quite often indirectly – concerned. In the foreground and centre of this genre we find the playful, experimental treatment of the genre's literary forms and strategies so as to undermine or destroy its rules and the reader's expectations. For instance, a detective who spends every waking hour searching relentlessly for a murderer only to discover that it is he himself who must, according to the genre's conventions, suffer from an extreme pathological split personality, which is made plausible to the reader. If this is not the case, the reader may have been subjected to a well-directed trick or metaphysical paradox, but it is no longer a crime story, in my opinion. In extreme cases, a 'metaphysical detective story' contains neither a detective nor a crime, but is instead limited to a game of hide-and-seek between author and reader, consisting of the literary presentation of mysterious signs, allusions and events that the reader must find and carefully connect in order to follow the text and profit from the read. The joy of reading is that the suspense is created neither by the solving of or threat of a crime or an escape from it, nor by the perpetrator's punishment or similar typical elements of crime stories, which are also found in gangster novels, psycho-thrillers, political thrillers and so on. Instead, the suspense is created by the way the author uses the conventions of the genre. Both may coincide, but this is seldom the case. I focus only on such 'metaphysical detective stories' that uphold the type of suspense that, to put it succinctly, works for crime stories. Among these are stories by Chesterton, Borges, Dürrenmatt and Eco, but not included are novels by Nabokov, Pynchon, Robbe-Grillet, Perec, Handke and many other writers of the decidedly highbrow genre of the 'metaphysical detective story'. One can parody, use irony, deconstruct a text and more, but a crime novel is only a text if it believes in the 'narratability of the world' (Thomas Wörtche).

References and Further reading:

Crime fiction

Block, Lawrence: *The Burglar Who Studied Spinoza*, New York 1981

De Santis, Pablo: *Voltaire's Calligrapher*, London 2010

Doody, Margaret: *Aristotle Detective*, London 1978

Doyle, Arthur Conan: 'The Speckled Band', in: Arthur Conan Doyle: *Sherlock Holmes. The Complete Stories*, Ware 2006, 558–578

Dürrenmatt, Friedrich: *The Judge and His Hangman*, New York 1963 (Original: *Der Richter und sein Henker*, Reinbek bei Hamburg 1958)

Dürrenmatt, Friedrich: *Inspector Barlach Mysteries: The Judge and His Hangman and Suspicion*, Chicago 2006. (Original: *Der Verdacht*, Zürich 1986)

Dürrenmatt, Friedrich: *The Pledge*, Chicago 2006. (Original: *Das Versprechen. Requiem auf den Kriminalroman*, 35th edition. Munich 2011)

Eco, Umberto: *Il nome della rosa*, Milano 1980 (English edition: *The Name of the Rose*, London 1984)

Fischer, Tibor: *The Thought Gang*, Edinburgh 1994

Johler, Jens: *Kritik der mörderischen Vernunft*, Berlin 2009 (English title: *Critique of Deadly Reason*)

Kerr, Philip: *A Philosophical Investigation*, London 1992

McCall Smith, Alexander: *The Sunday Philosophy Club*, London 2004

Poe, Edgar Allan: 'The Purloined Letter', *in: Edgar Allan Poe: Selected Writings*, 5th ed., Harmondsworth 1974, 330–349

Pouy, Jean-Bernard: *La pêche aux anges*, Paris 1986

Saylor, Steven: *Roman Blood*, New York 1991

Philosophical texts and literary theory

Aristotle: *Poetics*, London 2003; onlinebooks.library.upenn.edu/webbin/gutbook/

Auden, Wystan Hugh: 'The Guilty Vicarage: Notes on the Detective Story, by an Addict', in: Auden: *The Dyer's Hand and Other Essays*, London 1962, 146–158

Auden, Wystan Hugh: *Forewords and Afterwords*, New York 1973

Benjamin, Walter: 'Einbahnstraße', in: Benjamin: *Gesammelte Schriften Bd. IV 1*, Werkausgabe Vol. 10, Tillman Rexroth (ed.), Frankfurt am Main 1980, 83–148

Benjamin, Walter: 'Kriminalromane, auf Reisen', in: Benjamin: *Gesammelte Schriften Bd. IV 1*, Werkausgabe Vol. 10, Tillman Rexroth (ed.), Frankfurt am Main 1980, 381–383

Bloch, Ernst: 'Philosophische Ansicht des Detektivromans', in: Jochen Vogt (ed.), *Der Kriminalroman II. Zur Theorie und Geschichte einer Gattung*, Munich 1971, 322–343

Bronfen, Elisabeth: *Stanley Cavell zur Einführung*, Hamburg 2009

Camus, Albert: *Rebel: An Essay on Man in Revolt*, New York 1954

Cavell, Stanley: 'The Uncanniness of the Ordinary', in: *In Quest of the Ordinary*, Chicago/London 1988/1994, 153–178

Deleuze, Gilles: 'How Do We Recognize Structuralism?', in: *Desert Islands and Other Texts 1953–1974*, Semiotext(e) Foreign Agents Series, 2004

Deleuze, Gilles: 'The Philosophy of Crime Novels', in: *Desert Islands and Other Texts 1953–1974*, Semiotext(e) Foreign Agents Series, 2004, 81–85 https://theeveningrednessinthewest.wordpress.com/tag/gilles-deleuze/

Deleuze, Gilles: *Difference and Repetition*, 1994 [1968]

Derrida, Jacques : 'The Purveyor of Truth' , in: Yale French Studies 52, 1975, 31–113 (French edition: 'Le facteur de la vérité,' in: *La carte postale: De Socrate à Freud et au-delà*, Paris 1980, 439–524)

Derrida, Jacques: *Wie Meeresrauschen auf dem Grund einer Muschel... Paul de Mans Krieg Mémoires II*, Vienna 1988

Dürrenmatt, Friedrich: 'Monstervortrag über Gerechtigkeit und Recht, nebst einem helvetischen Zwischenspiel', *in: Philosophie und Naturwissenschaft. Essays, Gedichte und Reden*, Zürich 1980, 36–107

Eco, Umberto: *Postille a ‚Il nome della rosa'*, Milano 1983; www.artblog.comli.com/postille-nome-della-rosa-testo-integrale/ (English edition: *Postscript to 'The Name of the Rose'*, New York 1984)

Eco, Umberto: 'Die Enzyklopädie als Labyrinth', in: *Im Labyrinth der Vernunft*, 3rd edition. Leipzig 1995, 104–112

Eco, Umberto: 'Die aristotelische *Poetik* und wir', in: *Die Bücher und das Paradies*, Munich 2006, 238–257

Freeling, Nicolas: *Criminal Convictions*, Boston 1994

Hampe, Michael: *Die Macht des Zufalls*, Berlin 2006

Hügli, Anton/Lübcke, Poul (ed.): *Philosophielexikon*, Reinbek bei Hamburg 1991

Jameson, Fredric R.: 'On Raymond Chandler', in: Glenn W. Most/William W. Stowe (ed.): *The Poetics of Murder. Detective Fiction and Literary Theory*, San Diego/New York/London 1983, 122–148

Jaspers, Karl: *Einführung in die Philosophie*, 21st edition. Munich 1998 (English edition: *Way to Wisdom: An Introduction to Philosophy*, New Haven 2003)

Kiesow, Rainer Maria: *Das Alphabet des Rechts*, Frankfurt am Main 2004

Kracauer, Siegfried: *Der Detektiv-Roman. Ein philosophischer Traktat*, Frankfurt am Main 1979 (English edition: *Detective Novel. A Philosophical Treatise*, Oxford 2006)

Lacan, Jacques: 'Seminar on The Purloined Letter', in: Glenn W. Most/William W. Stowe (ed.): *The Poetics of Murder. Detective Fiction and Literary Theory*, San Diego/New York/London 1983, 21–54

Martens, Ekkehard: *Der Faden der Ariadne oder Warum die Philosophen spinnen*, Leipzig 2000

McGuinness, Brian (ed.): *Wittgenstein in Cambridge: Letters and Documents 1911–1951*, 4th edition. Malden/Oxford/Carlton 2008

Merivale, Patricia/Sweeney, Susan Elizabeth: 'The Game's Afoot: On the Trail of the Metaphysical Detective Story', in: Merivale/Sweeney (ed.): *Detecting Texts: The Metaphysical Detective Story from Poe to Postmodernism*, Philadelphia 1999, 1–24

Monk Ray: *Ludwig Wittgenstein: The Duty of Genius*, London 1991

Noller, Ulrich: 'Die Erzähltechniken der Kriminalliteratur. Was ist das überhaupt, ein Krimi? Interviews mit Jochen Vogt und Thomas

Wörtche', in: Christina Bacher/Ulrich Noller/Dieter Paul Rudolph (ed.): *Krimijahrbuch 2008*, Wuppertal 2008, 253–270

Ricœur, Paul: 'Narrative Funktion und menschliche Zeiterfahrung', in: Volker Bohn (ed.): *Romantik. Literatur und Philosophie*, Frankfurt am Main, 45–79

Sartre, Jean-Paul: *The Words: The Autobiography of Jean-Paul Sartre*. New York 1981

Sartre, Jean-Paul: *Les carnets de la drôle de guerre. Novembre 1939 – Mars 1940*, Paris 1983 (German edition: Sartre, Jean-Paul: Tagebücher November 1939 – März 1940, Reinbek bei Hamburg 1984)

Sayers, Dorothy: 'Aristotle on Detective Fiction', in: *Unpopular Opinions*, 2nd edition. London 1951, 178–190; english. oxfordjournals.org/content/1/1/23.full

Scaggs, John: *Crime Fiction*, London/New York 2010

Schadewaldt, Wolfgang: *Die Anfänge der Philosophie bei den Griechen*, Frankfurt am Main 1978

Sweeney, Susan Elizabeth: 'Crime in postmodernist fiction', in: Catherine Ross Nickerson (ed.): *The Cambridge Companion to American Crime Fiction*, Cambridge/New York u. a. 2010, 163–177

Thiele, Markus: *HirnStröme. Ein Theorie-Thriller*, Vienna 1992

Vogl, Joseph: 'Was ist ein Ereignis?', in: Peter Gente/Peter Weibel (ed.): *Deleuze und die Künste*, Frankfurt am Main 2007, 67–83

Waldmann, Günter: 'Kriminalroman – Antikriminalroman', in: Jochen Vogt (ed.): *Der Kriminalroman I: Zur Theorie und Geschichte einer Gattung*, Munich 1971, 206–227

Woolf, Virginia: *On Not Knowing Greek*, London 2008, 3–18

Žižek, Slavoj: *Liebe Dein Symptom wie Dich selbst! Jacques Lacans Psychoanalyse und die Medien*, Berlin 1991

Žižek, Slavoj: *Looking Awry: An Introduction to Jacques Lacan through Popular Culture*, Cambridge (Mass.)/London 1991

2

Crime Fiction's emergence from the Spirit of Western Philosophy

The definition of crime fiction and which texts it incorporates is highly controversial. Similarly, what constitutes philosophy, and which texts form a part of it, is equally controversial. What is more, there is also debate regarding which texts belong to the early phase of crime fiction and what may be considered the spirit of western philosophy. We are entering uncertain territory, but this should not hinder us in crossing it.

It is agreed that Edgar Allan Poe's (1809–1849) detective stories, published from 1841 onwards, are an important turning point. Consequently, the early phase of crime fiction must have begun prior to this period in order to come to a climax here. Which stories, then, can be considered as pioneering works of this genre? My approach in addressing this question is a pragmatic one. Probably the most widely read history of crime fiction is *Bloody Murder* by Julian Symons. In particular, Symons names Voltaire's *Zadig* (1747), William Godwin's *Caleb Williams* (1794) and Eugene Francois Vidocq's *Mémoires* (1828) as Poe's immediate predecessors. The first two works are different from the third in that they are obviously popular fiction, while Vidocq's memoirs resemble a documentary narrative while actually displaying the typical traits of a novel. Vidocq (1775 – 1857), a former criminal and convict, founded the criminal investigation department of Paris in 1810. His book may be viewed as an early work of criminology, which cannot be said of the other two. Another significant difference is the fact that Voltaire (1694 – 1778) and William Godwin (1756 – 1836) were well-known philosophers and developers of theories. Vidocq, on the other hand, was more practical in confronting and investigating crime. For this reason, his work yields few results in our context. Nonetheless, it shows that the beginnings of crime fiction are not only to be found in the spirit of philosophy, but also in the history of crime prevention and the police, as well as in the reporting of the same. Instead, I would like to introduce two writers that Symons may have missed, probably as a result of his lack of familiarity with German literature. Indeed, German crime fiction does not find any mention in *Bloody Murder*. For one thing, Friedrich von Schiller (1759 – 1805) is missing, who wrote *The Criminal from Lost Honour* (1785), as well as *The Ghost-Seer* (1788) and a prologue to the collection *Pitaval* (1792). Additionally, Schiller also composed philosophical texts alongside his plays and poems. The second absent writer is E. T. A. Hoffmann (1776 – 1822) with his crime story *Mademoiselle de Scuderi* (1819). Hoffmann was an academic who was familiar with philosophical ideas and writings of his time. His stories influenced Poe's own writing. Stephen Knight includes Schiller and Hoffmann in his history of crime fiction, but unfortunately he underestimates their influence on the genre. There is no denying that Poe is considered to be the main contributor to the modern crime and detective story. But what does Poe have to do with philosophy? Quite a lot, in my opinion, as I will demonstrate towards the end of this chapter. For now, it is sufficient to mention that Poe did, after all, compose a longer, rich text of nature philosophy in 'Eureka' (1848). So, in crime fiction's Voltaire, Godwin, Schiller and Poe we have already found four philosophers and thus the first sign of the emergence of modern crime fiction from the spirit of philosophy. There is also a second link, with regard to content. The American philosopher Thomas Nagel wrote a very brief introduction to philosophy entitled 'What Does It All Mean?' In this and other writings, he addresses typical topics and questions of philosophy: 'how do we know anything?', 'what is truth?', 'other minds', 'the mind-body problem', 'the meaning of words', 'free will', 'right and wrong', 'justice', 'death', and 'the meaning of life'. Most of these themes can also be found in crime fiction, albeit in a manner quite different to philosophical studies. For now, these are merely two clues. I shall discuss these themes further in order to prove that crime fiction has emerged from the spirit of philosophy.

For now, let us look at Voltaire's philosophical short novel *Zadig; or the Book of Fate*. At the centre of this novel we find a crime, the interpretation of clues and the solving of a mystery, and yet this is not a crime novel as such. The different elements of the narrative are joined in a way different from what we would expect in a detective story. Why, then, is it considered to be a precursor of the crime story? Zadig, the story's hero, displays investigative brilliance when the queen's dog and the king's horse both disappear at the same time. Zadig describes the animals to the search party without, he claims, ever having seen them. This leads to him being suspected of stealing them. Because the dog and the horse are found, the suspicions prove to be ill-founded. What remains is the accusation of having lied about seeing nothing. During the trial, Zadig explains in detail how he was able to deduce the animal's traits by examining their tracks on the forest path. 'I noticed the track of an animal in the sand,' he said, 'and it was easy to see that it was that of a small dog. Long faint streaks upon the little elevations of sand between the footmarks convinced me that it was a bitch with hanging teats, showing that she must have had puppies not many days since. Other scrapings of the sand, which seem to have grazed all the way beside the forepaws, indicated that she had very long ears; and, as the imprint of one foot was always fainter than those of the other three, I judged that the lady dog of our august Queen was, if I may venture to say so, a little lame.' Similarly, he explains how he was able to describe the horse based on its tracks, without ever having seen the animal himself. As a result, he is freed of any penalty.

From the point of view of the crime story it is apparent that Voltaire gives away a moment of suspense. Firstly, he should have accurately described the tracks found by Zadig, to allow the reader to wonder about the creature that caused them. Then he could have allowed Zadig to present the solution himself. However, Voltaire is not interested in this type of dramatic suspense, but rather in another. The novel carries the significant subtitle 'or the Book of Fate'. Zadig's adventures and misfortunes are constructed in such a way that the reader wonders whether a man like Zadig is punished or rewarded by fate for the brilliance, generosity, helpfulness and courage that sets him apart from others. The reader follows with interest the highs and lows of Zadig's skills and is finally rewarded with a happy ending. Within the frame of this novel, Voltaire presents his doctrine of strict determinism. All things, even human actions, are preordained by the necessity of natural law. There are no coincidences and no free will; only fate reigns. Towards the end of the novel, Voltaire explicitly refers to his view of fate: Zadig meets an angel disguised as a hermit carrying 'The Book of Fate'. On their journey, they spend the night at the home of a charitable widow who lives with her fourteen-year-old nephew. The next morning, the boy accompanies them to the bridge. There, the hermit throws him into the river, where he drowns. The hermit explains that, if that young man whose neck was broken by providence had lived, he would have killed his aunt a year later and, another year after that, would have murdered Zadig himself. Here

Voltaire appears to contradict himself, since the natural chain of events is broken by the actions of a celestial power. Still, the reader should not view the encounter with the angel of fate as real, but as an ironic narrative gesture that only serves to clarify the author's philosophical message regarding the irreversibility of fate. The angel says, 'But there is no coincidence, everything is a test or a punishment, a reward or providence.' Yet if everything in life is preordained so precisely, then dramatic suspense is pointless in which characters try to catch a criminal and have him penalised for his deeds. If fate determines whether a criminal is punished or not, and neither his nor his pursuers' free will and efforts nor coincidence have influence on the course of the matter, then an essential dramatic moment that characterises crime fiction is missing.

While Voltaire claims that God exists, this God does not have any power to interfere with the rules he created that govern the course of the world. He cannot bring about miracles. Voltaire, a philosopher of the Enlightenment, wrote at a time when the belief in miracles was prevalent. He, however, felt contempt for such beliefs. Even though Zadig can describe the missing animals thanks to his acute skills of observation and deduction and is thus proved innocent in court, some 'magi insist he is a warlock who must be burnt'. It was certainly common in the eighteenth century for religious explanations to be used instead of scientific observations, and it was the primary aim of prominent philosophers of the Enlightenment to promote reason and to replace religious myths with rational thought. The discovery of a murder victim in a seemingly locked room – a classic murder mystery case – might have led Voltaire's contemporaries to believe this to be the work of God or the devil, instead of finding a rational, technically possible solution. The modern crime story owes its strictly scientific and rational reasoning of cause and effect to writers of the Enlightenment, like Voltaire and others, who viewed religion critically. The element of detective investigation also played a part in such philosophies when philosophers revealed religious oracles not only to be improbable and irrational, but also most likely deceptions by priests. In his historico-philosophical observations, the German philosopher Ernst Bloch rightly emphasised that Enlightenment and detection are connected. It is Voltaire's aim to force the reader to think and judge for himself, which is why he often reverts to the telling of 'facts' in his writing. The actual cases are intended to expose the absurdity and ridiculousness of some theories. People should trust their own experience and intelligence and constantly replace generalised and unclear claims with certain, concrete ideas. Literature of this kind envisages a bond between the writer and the intelligent reader, which will become constitutive of the modern crime story.

Voltaire sees the world as a place of crime and catastrophe, a place in which murder, greed and ideological conflicts are the driving forces. Evil thrives next to the good, as shown in *Zadig* and the story 'The World as It Goes'. The fact that crime is everywhere means that a seemingly innocent, pleasant young boy can turn into a murderer at any moment. In Voltaire's world, improbable chains of events can occur both in nature and in human relationships. All that seems steady and unshakeable today can come to an end tomorrow. The universe, an incredible machinery of causal elements, is incomplete and random, disharmonic and bizarre. While the events in the story of Zadig appear to be governed by a higher power, and the tale has a conciliatory ending, with the virtuous Zadig becoming the benign ruler of Babylon, the later novel *Candide or Optimism* (1759) shows no sign of any hidden meaning behind the course of the world. The evil that man encounters is not caused by his evil deeds. Divine providence does not watch over us or deal out rewards to the virtuous and punishment to the wrongdoers. Yet the modern detective story does not adopt this deeply hopeless and pessimistic worldview; instead, it focuses on an instance of it, the uncertainty of who is good and who is evil and what will happen to the culprit. In fact, it is difficult to tell whether a character is evil or not, both in Voltaire's writing and the detective story. Even the highest ranking and most civilised protagonist might be the perpetrator. It is this uncertainty on which the classic whodunit bases its suspense. Voltaire forgoes this uncertainty and allows the culprit to immediately reveal his intentions through his deed. Only later crime stories of the Noir tradition come close to Voltaire's depressing worldview.

In the eighteenth century, philosophy was mainly concerned with how to justify God and his impact as the creator of the world in the face of evil. Voltaire dispensed with such a justification altogether. God and the world are what they are. Not even reason, God's gift to man, can deliver us from evil. So the question remains, how are we to deal with crime? Should we simply leave it be, since fate rules the course of the world anyway? Despite being a philosopher of the Enlightenment, Voltaire does not trust us to base our lives on the ideals of reasoning. Instead, he leans towards an entirely pragmatic kind of rationality. In his opinion, rationality errs too often because it neglects empiricism and it is too weak to drive us to humane actions. It is in our best interest to fight, pursue and punish criminals in order to prevent damage to our goods and to thrive together as a community. We can rely on God to punish those who are evil just as little as we can rely on the dominance of reason. What remains is not necessarily powerlessness. Despite his deterministic worldview, Voltaire considered the free will of the individual to be a useful belief, which we should be unwilling to relinquish for moral reasons and our general welfare. He gave his contemporaries an impressive example of this: he made his name in the fight for justice by defending the innocence and honour of people accused of crimes against the church. He condemned the absurd allegations and the cruel punishments that were carried out such as torture, maiming and execution. Voltaire campaigned for humane penal laws and propagated Cesare Beccaria's reformatory work *Dei delitti e delle pene* of 1764, which disputed any justification of the death sentence.

Voltaire's personal commitment is in line with the pleasanter parts of Zadig's story. As minister, for a time, Zadig brings out the truth and thereby shows people the power and sanctity of the law. He moderates harsh laws and creates new, just regulations. Laws are meant to protect, not intimidate us. The risk of acquitting a guilty person is preferable to convicting an innocent. Zadig carries out his office with penetrating reason and benevolence. Still, his sense of justice only becomes a blessing for his people towards the end, when he is the ruler of Babylon. In this instance, Voltaire pays homage to his monarchist day and age. His fictional hero could not yet be a detective despite his keen reasoning and infallible understanding of right and wrong. The division of power into legislative authority, judiciary and executive authority, including the police, did not yet exist and the division of labour in society had not yet produced police detectives or private investigators. It took almost a century before the detective could become the hero of a story.

Friedrich von Schiller took the next step towards the emergence of the modern crime story. A writer of the later German Enlightenment, with a sharp historical consciousness, he reflects the contradictions and limitations of the Enlightenment and expresses the crisis of moral consciousness, for morality – just like religious conviction – threatens to become the remnant of a kind of superstition as a result of the

Enlightenment. Young Schiller is fascinated by crime, murder, fraud and intrigue, which is particularly evident in his early poem *The Child Murderess*, his first play *The Robbers* (1781), the novella *The Criminal of Lost Honour* and the unfinished novel *The Ghost-Seer*. Influenced by the Enlightenment, Schiller seeks to understand the true and whole nature of humankind, of man as part of nature. As early as 1780 his medical dissertation concerns itself with the connection between the animalistic nature of man and his spiritual nature. By analysing crime, he also hopes to gain insight into the human soul and its influence in history.

As demonstrated by Michel Foucault in *Discipline and Punish* in 1975, there was a fundamental shift within criminal justice during the Enlightenment. Criminal proceedings focused on the punishment of the criminal's body. Confessions were often forced from the suspect through torture, and the convict was subjected to humiliating punishment in a public ritual of martyrdom. Later, such a spectacle in front of the crowds was deemed to be cruel, repugnant and – at least when the suspects were innocent – unlawful. For the most part, it was also considered to be ineffective and therefore should be replaced by subtler, more effective punishment. The effect on the criminal's conscience and soul becomes the centre of attention. The delinquent must be purged of sin, and it is this change in the perception of penal justice that is also expressed in crime fiction, particularly in the following story by Schiller.

The 'true story', which is the subtitle of *The Criminal of Lost Honour* begins with the words, 'In the whole history of man there is no chapter more instructive for the heart and mind than the annals of his errors. On the occasion of every great crime a proportionally great force was in motion. If by the pale light of ordinary emotions the play of the desiring faculty is concealed, in the situation of strong passion it becomes the more striking, the more colossal, the more audible, and the acute investigator of humanity, who knows how much may be properly set down to the account of the mechanism of the ordinary freedom of the will, and how far it is allowable to reason by analogy, will be able from this source to gather much fresh experience for his psychology, and to render it applicable to moral life.' A common vice that is suppressed and kept small by the narrow laws of the bourgeoisie might, under other circumstances, come close to the enormity of Borgia, Schiller suspects. This may remind some Chesterton readers of the psychology of Father Brown, who so easily empathises with criminals, because he finds in his own heart the same impulses to which they are subject. Schiller also wants to upset the reader's righteous sense of security that easily creates a distance between them and the criminal. To achieve this, there are only two ways to tell the (hi)story. Either the reader must become as warm as the hero, or the hero must become as cold as the reader. The young Schiller, as a defendant of Enlightenment's aesthetic, goes for the latter: 'The hero must become as cold as the reader or – what comes to the same thing – we must become acquainted with him before he begins to act; we must see him not only perform his act, but also will his action. His thoughts concern us infinitely more than his deeds, and the sources of his thoughts still more than the consequences of his deeds. [The soil of Vesuvius has been explored to discover the origin of its eruption; and why is less attention paid to a moral than to a physical phenomenon?] Why do we not equally regard the nature and situation of the things which surround a certain man, until the tinder collected within him takes fire?' Schiller searches for truth in the criminal act, 'in the unalterable structure of the human soul, and in the variable conditions by which it is influenced from without...' He discovers virtue and vice together in the same cradle, which is a concept similar to Voltaire's. With the help of this portrayal of moral transgressions, Schiller wishes to spread 'the mild spirit of toleration' among his readers, which should lead to reconciliation with the criminals. Schiller does not attempt to create suspense based on whether the perpetrator is caught or will be justly punished. In fact, he anticipates the ending: '...he perished by the hand of the executioner'. But Schiller raises doubts as to the entitlement of a human being to take the life of a criminal. '[B]ut the dissection of his crime will perhaps instruct humanity,' he continues, 'and possibly instruct justice also.' Whether or not this punishment is just or appropriate can now be decided by the enlightened reader himself.

In Schiller's prologue to the well-known collection of F. Gayot de Pitaval's criminal cases, we come across a similar justification for the reading of such cases. Since Schiller pays homage to the classical ideals of truth, goodness, and beauty, he feels obliged to justify the publication of entertaining criminal cases aimed at a wider readership and available without judicial details in a new German translation. Schiller starts by remarking that a number of soulless writings of bad taste and equally bad morals are in circulation among the devouring masses. He ascribes the great interest in such mediocre literature to man's general penchant for passionate and complex situations, which these inferior texts easily satisfy. Now, Schiller suggests that better writers should copy the plot devices used by popular writers in order to gain more readers. In this manner, a popular literature that contains some degree of reality for the mind will spread useful knowledge and serve to 'guide the reader's thoughts towards worthier matters'. This valuable characteristic is fulfilled by Pitaval's criminal cases. 'Here, we see man in the most complicated situations that heighten our expectations. Solving these predicaments leaves the reader pleasantly occupied. The secret game of passion unfolds before our eyes and some rays of truth shine through the concealed paths of intrigue and the machinations of worldly and spiritual fraud. Driving forces that usually remain hidden from the observer in everyday life emerge visibly in those situations in which life, freedom and property are threatened, and thus the judge is able to look deeply into the human heart. What is more, the judiciary's cumbersome legal process is much better able to bring forth the secret motives behind human actions than is otherwise the case. Whereas many complete stories leave us unsatisfied as to the ultimate causes of an event or the true motives of the protagonists, the criminal process often manages to unveil innermost thoughts and bring to light the most secret web of deceit… The entertainment that the mere content of such cases provides is further enhanced by the manner in which the topic is treated. Wherever possible, writers have tried to convey the doubtfulness of decisions, often embarrassing judges in the process, by carefully and artfully hiding final developments on both sides in order to increase the tension.'

There is hardly a better recommendation for a legal thriller, but not only this. Schiller's narrative of a crime is more comparable to the practices of writers such as James M. Cain, Georges Simenon or Patricia Highsmith, who dissect what it is that drives criminals, than the type of detective story whose primary interest is the reconstruction of the crime and the hunt for the perpetrator. Both narrative types appeal to the reader's interest in the deed and the criminal's development, and both leave the reader in a heightened state of expectation. In this context, Schiller speaks of the reader's gift of divining the truth. Taking 'divination' as the art of augury and prophecy, one would expect Schiller, as a man of the Enlightenment, to be sceptical of such a thing. What he means by 'divination', however, is an inkling and a prediction of events that are based on facts, the reader's experience and logical deduction. This gift of divination is an everyday aid we use to deal with people's behaviour and events in our surroundings and it gives the reader much pleasure in the reading process, which is something the detective story takes advantage of. In Schiller's work, too, we find traces of a deductive game with the reader, particularly in his unfinished novel *The Ghost-Seer* from 1788.

Having studied extensively the work of the German Enlightenment philosopher Immanuel Kant (1724–1804), especially in later years, Schiller derived the title *The Ghost-Seer* from Kant's *Dreams of a Spirit-Seer, Illustrated by those of Metaphysics* (1766), the German word 'Geisterseher' meaning both ghost-seer and spirit-seer. Although biographical research has not been able to prove definitively that Schiller actually read Kant's book, considering how well educated and interested Schiller was in philosophy it is hard to imagine he was unaware of this book and its contents. He did not only take the word 'ghost-seer' from Kant, but also the term 'metaphysical dreams', for which he shows as little respect as Kant does. Both texts even display similarities in their content. Kant's book, for instance, refers to the Swedish scientist and spiritualist Emanuel Swedenborg (1688–1772), who was said to have had supernatural gifts. It was believed that Swedenborg had visions of events long distances away and was able to predict them before news of them arrived by post. He claimed to be in direct contact with the spirits of the deceased and could receive their messages.

Schiller also writes about supernatural powers in his own text, the hero of which is a German protestant prince hiding incognito in Venice. There, the prince is confronted with a series of mysterious events that appear to be paranormal. At the time of the carnival, a man wearing an Armenian mask follows the prince and his companion, the Count of O**. Before disappearing, the masked man addresses the prince by his real name and says, 'Wish yourself good luck, prince… At 9 o'clock he died.' A few days later, the prince receives the news that his cousin died at exactly that time. This means that he moves up in line for the throne. At first, the prince cannot explain the Armenian's prophecy. Later on, he attempts to convince himself that such a prediction was possible due to his cousin's permanent ill health. The prince and his companion, the narrator of the story, meet the mysterious Armenian again at a séance with a Sicilian magician, which turns out to have been rigged with great technical expertise. Time and again, mysterious or unusual occurrences throughout the story are proved to be the results of clever and surprising technical tricks. Schiller supposedly used the Count of Cagliostro, a masterful con-man and schemer, as the prototype of his mysterious 'Armenian'. In the course of the story, we wonder whether the prince, who is all too easily influenced and who certainly does not embody the enlightened ideal of rational autonomy, will use common sense and reason, or whether he will be corrupted by deceivers and conspirators. The character of the prince is based on Prince Friedrich Heinrich Eugen, nephew of the Württemberg duke, Carl Eugen. The prince had defended the evocation of ghosts and supernatural incidences in an article and even admitted his affinity to 'speculative philosophy'. He did so with such religious fervour that there were rumours he was going to convert to Catholicism, which caused considerable friction in the protestant state of Württemberg.

At first, the prince in *The Ghost-Seer* appears sceptical and rational despite his fascination with the mysterious. In the manner of Sherlock Holmes he accuses his companion of preferring to believe in miracles rather than admitting to something that seems unlikely, but possible, or denying the powers of nature rather than accepting a combination of these powers. Both the prince and his companion consider it the duty of a philosopher to explain such mysterious phenomena. This illustrates that science and philosophy were not yet clearly differentiated and that exposing intrigues and tricks was not yet considered the task of criminal investigations and psychology, but instead philosophy. In a philosophical conversation within the story, the prince's companion stated it was the philosopher's task 'to think'. However, he immediately admits that the king, too, thinks when he reigns. From our perspective today, we could add that scientists and detectives think as well. But in Schiller's day, thinking was reserved for philosophers and the sovereign, so that, at least initially, the thinking prince in *The Ghost-Seer* becomes the philosophising detective or the investigating philosopher in a story of fraud and conspiracy.

In Schiller's day, religion, epistemology and politics were inextricably connected. The question was: if we were to lose our faith, could we possibly be certain of anything at all? Schiller repeatedly demonstrated in his text how something that seemed completely real could turn out to be merely an image, an illusion. In his introduction to *The Ghost-Seer*, Andrew Brown mentions that Schiller's prince did indeed proceed like a detective, using scientific models and strictly logical deduction. However, the cunning nature of reason is more suited to Machiavelli's prince and relies on the zigzagging course of masquerades and deceit to reach its goals. But not only is reason cunning; according to Brown, Schiller's narrative, much like G. K. Chesterton's, suggests that faith is also cunning, as inappropriate as it may seem.

In *The Ghost-Seer*, Schiller not only refers to Cagliostro and Swedenborg, but also to the secret societies of his day and their conspiracies. Before he composed *The Ghost-Seer*, Schiller – like many others – was preoccupied with the endeavours of the Freemasons and Illuminati, considered by some to be the secret force of the Enlightenment, but also with the powerful and influential Jesuit order that opposed the Reformation and was banned in many countries at the time. He took a reserved, even dismissive stance regarding the morally dubious and obscure behaviour displayed by such groups. Despite having been made an honorary citizen of the French Republic at the time of the revolution due to his rebellious early plays, he loathed conspiracies and violence and preferred the enlightened humanist upbringing of sovereigns who wished to bring about changes in state and society. Ultimately, he remained loyal to the monarchy despite all criticism. William Godwin, in contrast, took an entirely different stance regarding the French Revolution and it is he we can thank for taking the next step in the history of the modern crime story.

Some consider William Godwin to be the last representative of British Enlightenment philosophy. His main opus, which briefly brought him significant fame, was *An Enquiry concerning Political Justice and its Influence on General Virtue and Happiness* (1793). Godwin sympathised with the ideals of the French Revolution, which is clearly evident in the text. In his trilogy Godwin creates a social order based on liberty, justice, truth and reason. He dismisses all state institutions, considering them to be corrupt and attempting to corrupt their citizens. For this reason, he focuses on communication as a useful tool for change and revolution instead of the open violence of the French Revolution. Unlike similar texts, Godwin's only evaded censorship because the Prime Minister, William Pitt, was of the opinion that a book for 63 shillings would not cause much harm among members of the population who could not even afford 3 shillings. At least it met with great response from the intelligentsia.

Within 10 days of the publication of *An Enquiry Concerning Political Justice* in February 1793, Godwin began work on his novel *Things As They*

Are; or, The Adventures of Caleb Williams. The Enlightenment and its ideals underlie the novel, as he announces in a prologue that was only added in a later edition for fear of political repression: 'The following narrative is intended to answer a purpose more general and important than immediately appears upon the face of it. The question now afloat in the world respecting *Things As They Are*, is the most interesting that can be presented to the human mind… It is now known to philosophers that the spirit and character of the government intrudes itself into every rank of society. But this is a truth highly worthy to be communicated to persons whom books of philosophy and science are never likely to reach. Accordingly it was proposed in the invention of the following work, to comprehend, as far as the progressive nature of a single story would allow, a general review of the modes of domestic and unrecorded despotism, by which man becomes the destroyer of man.'

According to Julian Symons, *Caleb Williams* is the first novel to capture the characteristics of crime fiction. The book revolves around a murder, its discovery, and the murderer's relentless hunt for the person who discovered the crime. At the same time topics such as justice and injustice, liberty and a lack thereof, truth and lies, and reason are addressed. These are dealt with in a very mundane, secular manner without any concern for the hereafter. Such themes often enter into the subtext of crime stories, but here they are made explicit in some parts of the text. There is probably no other work of crime fiction that expresses an author's philosophy as clearly as this book does. The corrupting effect of existing social institutions is not only apparent from the fictional characters' fate, but is also expressed quite clearly in the narrator's own words: 'But of what use are talents and sentiments in the corrupt wilderness of human society? It is a rank and rotten soil from which every finer shrub draws poison as it grows. All that in a happier field and a purer air would expand into virtue and germinate into general usefulness, is thus converted into henbane and deadly nightshade.' While Godwin does depict the thoughts and motives of victims and offenders, he focuses much more on the outward social circumstances and constraints that influence their actions.

The two opponents in the novel, aristocratic estate owner Falkland and his secretary Williams, are actually benevolent people of noble character. It is the social circumstances and social institutions – in particular the criminal justice system and a false understanding of honour – which lead them, or even force them, to commit disgraceful acts. Godwin resists the idea of free will and pleads for the necessity of decisions derived from both emotions and reason. Williams notices that his employer, Falkland, is prone to extreme, dejected moods. Driven by curiosity and in the spirit of the Enlightenment he attempts to deduce the causes of this depression. In an entirely secular manner, Williams does not even bother looking for supernatural explanations, such as the demon which possesses Falkland, but instead discovers that the master he admires suffers from a heavy burden of guilt: in the heat of the moment, Falkland killed his rival Tyrrel and allowed two innocent people to be executed for the crime. In spite of this, Williams sympathises with Falkland: 'if he have been criminal, that is owing to circumstances.' As soon as Falkland discovers that Williams knows his secret, he fears that his safety and reputation are threatened. He tries to silence Williams in any way he can without actually killing him. In the end, he destroys Williams' reputation by planting false evidence of a theft on him, wrongly making him the victim of criminal justice. Williams describes impressively the suffering to which he and other inmates, some of whom are also innocent, are subjected: '[V]isit the scenes of our prisons! Witness their unwholesomeness, their filth, the tyranny of their governors, the misery of their inmates! After that show me the man shameless enough to triumph, and say, England has no Bastille!' This view is identical to that expressed by Godwin in the *Enquiry*, which he summarises succinctly as follows: 'Thus every consideration tends to show, that a man tried for a crime is a poor deserted individual with the whole force of the community conspiring his ruin.'

In the course of his numerous arguments against punishment and penal law, Godwin also speaks about the unreliability of evidence. He doubts in equal measure the reliability of witnesses, their objectivity and their meticulous reasoning. Evidence based on incriminating circumstances can lead to the wrong conclusions, as Godwin emphasises with the rhetorical question: 'Who does not know, that there is not a man in England, however blameless a life he may lead, who is secure that he shall not end it at the gallows?' He also criticises so-called direct evidence, by which the delinquent must be identified, with the words: 'How many instances are there upon record,' he asks, 'of persons condemned upon this evidence, who, after their death, have been proved entirely innocent?' Judges are unable to recognise the motives of suspects because the human heart ultimately remains unfathomable. *Caleb Williams* exemplifies the arbitrary way in which criminal justice pursues and destroys the innocent. English criminal law, according to Godwin, is devised and used by those in power with the simple purpose of upholding their political authority.

When Williams breaks out of prison, he temporarily finds refuge with a gang of thieves. Their leader justifies his deeds with the words, 'Our profession is the profession of justice. It is thus that the prejudices of men universally teach them to colour the most desperate cause, to which they have determined to adhere. We, who are thieves without a licence, are at open war with another set of men, who are thieves according to law.' This view of society and law is also shared by the criminal protagonists in Edward Anderson's popular crime novel *Thieves Like Us* (1937). Williams, however, does not subscribe to this view and leaves the gang to try and go into hiding. Unfortunately, he is chased by a former criminal who now works as a professional 'thief-taker'. The characterisation of the malevolent, vengeful and greedy 'sniffer dog' Gines clearly contrasts with the spiritualising legitimisation, indeed glorification of the master detective of later crime and detective fiction, who uncovers crimes and solves cases primarily with his superior powers of deduction and daring.

Towards the end of the novel, Williams can see no other way but to give himself up and bring Falkland before the court. In the direct confrontation Williams speaks very openly and honestly about his suffering and Falkland's crime, which deeply affects all who are present. Finally, Falkland surrenders and admits his guilt. One might now think that Williams would be delighted about his victory, but instead he reproaches himself for delivering Falkland to justice. Here, Godwin's philosophical ideals are displayed quite clearly. The motto of the Enlightenment, 'truth will out', should be private and personal rather than public and subject to the laws of the state. Williams accuses himself by saying, 'I am sure that, if I had opened my heart to Mr. Falkland, if I had told to him privately the tale that I have now been telling, he could not have resisted my reasonable demand… I despaired, while it was yet time to have made the just experiment; but my despair was criminal, was treason against the sovereignty of truth.' In his introduction, David McCracken rightly emphasises the core significance of this statement which can also be found in other words in Godwin's *Political Justice*.

Symons points out that what is remarkable about *Caleb Williams* is his refusal of all assumptions which underlie later detective stories. In the detective story, law and order are hailed as the epitome of good; in

Godwin's writing it is absolute evil. The lawless are often heroic while the malicious 'thief-taker', a forerunner of the detective, is an evil scoundrel. The reversal of the basic assumptions of good and evil compared to later detective stories is mainly related to developments in society. In a democracy, laws are legitimised and respected quite differently than in a despotic monarchy, which alters the perception of the criminal and of those who uphold the law. Another reason lies in Godwin's particular philosophy. This is based so strongly on the belief in man's perfection, in truth, justice and reason, that every unadorned glance at the wretched reality must surely appear to be a swamp of corruption compared to this ideal. The protagonist of the novel, with the mind of a detective, cannot be portrayed as the seeker of truth and defender of liberty and justice – in short, as the hero – since, according to Godwin's socio-philosophical premise, he remains merely a powerless individual in a complex system. No other crime writer after William Godwin had ideals that were as lofty and anarchic as his.

The German Romantic E. T. A. Hoffmann's crime novella *Mademoiselle de Scudéri* was first published in October 1819 at a time of upheaval. The noble ideals of the Enlightenment and the French Revolution had been belied or even discredited by the subsequent Napoleonic wars, the Restoration and the initial social grievances of the advancing industrial revolution. Writers of Romanticism turned towards new themes and ideas. The Enlightenment impulse of the first crime stories could not continue uninterrupted.

Hoffmann sets his novella in the time of Louis XIV and of the poet Madeleine de Scudéri. At the beginning, he describes Paris as the setting for the wickedest atrocities. The invention of a new deadly toxin that leaves no trace in the human body leads to a kind of epidemic of murder by poisoning, shaking people's trust in each other, even among the closest family members: 'The husband trembled before his wife; the father dreaded the son; the sister the brother.' Hoffmann had read about these murders by poisoning in Voltaire's *The Age of Louis XIV* and in the collection of Pitaval's criminal cases. Schiller's edited version also contains these cases of poisoning. In order to uncover and combat these crimes, the king set up his own court of justice, the *chambre ardente*. However, this chamber was not only successful in detecting and punishing delinquents, but rather developed into a cruel inquisition in its blind zeal. Anyone suspected of the smallest crime could fall victim to it without an opportunity to argue their innocence. Just as the deaths by poison decline in Hoffman's novella, murder committed by jewel thieves increases worryingly, so that anyone who carries jewels at night runs the risk of being stabbed to death. Old Mademoiselle de Scudéri is passed a box of stolen jewels because of indelicate verses that seem to express sympathy for the thieves. The jewels appear to be the work of the most prestigious goldsmith of the day, Master Cardillac, who does not want them back. The Mademoiselle sees this as a bridal gift to her and, some time later, Cardillac is found stabbed in his workshop. Since the house was locked at the time of the murder, Cardillac's assistant Brusson, who is found with the body, is suspected of the crime. The jewellery thieves' murders stop, which makes the imprisoned Brusson look even more suspicious, not only of committing this murder, but also others. Moreover, Brusson is engaged to Cardillac's daughter Madelon, who is, however, convinced of his innocence. She turns to Mademoiselle de Scudéri for help who must now find the true murderer and save Brusson from being executed. Hoffmann emphasises that she proceeds intuitively and with cunning, but it isn't the skill of a professional detective that brings things to a successful conclusion. The surprising confessions made by people in her presence due to her integrity are the reason why she manages to reveal the true murderer. She does not rely on facts or logical deduction to check the reliability of people's statements, but instead on her unerring intuition. To save Brusson from the machinery of justice, she defends him before the king so that he may be pardoned by sovereign decree.

While in Schiller's *The Ghost-Seer* all trust in the power of observation and common sense is shattered and thrown into doubt, Mademoiselle de Scudéri's trust in her knowledge of human nature and her intuition are put to the test here. Hoffmann does not share Godwin's optimistic belief that the truth can be found in an honest, personal and truthful dialogue. Like Schiller, he is sceptical when it comes to the power of the Enlightenment ideals in *The Ghost-Seer*. Hoffmann knew and held this book in high esteem and said that anyone who had any affinity to Romanticism carried this book in his pocket. He also uses the word 'ghost-seer' in his crime story. What Hoffmann does, however, share with Godwin is a negative view of the arbitrary and cruel criminal justice system, in this case the *chambre ardente*, whose similarities to the infamous dungeons of the Bastille he emphasised. Hoffmann himself had been a criminal court judge in Berlin, which lends a keener poignancy to his view of the inhumanity of the justice system. One might object that he is writing about a justice system of a previous century, but Hoffmann dealt with cases in which he himself was the judge who had to repeal unjust charges and verdicts. As judge, Hoffmann knew from personal experience that condemnation in certain situations ultimately boiled down to an inner conviction rather than brilliant evidence, such as contradicting witness testimonies. Mademoiselle de Scudéri argues in a similar vein before the king. Ultimately, with all the uncertainty that surrounds the judging of others, the individual must rely on human understanding, expressed by an inner conviction, because observation and reason alone no longer suffice. Since inner conviction is first and foremost attained through dialogue, Hoffmann approaches Godwin's own position without actually sharing his enlightened ideals.

As a Romantic, Hoffmann is particularly disinclined to follow the philosophy of Enlightenment in a direction that perceives the individual as a complex, rationally constructed machine, a philosophy represented, for example, by La Mettrie's *Man a Machine* (1747). Although Hoffmann was indeed fascinated by humanoid machines and delved into the subject at the time, he was appalled by the mechanical and calculable aspect of many people's behaviour. Already as a twenty-year-old he lamented to his friend in a letter that he wished to break through the machine men and the platitudes, where necessary with violence. His earlier tale 'The Sandman' (1816) deals with this gradual convergence of man and machine as well as man's approximation of machines and their schematic actions to the extent that it is difficult to tell them apart. In his story, one of the main protagonists is an automaton called Olimpia who is so human in her behaviour that the man who constructed her can pass her off as his daughter. Most people fall for it and Nathanael, the male protagonist who is prone to insanity, even falls in love with her and feels that only she can understand him completely. Once Olimpia's true nature is discovered, a deep-seated uncertainty takes hold of those who fell for the deception. Lovers demand from their partners to speak in such terms that will prove they are capable of thought and emotions. As well as a sarcastic social critique of the contemporary efforts to rationalise and discipline human behaviour, which Foucault depicted in *Discipline and Punish*, Hoffmann's story deals with the philosophical question, 'How much do you really know about what goes on in anyone else's mind?' This is a question posed not only by the philosopher, but also, in a different and more pragmatic way, by the investigating detective. Unlike Schiller, Godwin and Voltaire, Hoffmann does not explicitly refer to philosophical issues. This does not mean, however, that no philosophical references have been worked latently into his texts. In 'The Sandman', for instance, he is interested in showing how easily our everyday reality is dehumanised and how incomprehensible the mystery of all living things is in comparison. The crime story about Mademoiselle de Scudéri revolves constantly around questions of truth, justice and evil, which are each addressed from different angles throughout the story. Apart from the subject of legal philosophy, which he must have encountered in his studies of law, Hoffmann concerns himself with questions of aesthetics and natural philosophy, in particular by Gotthilf Heinrich Schubert (*Views of the Dark Side of the Natural Sciences*, *Symbolism of Dreams*) and F. W. J. Schelling. Schelling's romanticist natural philosophy regarded spirit and matter as different physical conditions in a polarised nature. It located a dialectic contrast within the natural subject, which suggests a psychosomatic notion of illness. What was then seen as part of natural philosophy would later become psychology, psychiatry or psychoanalysis. A standard psychiatric work of the time, with which Hoffmann was familiar, displays in its very title the connection with philosophy: *Traité médico-philosophique sur l'aliénation mentale; ou la manie* (*Treatise on Insanity*), by Philippe Pinel (1801). Hoffmann was interested in the latest discoveries of psychiatry not only as a poet, but also as legal practitioner, since criminal law has no meaning if it is no longer directed at a criminal who acts of his own free will. Ultimately, in Hoffmann's crime story, the jewel thief's murderous obsession, the 'evil star' under which his fate stands, is explained not with the help of a demon or a curse, but rather by prenatal trauma, which at the time was a highly modern, scientific view of conditioning.

The spectres perceived by Hoffmann are not always ghosts, fairies and goblins, as they appear in romantic fairy tales, but are instead the ghosts of an inhumane reality, the irrational abyss and the uncanny that exist beyond the laboriously managed routines of everyday life. The lurking of the dangerous and the deadly behind every seemingly harmless corner, creating suspects everywhere, is what creates an atmospheric suspense that is ideal for a crime story. The Enlightenment writers Voltaire and Godwin also confront us with a world full of criminals and injustice, in which evil seems to reign. Here, however, the cause of evil – as made evident by Godwin – lies in an incorrect social structure and in man's inadequate education and enlightenment. The world is what it is and there is nothing mysterious about it, but this is not a view shared by Romanticism. Evil is surrounded by an aura of the uncanny and mysterious that contrasts with the homely atmosphere of our everyday lives. While Enlightenment provided rational, comprehensible laws for the nature of man, the Romantic, in line with German philosophy at that time, perceives his self and his soul as a source of imaginative power and creative will. Imagination, not reason, is the root of creativity.

This results in E. T. A. Hoffmann's basic poetic and philosophical idea, which permeates his entire work. He differentiates between two spheres of being: the everyday world of prosaic conditions and the 'higher being' of poetry, fantasy and the spiritual. While the young Hoffmann was entirely devoted to the imaginative realm and the arts and despised bourgeois constraints, he discovered later in life the right of both to coexist. The artist's duty is to endure the tension between both of these aspects of life and to accept them as the basis of his art. Thus, *Mademoiselle de Scudéri* is not only a crime story, but also a story about the artist's status and responsibilities in society. Two artists form the core of the action, the poet de Scudéri and the goldsmith Cardillac. Cardillac is the egocentric and obsessive creator, as if possessed by a devil. He is unable to detach himself from his creations and does not shy away from murder in order to retrieve them. Mademoiselle de Scudéri, on the other hand, is an especially virtuous person and a responsible poet who is appalled by the consequences of the light verses that she somewhat carelessly released and which are now being read as an incentive to murder. Her poetic talent to see what lies in the hearts of people enables her to recognise Brusson's innocence and take his side. Although both artists, Cardillac and the Mademoiselle, are distanced from any hierarchical authority, de Scudéri is not a criminal like Cardillac who breaches the basic norms of coexistence in society, but she rather uses her reputation as a poet and her connections to the court and the sovereign to save the victims, Madelon and Brusson.

As a poet, Mademoiselle de Scudéri is doubly talented in that she can see the inner, visionary shows of imagination, and also has keen observational skills which, together with her power of imagination and abilities of deduction, enable her to see through social interrelationships and into the human character. Hoffmann particularly emphasised this skill of seeing in his later short story 'My Cousin's Corner Window'. The first requirement of a writer must be that he has an eye that actually does observe. At the same time, Hoffmann is aware of the fact that such observation is fictional and possibly flawed when he has the sceptical first-person narrator say ironically to the cousin, the writer, that he must believe everything his cousin has deduced because of his vivid depiction, even though not a word may be true. Whether what was deduced from observation corresponded to what really happened always remains uncertain to Hoffmann the Romanticist, whereas with Poe and Doyle, the 'modern' crime writers, the striking resolution of a case based on the detective's observation and deduction is presented as being infallibly true.

The constellation showing that both the detective and the criminal are of artistic nature can also be found in Poe's 'The Purloined Letter'. The combination of both assets, the rational mind and imagination, is characteristic of the later master detective Dupin, who not only draws everyday logical conclusions, but also – in his first case – cultivates the fantastical idea that an ape could have killed the two victims in the Rue Morgue. Creative imagination, not just his keen intellect, elevates the master detective above the common police investigator.

Mademoiselle de Scudéri, however, is no such detective. Despite the investigation of a mysterious murder and the systematically hidden clues, Hoffmann's story is not a crime or detective story in the modern sense of the word, simply because the narrative manipulates both events and the reader with the help of well-placed effects, thus providing him with no opportunity to logically reconstruct and follow the chain of events and the murderer's discovery during the course of the action. It is not just the crime story, but also the detective who differs from the romanticist conception of reality. While a German romanticist senses a delightful or terrifying secret behind anything that deviates from the norm, the later detective, through keen observation, sees any deviation as something suspicious. Anything presented to the detective as a miracle is investigated distrustfully and critically analysed from a distance until he comes to a rational conclusion. For the creation of Edgar Allan Poe's modern crime and detective story, it was necessary for elements taken from the Enlightenment *and* Romanticism *and* empirical science to come together.

Before we come to Poe, let us make a brief detour to look at Thomas De Quincey's essay 'On Murder, Considered as One of the Fine Arts'. The first main section of this text, published in 1827, is concealed in the style of a lecture on philosophy and aesthetics. Therefore, it is not a fictional narrative. So what does it have to do with the emergence of the crime story? Symons briefly mentions De Quincey's essay and Knight discusses it at length. What points towards the modern crime and detective story is the particular view of the crime, the murder. 'People begin to see,' De Quincey writes, 'that something more goes to the composition of a fine murder than two blockheads to kill and be killed – a knife – a purse – and a dark lane. Design, gentlemen, grouping, light and shade, poetry, sentiment, are now deemed indispensable to attempts of this nature.' It is indeed true that the crimes portrayed in the stories examined so far were comparatively simple. Only perhaps in Hoffmann's *Mademoiselle de Scudéri* do we find a certain degree of artistry in the deadly stab into the victim's heart. The simplicity of the type of murder does not harm the narrative, since its main interest does not lie in the deed's cleverness, but in the fate of the characters involved. All precursors of crime literature are stories of fate. Who or what guides the fate of an individual? What does fate have in store for them? Is it a just fate? These are the questions that concern writers and readers alike. De Quincey shifts our attention to the fascination of a cold-blooded and cunningly committed crime that seems even more mysterious for this very reason. 'In the grand feature of *mystery*, which in some shape or other ought to colour every judicious attempt at murder, it is excellent [the murder of Sir Edmondbury Godfrey – author's note]; for the mystery is not yet dispersed.' If a murder has been thought through cleverly, thus posing a mystery, it requires a cunning person to reconstruct the crime and reveal the perpetrator. The master detective is the person to uncover the secret. It is no coincidence that detective stories were also called mystery stories. De Quincey, however, did not take this step towards the detective: he upholds the romanticist fascination for the emotion, be it fear or horror, and for the sublime (here, the crime), referring to Kant's idea of the sublime. In his essay, he explicitly emphasises that he has 'traced the connection between philosophy and our art'. He also gives attention to attempted assassinations of philosophers and occasionally refers to classical philosophical texts. This is evidence enough that philosophy was also a source of inspiration for De Quincey in this manner of addressing crime.

Now let us finally come to Edgar Allan Poe, who perfected the narrative model of modern crime and detective stories. Even in his lifetime, the poet and literary critic James Russell Lowell honoured Poe as the most philosophically profound literary critic ever produced by America, in *Graham's Magazine* in 1845. Even though his foster father forced Poe to end his studies at the University of Virginia after just eight months, he managed to gain extensive philosophical knowledge. He repeatedly returns to philosophers and their writings in his own essays and stories. Poe was not only familiar with the philosophers of antiquity and those writing in English; he also knew French writers such as Rousseau, Fourier and Comte and German intellectuals such as Leibniz, Kant, Herder, Fichte, the Schlegel brothers, Novalis, Schelling, Hegel, Alexander von Humboldt (cf. 'Eureka' and 'Morella'). He also refers to philosophers in his three detective stories with master detective C. Auguste Dupin and raises philosophical questions. In 'The Murders in the Rue Morgue' from 1841 Poe mentions Epicurus and ends his story with a quote by Rousseau; in 'The Mystery of Marie Roget' in 1842 he chooses a maxim from the German Romanticist Novalis' moral philosophy; furthermore, 'The Purloined Letter' from 1845 begins with a line from the Roman philosopher Seneca. Poe obviously loved the word 'philosophy', which appears repeatedly in his work. He not only formulated a 'Philosophy of Composition' (1846), but also a 'Philosophy of Furniture' (1840), although in German translations the word 'philosophy' is often replaced by 'theory' or 'art'. By referring to philosophy Poe not only intends to show off his knowledge or to use philosophy as decorative padding for his writing. Rather, it also shapes his way of thinking in approaching the investigation of a crime or mystery in detective stories, which he calls 'tales of ratiocination'. How serious Poe was about the philosophical and scientific content of these 'tales of ratiocination' is demonstrated by a footnote he added to his highly respected natural philosophical essay 'Eureka', referring to 'The Murders in the Rue Morgue'.

So what are Poe's philosophical thoughts in his detective stories? The first story contains thoughts regarding analytical thinking, which requires acumen that may appear to some to be unnatural. It requires method and intuition. The analyst is able to put himself into his opponent's position in a game of draughts or whist, forcing both minds to battle one another. Resources needed for this intellectual endeavour 'lie frequently among recesses of thought altogether inaccessible to the ordinary understanding'. Based on observations and memories, conclusions are drawn. Poe also speaks of 'deductions' and warns against equating analytical powers with resourceful sense, which construes and deduces: 'Between ingenuity and the analytic ability there exists a difference far greater, indeed, than that between the fancy and the imagination, but of a character very strictly analogous. It will be found, in fact, that the ingenious are always fanciful, and the *truly* imaginative never otherwise than analytic.' In this vein, the hero of the story, Monsieur C. Auguste Dupin, is introduced and 'the wild fervor, and the vivid freshness of his imagination' is emphasised. The narrator describes that Dupin possessed such 'peculiar analytical ability [...] that most men, in respect to himself, wore windows in their bosoms'. Moreover, Dupin's dissecting ability is paired with a creative ability; the narrator speaks of the 'old philosophy of the Bi-Part-Soul'. To prove this, a situation is portrayed in which Dupin reproduces the (unspoken) thoughts of the narrator by means of precise observation and the resulting conclusions. Further proof of Dupin's extraordinary intellectual abilities is the resolution of the Rue Morgue murder mystery. The police of Paris are clueless, which does not surprise Dupin. To him, all Parisian policemen are 'cunning, but no more'. He also refers disapprovingly to Vidocq: '...without educated thought, he erred continually by the very intensity of his investigations. He impaired his vision by holding the object too close. He might see, perhaps, one or two points with unusual clearness, but in so doing he, necessarily, lost sight of the matter as a whole. Thus there is such a thing as being too profound. Truth is not always in a well. In fact, as regards the more important knowledge, I do believe that she is invariably superficial. The depth lies in the valleys where we seek her, and not upon the mountain-tops where she is found... By undue profundity we perplex and enfeeble thought; and it is possible to make even Venus herself vanish from the firmament by a scrutiny too sustained, too concentrated, or too direct.' The murders in the Rue Morgue display all signs of the extraordinary. Murder is committed in a locked room in which the culprit cannot be found. One of the bodies has been pushed head-first into the fireplace with sheer inhuman strength. One of the voices heard by the witnesses – apparently that of the murderer – cannot be attributed to any known group of languages, and there are further confusing details. Dupin expressly insists that he excludes the supernatural: 'Madame and Mademoiselle L'Espanaye were not destroyed by spirits. The doers of the deed were material, and escaped materially.' The special circumstances surrounding the case and the deliberations involved have paralysed the authorities '...by putting completely at fault the boasted *acumen*, of the government agents. They have fallen into the gross but common error of confounding the unusual with the abstruse. But it is by these deviations from the plane of the ordinary, that reason feels its way, if at all, in its search for the true. In investigations such as we are now pursuing, it should not be much asked "what has occurred," as "what has occurred that has never occurred before." In fact, the facility with which I shall arrive, or have arrived, at the solution of this mystery, is in the direct ratio of its apparent insolubility in the eyes of the police.' At another point, Dupin continues, 'The impossibility of egress, by means already stated, being thus absolute, we are reduced to the windows. Through those of the front room no one could have escaped without notice from the crowd in the street. The murderers *must* have passed, then, through those of the back room. Now, brought to this conclusion in so unequivocal a manner as we are, it is not our part, as reasoners, to reject it on account of apparent impossibilities. It is only left for us to prove that these apparent "impossibilities" are, in reality, not such.' Dupin refers to his thoughts about the sound of the voice that was heard, whose language could not be identified by a number of speakers of other languages, as 'legitimate deductions'. They lead him to suspect that he is dealing not with a person, but rather with an animal – an ape, to be precise. After examining the windows through which the murderer(s) must have escaped, Dupin speaks of 'inductions' that have brought him to the end of the mystery: a broken nail that is stuck in the window. The detective warns against being misled by anything that may seem coincidental in the case: 'Coincidences ten times as remarkable as this (the delivery of the money, and murder committed within three days upon the party receiving it), happen to all of us every hour of our lives, without attracting even momentary notice. Coincidences, in general, are great stumbling blocks in the way of that class of thinkers who have been educated to know nothing of the theory of probabilities – that theory to which the most glorious objects of human research are indebted for the most glorious of illustration.'

After Dupin presents the narrator with all the observed and ordered facts, he asks, 'What result, then, has ensued? What impression have I made upon your fancy?' The narrator fails to come to the conclusion that an ape might be the murderer. Based on an experiment with a drawing of fingerprints taken from the victim's throat, which is then wrapped around a throat-sized piece of wood, Dupin convinces the narrator that a human cannot have committed the murder and that only a large animal comes into question. The legitimate and logical conclusion, be it deductive or inductive, which is not explained literally or formally in the story, must be as follows: every person has certain traits such as a certain finger size and a particular way of speaking. The creature that killed the two women has neither of these. As a result, it is not human. Since only humans and animals can be the killer, and not spirits, it must be an animal. The strangle marks on the throat of one of the victims are too large to come from a human hand, so it must be an animal with large fingers. Apes have such large fingers and therefore it is highly likely that an ape, such as an orang-utan, is the perpetrator. Dupin further concludes that the murderer(s) must have escaped through the windows of one particular room, so as not to be seen by the crowd of witnesses present. At first appearance, all windows were firmly locked from the inside. This appearance must be deceptive. At least one of the windows must have been able to have been closed from the outside. Dupin first examines a window, but finds no way to close it from outside. Consequently, it must be the other window through which the murderer(s) escaped. Dupin confirms his assumption when he finds the broken nail. Still, Dupin refuses to let the matter rest on his observations and the conclusions drawn. To prove the result, he conducts an experiment by placing an ad in the papers, saying that the owner of an escaped and now captured orang-utan could come and collect it from him. Dupin's prediction that the owner would come forward, thereby confirming his assumptions regarding the murder, proves to be correct. The case is solved thanks to rational deductions based on precise observation and the police release an innocent suspect. But this fact, or whether the ape's owner is held responsible, is no longer of importance to Dupin. 'My ultimate object,' he says, 'is only the truth.'

The search for truth is one of philosophy's aims, which is also true of each science, including that of criminology, which was still in its infancy. Logic is an integral part of philosophy and of scientific reasoning. One objection to the thesis that the detective story developed from the spirit of philosophy, especially in the case of Poe, might be that these are scientific methods which have nothing to do with philosophy. In his professorial dissertation 'Le 'Detective Novel' et l'Influence de la Pensée Scientifique' from 1929, Regis Messac claimed that a rounded detective story is unimaginable without the 'esprit scientifique' of positivistic scientific reasoning. But where is the spirit of philosophy in this?

We can answer the question as follows: then as well as now, there is indeed the common belief that philosophy can be treated strictly as a science. Furthermore, in the first half of the nineteenth century, individual scientific disciplines were not quite distinguished from each other and had not yet separated from philosophy so as to be clearly different and apart from it. Most of all, however, Poe himself viewed the reasoning he depicted in his detective novels as an element of philosophy. This becomes especially clear in 'The Mystery of Marie Roget'. At one point in his argumentation, Dupin considers it *particularly unphilosophical* to attempt to refute a general claim regarding the likelihood that a corpse will resurface in the water after a certain time with special, contradicting cases. The number of examples to the contrary is too small to justify a different rule. A short time later, Dupin mentions that he and the narrator now have before them 'the whole philosophy of this subject'.

In Poe's second detective story, similar lines of thought that we have come to know from the first are picked up again. Looking back at the solution of the Rue Morgue case, only inductions are now spoken of, while deductions are suppressed, perhaps so as to emphasise the greatest possible proximity to scientific methods. Yet at first Dupin does not consider the facts when reflecting on his second case. Instead, he focuses his attention on assumptions found in the press, which he eyes critically. Furthermore, Dupin goes against the common line of argument used in the justice system: in producing evidence, courts rely too heavily upon generally accepted principles and do not accommodate the particularity of the case, so that in individual cases 'vast individual error' may result. Poe quotes Landor in a footnote: 'Thus the jurisprudence... will show that, when law becomes a science and a system, it ceases to be justice. The errors into which a blind devotion to *principles* of classification has led the common law, will be seen by observing how often the legislature has been obliged to come forward to restore the equity its scheme had lost'. Criticism of the judicial quest for truth is intensified in a later passage: 'It is the malpractice of the courts to confine evidence and discussion to the bounds of apparent relevancy. Yet experience has shown, and a true philosophy will always show, that a vast, perhaps the larger, portion of truth arises from the seemingly irrelevant. It is through the spirit of this principle, if not precisely through its letter, that modern science has resolved to *calculate upon the unforeseen*... The history of human knowledge has so uninterruptedly shown that to collateral, or incidental, or accidental events we are indebted for the most numerous and most valuable discoveries, that it has at length become necessary, in prospective view of improvement, to make not only large, but the largest, allowances for inventions that shall arise by chance, and quite out of the range of ordinary expectation. It is no longer philosophical to base upon what has been a vision of what is to be. *Accident* is admitted as a portion of the substructure. We make chance a matter of absolute calculation. We subject the unlooked for and unimagined to the mathematical *formulae* of the schools.' At the end of the story, Poe returns to the consideration of the scientific-mathematical treatment of probability and coincidence, using the example of a game of dice. He points out that it is unlikely to roll a six every time in a greater number of throws. This makes sense to the philosophically and scientifically thinking person, but not to the average reader whose eye is fixed on the individual rolling of the die. Such misapprehension 'forms one of an infinite series of mistakes which arise in the path of Reason through her propensity for seeking truth *in detail*.'

It is time to summarise Poe's remarks regarding philosophy, science and the correct method of finding the truth. We have seen that he does not separate philosophy and science, or even strictly differentiate between them, since they merge into one another seamlessly. If it is a mistake to seek the truth in isolated details or, as it is written elsewhere, in the event itself instead of (also) in its surrounding circumstances, then this means that attention must be focused on lawful connections and relationships. Such connections, however, should not be wild guesses or presumptions, but must instead be based on keen observation and hard facts. In the process it is important also to notice coincidences and seemingly negligible things, and take them seriously. Nonetheless, we would be misunderstanding Dupin and Poe if we attempted to base a hypothesis or theory on a single minor point alone. The greater context, the big picture, should not be forgotten. The causes of events of various kinds must be found on the surface of reality. There are no hidden, mysterious beings or powers, be they God, a demon or a spirit (as defined by Hegel), that influence our everyday reality. In the final passage of his story, Poe makes explicit mention of this: 'In my own heart there dwells no faith in praeternature. That Nature and its God are two, no man who thinks will deny. That the latter, creating the former, can, at will, control or modify it, is also unquestionable. I say "at will"; for the question is of will, and not, as the insanity of logic has assumed, of power. It is not that the Deity *cannot* modify his laws, but that we insult him in imagining a possible necessity for modification. In their origin these laws were fashioned to embrace *all* contingencies which *could* lie in the Future. With God all is *Now.*' Ultimately, therefore, the unhappy fate of the murdered Marie Roget is predetermined by God's will.

Even though Poe refers to God as the final cause, He has no further part in the lives of individuals in the sense that God allows nature to take its course. An individual's close relationship with his God, whose commandments he follows and to whom he prays, especially in times of need, seems pointless. Similar thoughts to the ones quoted above are found in the essay 'Eureka'. As far as the nature of God and His perceptibility are concerned, Poe stipulates that, 'Of this Godhead, in itself, he alone is not imbecile, he alone is not impious who propounds – nothing… We know absolutely nothing of the nature or essence of God: in order to comprehend what He is, we should have to be God ourselves.' Poe, therefore, does not believe in a divine revelation before man. Still, he somewhat modifies his strictly agnostic position later. Poe tentatively assumes that God is spirit rather than matter, which has created the universe, nature and all its laws in an original act of volition. Hence it is silly to assume that God would interfere with His own laws and correct worldly events: 'That Nature and the God of Nature are distinct, no thinking being can long doubt. By the former we imply merely the laws of the latter.' Poe's understanding of the obduracy of the laws of nature justifies observing these laws of nature when uncovering mysteries and solving crimes. The tools required for this, apart from keen observation, are deductive and inductive logic and, most of all, imagination, intuitively guessing which laws are involved. Poe ridicules John Stuart Mill and philosophers and scientists of his kind who regard only deductive and inductive methods as scientifically viable. He refers to such approaches as 'creeping' and 'crawling'. Unlike them, Poe takes it for a fact that true science, 'makes its most important advances, as all history will show, by seemingly intuitive leaps.' His prime example is Kepler, who originally simply guessed – or, as Poe called it, imagined – the laws he discovered. Poe's praise for the capabilities of scientific imagination and the derision for the stubborn reasoning that relies on deduction and induction not only stem from a romanticist understanding of philosophy and science, but are also precursors of Charles S. Peirce's theory of abduction and Paul Feyerabend's critique of the scientific method. In Auguste Dupin, Poe created a keen thinker who not only possesses the ability to analyse but also a talent for imagination. In this context, Boileau-Narcejac says that the wonderful still reigns, but that a miracle of logic emerges, replacing divinatory intuition with a rational approach in a playful and naïve manner.

This is made particularly clear in Poe's third detective story 'The Purloined Letter'. Minister D, a clever schemer, steals a letter from a high-ranking person, and uses it to blackmail her constantly. The Parisian police have been unable to find the letter despite a thorough search of the minister's offices and his own person. In his despair, the police prefect turns to Dupin who, right from the start, surprises him with his assumption: 'Perhaps it is the very simplicity of the thing which puts you at fault... Perhaps the mystery is a little *too* plain.' Dupin is particularly intrigued by the case because the minister is both a mathematician and poet and therefore an analyst, which makes him a worthy opponent. At the beginning of the first detective story, Poe defines the capability of an analyst as being able to put himself in someone else's shoes, identify with him, see through him, even mislead him. Now Dupin has the perfect opportunity. His friend, the narrator, assumes that the intellectual identification with the opponent depends on the precision with which the opponent's intellect is assessed. 'For its practical value it depends on this,' Dupin confirms. In view of the minister's superior intellect and the general comprehension of the police, he assumes that the letter must be placed somewhere where it is visible to everyone without anyone suspecting it to be the purloined letter. Except for Dupin, that is, who discovers the letter in the minister's easily accessible card rack. Philosophical and scientific considerations regarding mathematical axioms and ethics only play a minor part in the story and are not an integral aspect of the investigation or the plot.

If we examine Poe's remarks about the method of detection in his first two detective stories, we are reminded of Auguste Comte's positivistic method. In 'Eureka', Poe agrees with 'philosopher Comte' and we assume that Poe is referring to the second volume of *Cours de philosophie positive* (Paris 1830–42), entitled *Philosophie astronomique et philosophie de la physique*. It might also be the case that Poe knew of Comte's positivistic philosophy from a secondary source instead of the original.

In 'Eureka', Poe is disparaging of John Stuart Mill's *A System of Logic, Ratiocinative and Inductive* (1843). Mill was an early supporter of Comte and propagator of his ideas. Comte greeted his book on logic with the words that one could inform oneself to great advantage about the general appreciation of the spirit and the development of the positive method in the work of his friend John Stuart Mill. Incidentally, Alexander von Humboldt, whom Poe admired so much that he dedicated 'Eureka' to him, had also attended Comte's lectures. Comte began delivering his lectures to a select audience in 1826. These were later published in the aforementioned six volumes beginning 1830. When Poe wrote his detective stories, therefore, he may well have been familiar with Comte's ideas.

So what do Comte's philosophy and Poe's ideas have in common and what differentiates them? Comte famously claimed that the human intellect develops in three stages. At its beginning is the theological or fictitious stage that is then replaced, for the most part, by the metaphysical or abstract stage; this in turn is followed by the positive or real stage in which the human intellect finally prevails. During the first stage, the causes of different events are sought primarily in God or the gods; the human mind demands absolute knowledge, which is still the case during the metaphysical stage. Metaphysics attempts to explain the innermost nature, origin and purpose of all things. During the positive stage, the human mind does away with absolute analysis and restricts itself from this point on to the rapidly developing area of true observation instead. Whereas before a more or less indiscriminate speculative imagination dominated the early stages, positive philosophy subordinates imagination to observation. This by no means implies the relinquishing of imagination. On the contrary, the positive method of imagination offers a wide and fertile area, especially for the discovery and perfection of connections between observed facts. Yet Comte does not quite do justice to his positive scientific method when he speaks of the subordination of imagination to observation. Observed facts alone lead only to a random collection of facts that shows no definitive connection between isolated events. And yet it is precisely the determination of clear rules that is important to Comte. He requires the power of imagination in order to see the connections or at least to assume them to begin with, connections that determine what and how something must be observed. For Comte, the ultimate scientific test is whether predictions come true when based on observation and discovered laws. Although he developed a scientific method according to his own understanding, he still considers philosophy necessary and claims that all science ends in a philosophy. Comte is attracted by the ordinary, the general. Ideally, he would have one single law that explains every move and every circumstance in the world, including the social field.

Dupin's scientific approach in the first two stories complies mainly with Comte's ideas. In his analyses he allows himself to be guided by his observations. The connections he imagines or deduces are confirmed with the help of established fact, experiments and natural laws. The prediction that the owner of the escaped orang-utan would contact him on reading his ad in the papers comes true. Dupin claims the right to proceed both philosophically and scientifically. So far, there is great similarity between Comte and Dupin. In the third story, however, Dupin's imagination comes increasingly to the fore, and hardly any methodical investigation takes place. The later essay 'Eureka' makes clear that Poe, unlike Comte, has not moved away from metaphysics and has therefore not become a follower of pure positivism.

Although Poe's detective stories are influenced by the spirit of philosophy, a very pragmatic rationality clearly prevails. Philosophical questions become questions of criminal science as long as they are not casual reflections, but are instead important for the plot and the closing of a case. While the crime fiction of Godwin and even Hoffmann contains questions that are central to the story such as 'What is justice?' and 'How can justice be made victorious?' they are missing in Poe's own detective stories. Despite Dupin's distance from the police, it seems only natural to help them along the way, even if only 'for the purpose of justice' as implied casually at one point in the second story. Implicitly, a civic legal system is presumed in which all citizens have a fundamental right to be protected from criminals by the police and the judiciary, and judicial authority is not just reserved for the ruling classes. Dupin does not address the legality or expound the problems of existing national institutions. On closer observation, even his search for truth springs from an intellectual pleasure in solving a mystery rather than any noble demand for truth. It is a purposeless game of his autonomous reasoning. In this respect, Dupin is a worthy precursor of Sherlock Holmes, who only plays the game for the game's sake. On 16 July 1857, the brothers Goncourt noted in their diary that they had discovered a new literary world when reading Poe's detective stories. According to them, it was a sign of the literature of the coming twentieth century, in which deductions take the place of love at the core of the novel's plot, and the story's interest shifts from the heart to the mind, from the drama itself to its resolution.

But the traces of philosophy in crime literature reach back even further than to the Enlightenment. In fact, they reach back to the early beginnings of Greek philosophy. If we follow Giorgio Colli's studies in *The Birth of Philosophy* (1975), the challenge of the riddle stood at the very beginning of philosophy. In early Greek culture posing a riddle contained 'a terrifying potential for animosity' and involved a fight to the death. This is particularly evident in the riddle given by the Sphinx to Oedipus. Had he failed to solve it, death would have been certain, but the fact that he solves it condemns the Sphinx to the abyss. Homer also subjected himself to an ultimately deadly contest with young fishermen whom he asked on the beach if they had anything with them. Their mysterious reply was that what they caught, they had left behind, and what they did not catch, they carried with them. Their riddle referred to the fact that they had caught no fish, but instead their own lice, some of which they had killed and left behind, while the ones they did not catch were still with them in their clothes. Unable to solve this riddle, Homer died in a depressed state, as Aristotle reports. In the agonism between the one posing the riddle and the one who accepts and tries to solve it, the dialectic develops in the course of history as a question-and-answer game between two people as to who has the greater intellectual capacity. Arguments are made with the help of deductions that will corner the opponent, weaken his thesis and prove one's own. It is therefore again a contest, though one in which the aim is to destroy not the opponent, but his thesis.

Let us return to the detective story. Here, too, a riddle forms the focus of a contest, a battle between the detective and the criminal who has created the riddle. The detective attempts to corner the perpetrator by means of relentless questioning and conclusions drawn from answers and observations, until the detective has destroyed his supposed innocence and secured a death penalty, at least in older crime stories. Even the one who solves the mystery often exposes himself to danger since he may be killed by the murderer he is tracking. According to Boileau-Narcejac, the oracle that must be solved is 'the archaic form of the detective novel'. The philosophical themes of the 'search for truth', the 'search for justice', 'evil', and 'death' form a self-contained narrative model of the riddle or mystery. At the beginning of a narrative we find death in the form of a mysterious murder. The detective searches for the truth about the deed and the murderer – in other words, about evil. He secures justice by handing over the murderer to his executioner and thereby removing evil from the world.

The ratiocination of Poe's crime stories, which serves to create calculated suspense in the reader, still carries traces of its philosophical origins, but no longer aims at philosophical insight. In his very brief introduction to philosophy, Thomas Nagel writes that this is characterised by a specific question: while a historian asks what happened at a certain time in the past, the philosopher asks, what is time? So let us turn to the philosophical issues that Nagel considers characteristic. He asks, how do we know anything (of the world outside our own consciousness)? The detective asks, how do I get the information I need to solve the case? Nagel asks, how much do we really know about what is happening in someone else's consciousness? The detective asks, how do I see through a suspect? How do I know if a witness is lying? The philosopher asks, what is the relationship between consciousness and the brain? The detective asks, what makes someone commit a crime? What is his motive? Nagel asks, how can a word – a sound or a series of squiggles on paper – *mean* anything? The detective asks, how are certain words to be interpreted, for instance, in the case of codes, the final words of a murder victim or evidence given by a witness? The philosopher asks, is there such a thing as free will? The detective asks, was the murderer sane when he committed the crime or is he subject to an underlying pathological compulsion? The philosopher asks, what is right, what is wrong? The detective asks, which rights have been violated? How can the criminal be proved guilty? The philosopher asks, what is justice? The detective asks, how can justice be made victorious? How can the criminal be punished justly? Nagel asks, what is the nature of death? What does death mean to us as humans? The detective asks, how did a person come to his or her death? What was the sequence of events? The philosopher asks, what is the meaning of life? The detective asks, what remains for me after the case has been solved?

Admittedly, the questions in Poe's detective stories have not yet shifted completely towards pragmatic criminalistic reasoning; the stories have not quite emerged from the eggshell of philosophy, so to speak. In addition, they left traces – unexpected at the time of their origin – in the writings of many philosophers of the twentieth century. Lacan, the philosopher amongst psychoanalysts, Derrida, Deleuze, Cavell, Žižek, to name only a few, all refer to his story of the purloined letter. Despite their philosophical inspiration, Poe's detective stories are situated at the turning point towards a new rationality of the crime and detective story which is

65

constructed without references to philosophy. This does not necessarily mean that no philosophically minded crime writer ever incorporates philosophical ideas in his fiction, but the narrative model is not reliant upon them and can entirely do without philosophy. From an abstract point of view, however, something that the detective story and philosophy do have in common is a certain approach: philosophers and detectives alike draw conclusions about essential, invisible contexts from sensorially perceptible appearances and visible things. Both therefore refer back to the tradition of differentiating between appearance and reality.

How closely the investigative was connected with philosophy in the early stages of criminology becomes evident in a certain detail from the early history of Scotland Yard. Inspector Williamson, assistant to the legendary Jonathan Whicher and himself superintendent of the detective branch after 1869, was known by the nickname 'the philosopher'.

References and Further reading:

Fiction
Godwin, William: *Caleb Williams*, Oxford/New York 1982
Hoffmann, E. T. A.: *Des Vetters Eckfenster*, Stuttgart, 1980
Hoffmann, E. T. A.: *Der Sandmann*, Frankfurt am Main, Leipzig 1986
Hoffmann, E. T. A.: *Das Fräulein von Scudéri*, Stuttgart 2002 (English edition: Hoffmann, E. T. A.: *Mademoiselle de Scudéri*, London 2002)
Poe, Edgar Allan: *The Complete Tales and Poems of Edgar Allan Poe*, New York 1965
Poe, Edgar Allan: *Selected Writings: Poems, Tales, Essays and Reviews*, ed. by David Galloway, 4th edition. Harmondsworth 1974
Schiller, Friedrich von: *Werke in drei Bänden*, Vol. I, Herbert G. Göpfert (ed.), Munich 1966
Schiller, Friedrich von: *The Ghost-Seer*, London 2003
Schiller, Friedrich von: *Pitaval. Merkwürdige Rechtsfälle*, Munich, undated.
Voltaire: *Candide oder Der Optimismus*, in: *Sämtliche Romane und Erzählungen*, Frankfurt am Main/Leipzig 1976, 283–390 (English edition: Voltaire: Candide, ou l' Optimisme (1759), translated by Tobias Smollett, http: //en.wikisource.org/wiki/Candide)
Voltaire: *Die Welt, wie sie ist*, in: *Sämtliche Romane und Erzählungen*, Frankfurt am Main/Leipzig 1976, 213–231 (French edition: Voltaire: Le Monde Comme Il Va, Vision De Babouc, http://www.gutenberg.

org/e books/5138)

Voltaire: *Zadig oder das Schicksal*, in: *Sämtliche Romane und Erzählungen*, Frankfurt am Main/Leipzig 1976, 127–211 (English edition: Voltaire: *Zadig, or, The Book of Fate*, London 1749)

Philosophical, literary theory and essays

Alewyn, Richard: 'The Origin of the Detective Novel', in: Glenn W. Most/William W. Stowe (ed.): *The Poetics of Murder. Detective Fiction and Literary Theory*, San Diego/New York/London 1983, 62–78

Alt, Peter-André: *Schiller: Leben – Werk – Zeit*, Vol. 1, Munich 2000

Ayer, Alfred J.: *Voltaire. Eine intellektuelle Biographie*, Frankfurt am Main 1987 (English edition: Ayer: Alfred J.: *Voltaire*, London 1986)

Beccaria, Cesare: *Über Verbrechen und Strafen*, Frankfurt am Main/Leipzig 1998

Berlin, Isaiah: 'Die Apotheose des romantischen Willens: Die Revolte gegen den Mythos einer idealen Welt', in: *Das krumme Holz der Humanität*, 2nd edition. Frankfurt am Main 1992, 260–296 (English edition: Berlin, Isaiah: *The Crooked Timber of Humanity*, London 1990)

Berlin, Isaiah: *The Roots of Romanticism*, Berkeley 1999

Bitter, Rudolf von: Afterword, in: Voltaire, *Philosophische Briefe*, edited by Rudolf von Bitter, Frankfurt am Main/Berlin/Vienna 1985, 140–149

Bloch, Ernst: 'Utopische Funktion im Materialismus', in: *Tendenz – Latenz – Utopie*, Frankfurt am Main 1985, 265–285

Boileau-Narcejac: *Der Detektivroman*, Neuwied/Berlin 1964 (French edition: Boileau-Narcejac: *Le Roman policier*, Paris 1964)

Brown, Andrew: Introduction, in: E. T. A. Hoffmann: *Mademoiselle de Scudéri*, London 2002, xi-xviii

Brown, Andrew: Introduction, in: Friedrich von Schiller: *The Ghost-Seer*, London 2003, xi-xvii

Colli, Giorgio: *Die Geburt der Philosophie*, Frankfurt am Main 1975

Comte, Auguste: *Rede über den Geist des Positivismus*, 2nd edition. Hamburg 1966

Comte, Auguste: *Die Soziologie. Die positive Philosophie im Auszug*, edited by Friedrich Blaschke, 2nd edition. Stuttgart, 1974

Danto, Arthur C.: *Wege zur Welt. Grundbegriffe der Philosophie*, Munich 1999 (English edition: Danto, Arthur C.: *Connections to the World – The Basic Concepts of Philosophy*, New York 1989)

De Quincey, Thomas: 'On Murder, Considered as One of the Fine Arts', in: Thomas De Quincey: *The English Mail-Coach and Other Essays*, London/New York 1933, 47–133

Dittberner, Hugo: 'Das höhere Sein. Über E. T. A. Hoffmann', in: *E. T. A. Hoffmann*, edited by Heinz Ludwig Arnold, *edition text + kritik*, Munich 1992, 5–19

Drux, Rudolf (ed.): *Erläuterungen und Dokumente E. T. A. Hoffmann Der Sandmann*, Stuttgart 2003

Feldges, Brigitte/ Stadler, Ulrich: *E. T. A. Hoffmann: Epoche – Werk – Wirkung*, Munich 1986

Foucault, Michel: *Überwachen und Strafen. Die Geburt des Gefängnisses*, 3rd edition. Frankfurt am Main 1979 (English edition: Foucault, Michel: *Discipline and Punish*, London 1977)

Fühmann, Franz: *Fräulein Veronika Paulmann aus der Pirnaer Vorstadt oder Etwas über das Schauerliche bei E. T. A. Hoffmann*, Munich 1984

Gerber, Richard: 'Verbrechensdichtung und Kriminalroman', in: Jochen Vogt (ed.), *Der Kriminalroman II*, Munich 1971, 404–420

Godwin, William: *Enquiry concerning Political Justice and its influence on Morals and Happiness*, edited by F. E. L. Priestley, Vol. I, II; University of Toronto Press, 1969, 1970

Gröble, Susanne: *Literaturwissen, E. T. A. Hoffmann*, Stuttgart 2000

Groethuysen, Bernhard: *Philosophie der Französischen Revolution*, Frankfurt am Main/New York, 1989

Hofmann, Michael: *Schiller: Epoche – Werk – Wirkung*, Munich 2003

Huch, Ricarda: *Die Romantik*, Tübingen 1951

Jonas, Friedrich: *Geschichte der Soziologie 1. Mit Quellentexen*, 2nd edition. Opladen 1981

Kant, Immanuel: *Träume eines Geistersehers, erläutert durch Träume der Metaphysik*, Stuttgart 1976 (English title: Kant, Immanuel: *Dreams of a Spirit-seer, elucidated by Dreams of Metaphysics*)

Kanzog, Klaus: "Das Fräulein von Scudéri' als Kriminalgeschichte', in: Helmut Prang (ed.), *E. T. A. Hoffmann*, Darmstadt 1976, 307–321

Kempski, Jürgen von: Einleitung, in: Comte, Auguste: *Die Soziologie. Die positive Philosophie im Auszug*, edited by Friedrich Blaschke, 2nd edition. Stuttgart, 1974, IX-XXXVII

Kerlen, Dietrich: *Edgar Allan Poe. Elixiere der Moderne*, Munich 1988

Kerlen, Dietrich: *Edgar Allan Poe. Der schwarze Duft der Schwermut*, Berlin 1999

Klemperer, Victor: 'Voltaire und seine kleinen Romane', in: Voltaire:

Sämtliche Romane und Erzählungen, Frankfurt am Main/Leipzig 1976, 9–38

Knight, Stephen: *Crime Fiction 1800 – 2000: Detection, Death, Diversity*, Houndmills, Basingstoke/New York 2004

Kuczynski, Ingrid u. Peter: Afterword, in: William Godwin, *Caleb Williams oder Die Dinge wie sie sind*, 2nd edition. Leipzig 1985, 403–413

Lepenies, Wolf: *Die drei Kulturen. Soziologie zwischen Literatur und Wissenschaft*, Reinbek bei Hamburg 1988

Lindken, Hans Ulrich (ed.): *Erläuterungen und Dokumente – E. T. A. Hoffmann Das Fräulein von Scudéri*, Stuttgart 2001

Marsch, Edgar: *Die Kriminalerzählung*, 2nd edition. Munich 1983

McCracken, David: Introduction, in: William Godwin, *Caleb Williams*, Oxford/New York 1982, vii-xxii

Nagel, Thomas: *What Does It All Mean? A Very Short Introduction to Philosophy*, New York/Oxford 1987

Neiman, Susan: *Das Böse denken. Eine andere Geschichte der Philosophie*, Frankfurt am Main. 2004 (English edition: Neiman, Susan: *Evil in Modern Thought*, Princeton 2002)

Poe, Edgar Allan: *Brief an B. Essays*, 2nd edition. Leipzig 1992

Poe, Edgar Allan: 'Zum Geleit', in: *E. A. Poe, Brief an B. Essays*, 2nd edition. Leipzig 1992, 5–11 (English edition: Poe, Edgar Allan: *Exordium*, http://www.eapoe.org/works/essays/exordm.htm)

Poe, Edgar Allan: *Eureka*, London, 2002

Safranski, Rüdiger: *E. T. A. Hoffmann*, Frankfurt am Main 1987

Schmidt, Dirk: *Der Einfluss E. T. A. Hoffmanns auf das Schaffen Edgar Allan Poes*, Marburg 1996

Skotnicki, Irene: Nachwort, in: Poe, E. A.: *Brief an B. Essays*, 2nd edition. Leipzig 1992, 196–216

Starobinski, Jean: *Aktion und Reaktion*, Frankfurt am Main. 2003

Symons, Julian: *The Tell-Tale Heart*, London 1978

Symons, Julian: *Bloody Murder. From the detective story to the crime novel: a history*, 3rd edition, London 1992

Thorwald, Jürgen: *Das Jahrhundert der Detektive Bd. I: Das Zeichen des Kain*, Munich/Zurich, 1969

Ward, Ian: 'The Abode of Moral Truth: William Godwin's 'Enquiry Concerning Political Justice'', in: *Archiv für Rechts- und Sozialphilosophie* 2003, 349–371

Wolf, Burkhardt: 'Grundzüge einer historischen Gattungsbestimmung der 'Kriminalliteratur'', in: *Die Alligatorpapiere*; *http://www. alligatorpapiere.de/spexial2gattungsbestimmung%20wolf.html*; Viewed: 9th December 2004

Important writings on the philosophical reception of Edgar Allan Poe's short story 'The Purloined Letter'
Cavell, Stanley 'The Uncanniness of the Ordinary', in: *In Quest of the Ordinary*, Chicago/London 1988/1994, 153–178
Deleuze, Gilles: 'How Do We Recognize Structuralism?', in: *Desert Islands and Other Texts 1953–1974*, New York 1972
Derrida, Jacques 'The Purveyor of Truth', in: Yale French Studies 52, 1975, 31–113
Lacan, Jacques: 'Seminar on 'The Purloined Letter', in: Glenn W. Most/William W. Stowe (ed.): *The Poetics of Murder. Detective Fiction and Literary Theory*, San Diego/New York/London 1983, 21–54
Zizek, Slavoj *Liebe Dein Symptom wie Dich selbst!*, Berlin 1991
Zizek, Slavoj *Looking Awry*, Cambridge (Mass.)/London 1991

Further writings and the texts by Lacan and Derrida can be found in the collection:
John P. Muller/William J. Richardson (eds.): *The Purloined Poe: Lacan, Derrida, and Psychoanalytical Reading*, Baltimore/London 1988

3

The Rational World of
Sherlock Holmes

Dr. Watson made the following list of Holmes' skills: 'Sherlock Holmes –
his limits. 1. Knowledge of Literature. – Nil. 2. Knowledge of Philosophy.
– Nil. 3. Knowledge of Astronomy – Nil… 7. Knowledge of Chemistry. –
Profound. 8. Knowledge of Anatomy. – Accurate, but unsystematic …'
Before he presents this list, Watson emphasises that '[o]f contemporary
literature, philosophy and politics he appeared to know next to nothing.'
Is it not therefore quite daring or even pointless to look for philosophical
content in the fictional world of Sherlock Holmes? After all, there is a
reason why the chapter including the above quotes is entitled 'The *Science*
of Deduction'. The title is repeated in the second Sherlock Holmes novel,
thus appearing to be very significant and meaningful. Holmes' cases are
not concerned with 'The Philosophy of Deduction', but with 'science'. At
the same time, it cannot be denied that deduction as a part of logic is
traditionally attributed to philosophy and goes back to Aristotle's
Organon. Moreover, Watson underestimates his friend's skills, as his
occasional comments on literature and philosophy demonstrate.

On logic in crime investigation
Holmes makes at least 217 deductions, which can be clearly identified as
such, in the sixty crime stories that form the canon. Yet, according to
Marcello Truzzi, the majority of logical conclusions presented by Holmes
and which make a great impression on his clients, on Watson and
probably on most of his readers do not fulfil the criteria of logical
deduction. Further the primary weakness lies in the fact that Holmes does
not attempt to prove empirically the hypotheses he formulates based on
his deductions, but instead takes them as proven. Only in perhaps 28 cases
is the validity of a hypothesis tested. As the term 'hypothesis' illustrates –
for instance in 'The Norwood Builder' – Holmes' conclusions do not
restrict themselves to deductions. In this respect, the general use of the
term 'deduction' is misleading.

71

Charles S. Peirce differentiates deduction from induction and abduction (hypothesis). In the case of *deduction*, we assume a 'rule' such as 'All beans in the bag are white'. A 'case' emerges: 'These beans are from this bag'. The 'result' follows that these beans are white. In contrast, *induction* begins with a case: these beans are from this bag. The result is established that these beans are white. Based on this, the rule is that all beans from the bag are white. Finally, *abduction* assumes that all beans from this bag are white. The result established is that these beans are white. What follows is the case that the beans are from the bag. Reading the Sherlock Holmes stories, we can see that he proceeds deductively as well as inductively, but primarily, he establishes hypotheses. Therefore, the title 'The Science of Deduction' is misleading.

A famous example of the way that Holmes makes deductions shows that it is not all about drawing deductive conclusions. In *The Sign of Four* we find the following dialogue between Holmes and Watson:

'For example, observation shows me that you have been to the Wigmore Street Post Office this morning, but deduction lets me know that when there you dispatched a telegram.'

'Right!' said I. 'Right on both points! But I confess that I don't see how you arrived at it. It was a sudden impulse upon my part, and I have mentioned it to no one.'

'It is simplicity itself,' he remarked, chuckling at my surprise – 'so absurdly simple that an explanation is superfluous; and yet it may serve to define the limits of observation and of deduction. Observation tells me that you have a little reddish mould adhering to your instep. Just opposite the Wigmore Street Office they have taken up the pavement and thrown up some earth, which lies in such a way that it is difficult to avoid treading in it in entering. The earth is of this peculiar reddish tint which is found, as far as I know, nowhere else in the neighbourhood. So much is observation. The rest is deduction.'

'How, then, did you deduce the telegram?'

'Why, of course I knew that you had not written a letter, since I sat opposite to you all morning. I see also in your open desk there that you have a sheet of stamps and a thick bundle of postcards. What could you go into the post office for then, but to send a wire? Eliminate all other factors, and the one which remains must be the truth.'

Holmes is making it too easy for himself. Watson could have visited the post office to buy special issue stamps or to meet with someone. The dispatch of the telegram is not really a truly deductive conclusion as such, but a hypothesis, the validity of which requires proof.

Massimo A. Bonfantini and Giampaolo Proni have reconstructed in detail Holmes' criminal investigation in *A Study in Scarlet*. They found twelve investigative phases which may be differentiated even further. Their findings with regard to the conclusion procedures used can be summarised as follows: first there is the observation, recording and combination of the information gathered, as characterised by the inductive approach. Once this has been done, Holmes develops a hypothesis with the intention of explaining or interpreting the observed facts. In this manner, the possible causes of resulting events are to be determined. Such an approach is typical of abduction. What follows is an analytical presentation of the consequences that must necessarily follow from the hypotheses that have been developed. This, then, is deduction. Finally, the hypotheses and their deduced consequences are put to the test by observation or an 'experiment' so that induction forms the final part of the investigation. The hypotheses that Holmes develops, selects and possibly even tests throughout the course of the investigation lead to the construction of a net that aims at the confirmation of the main hypothesis, which is the murderer's identification.

It is the purpose of a criminal investigation to get from a *particular event* back to its *particular cause*. Holmes calls this 'to reason backwards' in the final chapter of *A Study in Scarlet* and 'analytical reasoning from effects to causes' in the first chapter of *The Sign of Four*. He explains his approach to Watson as follows: 'In the everyday affairs of life it is more useful to reason forwards, and so the other comes to be neglected... Most people, if you describe a train of events to them, will tell you what the result would be. They can put those events together in their minds, and argue from them that something will come to pass. There are few people, however, who, if you told them a result, would be able to evolve from their own inner consciousness what the steps were which led up to that result. This power is what I mean when I talk of reasoning backwards, or analytically.' (*A Study in Scarlet*) It is surely no coincidence that this passage harks back to the title of the lecture 'Retrospective Prophecy as a Function of Science' by one of Doyle's university lecturers, Thomas Henry Huxley.

In this context and on other occasions, Holmes emphasises to Watson how simple and elementary his approach is. Holmes' abductions lack any kind of extraordinary creativity and risk. Even his analyses are simple and straightforward. He is completely aware of this as he describes his professional approach in chapter three of *A Study in Scarlet*: 'They say that genius is an infinite capacity for taking pains… It's a very bad definition, but it does apply to detective work.'

Holmes usually bases his approach on experience and uses science that relies on observation and common sense rather than the theoretical elaborations of modern physics. Holmes' investigations are dominated by the keen observation of spontaneously emerging facts: 'It is a capital mistake to theorise before one has data. Insensibly one begins to twist facts to suit theories, instead of theories to suit facts.' He warns a policeman against drawing hasty conclusions by pointing out, 'You are not quite in possession of the facts yet.'(*The Sign of Four*) Investigative work requires the same attention, overview, diligence and patience that it takes to piece together a puzzle. The hypotheses that have been developed based on the given facts must be compared and sorted until an interpretation has been achieved that presents the only possible solution given the evidence. When Watson protests, 'But this is mere speculation', Holmes replies that 'it is more than that. It is the only hypothesis which covers the facts.' The entire process is neither mysterious nor surprising; it is, despite some unsatisfying conclusions in some situations, a solid approach aimed at certainty. Even though he evidently and repeatedly does so successfully, one of Holmes' principles is, as he says, 'I never guess.' (*The Sign of Four*)

There is no evidence that Doyle was familiar with Peirce's logic. Holmes uses the terms deduction, hypothesis and analysis, but not abduction. On closer examination, Holmes' abductions (hypotheses) as described by Watson are different from those Peirce preferred, which are bolder and more creative. They contain a moment of intelligent guesswork and invention. They strive to gain scientific knowledge and bold theories that must still be proved with experiments rather than to gain the pragmatic everyday knowledge that characterises the detective's work. In short, such abductions are random and for this reason useless to the police in a constitutional state: any arbitrary conviction that ignores the possibility that the accused may be innocent is impermissible. All of this indicates that Doyle cannot have been influenced by Peirce's logic.

Doyle himself names Professor Dr Joseph Bell, under whom he studied medicine, as the role model for Holmes' type of logical reasoning. He used his astounding diagnostic skills not only to interpret a patient's symptoms; he also used them on observable details that allowed him to draw conclusions regarding profession, social standing, preferences, lifestyle and more. Bell's conclusions were extraordinarily precise, which impressed his students, among them Doyle. There is a certain degree of similarity to Peirce's logic to the extent that Peirce's thinking was particularly influenced by medical diagnostics. The chapter 'Sherlock Holmes gives a demonstration' in *The Sign of Four* contains an allusion to Holmes' role model Dr Joseph Bell: "Surely,' said he, with something of the air of a clinical professor expounding to his class.'

As mentioned earlier, the physician and scientist Thomas Henry Huxley is another academic from the University of Edinburgh who influenced Doyle. In 1862 he gave a series of lectures to workers on the topic 'Our Knowledge of the Causes of the Phenomena of Organic Nature', which was also published. The third lecture dealt with 'The Method of Scientific Investigation'. Huxley is of the opinion that basic scientific methods can also be utilised in everyday life. He demonstrates this using the example of a stolen teapot and some spoons. Inductive and deductive conclusions are used to determine realistically what happened. The resulting hypothesis – that there has been a burglary – is only verified once the police have caught the burglar and recovered the stolen items. In the context of these deliberations, Huxley also speaks of the significance of 'missing links' and the necessary exclusion of supernatural interference with the laws of nature. Thus the fundamental scientific instruments required by a detective like Sherlock Holmes are set out. We must assume that Doyle was familiar with this popular lecture by his admired teacher.

In his memoirs, Doyle mentions not only Huxley's philosophy but also that of John Stuart Mill, which influenced his day and age. Mill's most successful book – at least in England – was *A System of Logic, Ratiocinative and Inductive*, published in 1843 and reprinted many times in subsequent years. In his contribution to *The Baker Street Journal* (first issue, I (2): 113–117) in 1946 entitled 'Sherlock Holmes the Logician', J. L. Hitchings was of the opinion that, for the most part, Holmes' logic corresponded to that understood by Mill. This may be true in part, but not entirely. There are indeed remarkable similarities between the two types of logic, but also clear differences. What Mill and Holmes share is a scientific basis of logic that relies on the gaining of new insights about reality, be they scientific or pragmatic investigations. In this respect they contradict logic experts who view logical truths as tautologies and see no relevance of information in logical deductions.

Furthermore, Mill and Holmes both lean towards naturalism. Because the individual is part of the causal order of nature and should be analysed as such, the natural scientist plays a dominating role. Only the natural sciences are able to determine what exists. Their methods are the methods of all reasonable analysis. There is nothing that cannot be explained with the means of natural science. 'Detection is, or ought to be, an exact science,' as Holmes emphasises (*The Sign of Four*). The humanities and social sciences do have their justification, but the differences between the separate strategies used to answer physical or social questions are only gradual. Therefore causal reasoning may also be used to explain human actions based on motives and intentions, just as it is in the sciences.

Mill and Holmes are empiricists, or strive to be. Ultimately, all sciences are empirical sciences that are based on the precise observation and processing of data supplied by our senses, and the same can be said for scientific detection. Holmes is especially an expert in perceiving and using the smallest, seemingly most insignificant details. 'You know my method,' he says to a repeatedly surprised Watson, 'It is founded upon the observation of trifles.' (The Boscombe Valley Mystery.)

In view of the significance of observed facts for the investigation, it is surprising that Holmes and Watson speak of deduction instead of induction. This wording does not represent Holmes' method of investigation correctly since it extends to deduction, induction and abduction. Nonetheless, a significant difference between Holmes' and Mill's logic is demonstrated here. Mill's acceptance of exclusively empirical methods places the focus on inductive methods, which is why he devotes the entire third book of the *Systems of Logic* to induction.

Mill prefers inductive conclusions since they serve to provide new insights, and this is particularly the case with enumerative induction. In such an inductive generalisation, a finite number of circumstances lead us to one universal proposition. For instance, if we observe 10,000 swans, all of which are white, we conclude that all swans are white, which is evidently incorrect. If we know that a certain serial killer with a unique style has committed murder on Christmas Eve every year, we may conclude that the murderer will strike again every year on Christmas Eve unless he is discovered and caught. These examples illustrate how susceptible inductive generalisations are to errors, despite their frequent successful use in everyday as well as scientific analyses. It is therefore a pragmatic method used to gain insight.

Mill admits there is a certain degree of validity in the method that provides the best explanation. In this process, a hypothesis is accepted as the best explanation for a series of phenomena, which in turn proves the validity of the hypothesis. For example, in 1860 someone in London sees how a certain member of parliament who tends to use coaches and is known for his punctuality arrives late in parliament. The observer concludes that the MP was unable to get a coach. If there is no equally good or better explanation for his lateness than his missing a coach, then we must assume that this explanation is correct. Holmes also uses the same method when he is accused of speculating as he illustrates, 'It is the only hypothesis which covers the facts.' (*The Sign of Four*)

Mill presents four – some say five – methods of experimental analysis. All methods allow for conclusions drawn on causal relationships, i.e. on evidence regarding a certain type: events of type A cause events of type B. Such methods serve to eliminate causes and effects in a presupposed list of possible causes and effects. This means that we identify circumstances among the ones that precede or follow a particular phenomenon with those that are actually related according to an invariable law. It should be clear that such methods are essential in criminal science, where, say, it is important in the case of murder to ascertain the cause of death (e.g. poisoning) among a myriad of possibilities. We need to be able to specify, for instance, what type of poison was used, how it acts and what kind of traces it would leave in the body.

The 'method of agreement' is Mill's first method. A specific outcome is examined based on the circumstances of its creation. The point is to find a common factor in all of these circumstances, an aspect according to which they all match. This factor is then the cause. However, there is a problem if the resulting similarity is not the only one. Additionally, a phenomenon may have more than one cause. For instance, an illness may subside thanks to the administration of a drug or simply the body's self-healing process.

The second rule is the 'method of difference'. If circumstances that lead to a certain event coincide with all but one of the aspects of circumstances that do not result in that event, in other words, they differ only in this single aspect, then this differentiating factor is the cause. While the method of agreement eliminates circumstances that may be missing without having any effect, the method of difference eliminates all circumstances but the one that must not be missing without also changing the effect. Both methods can be connected and result in the so-called 'combined method of agreement and difference' which is often considered to be the fifth method. To illustrate the method of difference, Mill uses a criminological example that could just as well have come from Holmes himself. In it, someone is shot in the heart and the wound looks as one would expect in such a case. According to the method of difference we know that the shot through the heart killed the person since he was alive before and all conditions were the same apart from the shot wound.

Mill's third method is the method of residues. Once particular causes of particular effects have been identified from a given number of circumstances with the help of the first two methods, a causal relationship between the remaining circumstances and effects can be assumed without the need to recreate the effect. Hitchings is of the opinion that Mill's third method is essentially Holmes' method. This theory is supported by Holmes' well-known sentence, 'How often have I said to you that when you have eliminated the impossible, whatever remains, *however improbable*, must be the truth?' (*The Sign of Four*). This rule is not entirely identical to the method of residues, but it is based on the same principle of elimination.

The methods mentioned so far cause problems with regard to phenomena in which repetition is difficult to observe or bring about (which does not necessarily apply to the method of residues). Further difficulties arise if factors cannot be isolated in a case. The fourth method offers a solution, if a complicated one. This method requires that we vary factors that cannot be eliminated, or observe them while they are diversifying. If there is covariance, we can draw conclusions regarding the cause. The two covariance factors need not be part of the same cause-and-effect relationship, but both effects can nonetheless have a joint cause. Mill refers to this method, the detail of which depends on further requirements, as the 'method of concomitant variations'. It is better suited to complex scientific analyses than to crime investigation.

After all this, the question that remains is: what is Mill's opinion of deduction, the type of logical deduction that Holmes, according to Watson, primarily uses? In Mill's opinion, deduction must be combined with observation, experiment and induction. He is interested in logical conclusions as long as they lead to new insights, in other words, where new, unknown propositions can be deduced from known ones. For this reason, he differentiates between deductions that only appear to be deductions and those that have an epistemic use. He refers to the latter as ratiocination, a word that Poe used to characterise his detective stories. Such deductions have an important function in securing the consistency of the type of knowledge that is gained by observation and induction. These are Aristotelian syllogisms such as the following:

Major premise: A person who thinks is discerning. Minor premise: Some people are not discerning. Conclusion: Some people do not think.

The conclusion's content may not extend beyond the premise's content, but neither is it the case that the conclusion is included in the two premises. The conclusion serves to clarify existing knowledge. If other propositions are derived from universal propositions with the help of syllogisms, this does not necessarily mean that these conclusions follow from these universal propositions. Ultimately, conclusions follow inductively from singular propositions and universal propositions merely take note of the fact that the induction in question is justified and, in other words, there is sufficient evidence for the conclusion. Basically, the sentence 'All men are mortal' does not lead us to conclude that George is mortal because he is human. Instead, we draw this conclusion from the statement that 'Adam, Eve, Hans, Grete, Kevin (and here follows a great number of other people) have died, so George will also die.' (Ralph Schumacher.) According to Mill, and this is his motto, all conclusions regarding particulars are drawn from particulars.

Ultimately, Holmes does exactly this, but he does refer to induction as deduction. Further, he uses the term deduction in a broad sense and one might say that it is partially incorrect. Since Conan Doyle, as mentioned earlier, explicitly refers to Mill in his autobiography, such a mistake is surprising. Most likely, he never read Mill's book *System of Logic* and gains his information about logical conclusions from popular writings or only from Dr Joseph Bell's lectures.

The success of inductive methods – especially of inductive generalisation – presupposes nature's uniformity which would make measurable and applicable knowledge more likely. According to Mill, every induction contains the assumption that there are similar cases in nature. This means that what happens once will happen again if the circumstances are sufficiently similar, and this will be the case as often as this degree of similarity persists. To assume a uniformity of nature means claiming that all empirical phenomena occur according to uniform causal laws.

Particularly, Holmes assumes an *extreme uniformity* of nature. He published a magazine article entitled 'The Book of Life' as testimony to this. In *A Study in Scarlet*, Watson summarises the article's content as follows: 'The writer claimed by a momentary expression, a twitch of a muscle or a glance of an eye, to fathom a man's inmost thoughts. Deceit, according to him, was an impossibility in the case of one trained to observation and analysis. His conclusions were as infallible as so many propositions of Euclid. So startling would his results appear to the uninitiated that until they learned the processes by which he had arrived at them they might well consider him as a necromancer.'

'From a drop of water,' said the writer, 'a logician could infer the possibility of an Atlantic or a Niagara without having seen or heard of one or the other. So all life is a great chain, the nature of which is known wherever we are shown a single link of it. Like all other arts, the Science of Deduction and Analysis is one which can only be acquired by long and patient study, nor is life long enough to allow any mortal to attain the highest possible perfection in it. Before turning to those moral and mental aspects of the matter which present the greatest difficulties, let the inquirer begin by mastering more elementary problems. Let him on meeting a fellow-mortal, learn at a glance to distinguish the history of the man, and the trade or profession to which he belongs. Puerile as such an exercise may seem, it sharpens the faculties of observation, and teaches one where to look and what to look for. By a man's finger-nails, by his coat-sleeve, by his boot, by his trouser-knees, by the callosities of his forefinger and thumb, by his expression, by his shirt-cuffs – by each of these things a man's calling is plainly revealed. That all united should fail to enlighten the competent inquirer in any case is almost inconceivable.'

When Watson mentions that this approach is impossible to put into practice, Holmes replies: 'Here in London we have lots of Government detectives and lots of private ones. When these fellows are at fault, they come to me, and I manage to put them on the right scent. They lay all the evidence before me, and I am generally able, by the help of my knowledge of the history of crime, to set them straight. There is a strong family resemblance about misdeeds, and if you have all the details of a thousand at your finger ends, it is odd if you can't unravel the thousand and first.' (*A Study in Scarlet*)

For this reason, Holmes advises a criminal investigator: 'Mr Mac, the most practical thing that ever you did in your life would be to shut yourself up for three months and read twelve hours a day at the annals of crime. Everything comes in circles... The old wheel turns and the same spoke comes up. It's all been done before and will be again.' (*The Valley of Fear*)

By his own admission, only the uniformity of natural phenomena allows Holmes to analyse, conclude and predict realistically. This even applies to criminal actions. Holmes uses the term family resemblance as a scientific metaphor for this, which, as a rule, is an innovation attributed to the later Wittgenstein in his *Philosophical Investigations* (§ 67). It becomes clear that Holmes' understanding of nature is influenced by evolutionary theories, which is consistent with the spirit of the age as described in Conan Doyle's autobiography. According to his memoir, his times were influenced by the philosophy of Thomas Henry Huxley, John Tyndall, Charles Darwin, Herbert Spencer and John Stuart Mill. All of them were followers of evolutionary theory in one form or another. Of course, Darwin's theories were the most significant ones, scientifically, and Conan Doyle studied them in great detail. Nonetheless, it comes as no surprise that Huxley, who was generally known as 'Darwin's bulldog', takes pride of place. Conan Doyle studied under him at the University of Edinburgh, admired him and adopted his agnosticism as a student. Huxley considered himself a natural scientist and philosopher. He searched for a 'greater principle' that would do justice to the connection between all beings. Darwin's doctrine contained a well-founded hypothesis for nature's arrangement, but Huxley did not concern himself with natural selection; instead he was interested in the 'missing links' in the history of evolution and the construction of family trees. This demonstrates an intellectual affinity to Holmes' understanding that all of life is 'a great chain', the nature of which is known to us as soon as we examine even a single link. Yet Holmes' nature philosophy goes beyond Huxley's views when he extends the chain of natural relationships to the inorganic field of water on the one hand and human society on the other. This rather indicates the influence of Herbert Spencer's cosmic evolutionary theory, which Huxley criticised.

According to Holmes' view of nature, everything is related. Such a view can be found quite often in literature, independently of scientific evolutionary theories. Balzac and Emerson are just two of the writers who have incorporated this view in their work. The famous literary scholar Ernst Robert Curtius refers to this spiritual view as the 'theory of the unity of the all' (*All-Einheits-Lehre*). This theory is a constant in the history of humanity and seems to have its origin in magical thinking: reality is understood as an infinitely varied everything that is a single acting relationship of life, an animate unity. *Similia similibus* is the formula for its perceptibility. These teachings are neither philosophy nor religion, nor indeed science, because their origin lies deeper, is more unified and irrefutable. Despite his opinion to the contrary, Holmes is no real empiricist. Watson, whose seemingly stubborn approach relies on healthy common sense, is not entirely wrong in criticising Holmes' kind of logic, even though Holmes usually tends to win the dispute.

On rationalism in the Sherlock Holmes stories

TCOT is a common abbreviation in catalogues and bibliographies, which often appears at the start of the title of a crime story. This acronym stands for 'The Case of the'. Even though Conan Doyle never used these words in the title of his Sherlock Holmes stories, this kind of thinking and rationality are important aspects of Holmes' cases because he expands his understanding of the world with the help of his cases. One of his standard phrases – partly literally and partly metaphorically – is 'I have never seen such a singular case.' 'A Case of Identity' is the title of one short story and *The Casebook of Sherlock Holmes* is the final collection with the master detective. The second chapter of *The Sign of Four* is entitled 'The Statement of the Case'. In Julian Symons' history of crime fiction the chapter relating to Holmes bears the title 'The Case of Sherlock Holmes'. Watson repeatedly emphasises that Holmes regularly focuses entirely on his case, but that he is sluggish and passive and indulges in cocaine when he is not working on one. 'The world is all that is the case' is Holmes' answer to Watson's appeal to open himself up to other aspects of the world. When Watson mentions that there are things beyond a case, such as the beauty of a female client, Holmes responds, 'The world is the totality of facts, not of things.' Watson is indignant: 'You really are an automaton – a calculating machine.' With a smile, Holmes says, 'It is of the first importance, not to allow your judgement to be biased by personal qualities. A client is to me a mere unit, a factor in a problem. The emotional qualities are antagonistic to clear reasoning.' He invites Watson to '[s]tand at the window here. Was ever such a dreary, dismal, unprofitable world…? What could be more hopelessly prosaic and material? What is the use of having powers, doctor, when one has no field upon which to exert them? Crime is commonplace, existence is commonplace, and no qualities save those which are commonplace have any function upon earth.' (*The Sign of Four*)

Now, every reader familiar with philosophy will know that the words 'The world is…' may be Holmes' own, but that, in reality, they are the first two lines from Wittgenstein's *Tractatus Logico-Philosophicus*, one of the most famous and widely read philosophical texts of the twentieth century. It is unlikely that Conan Doyle was aware of this text from 1921. In any case, Holmes is set some decades earlier. Furthermore, the two sentences of the *Tractatus* in the context of Wittgenstein's argumentation have a different meaning from that of a fictional detective's speech. A case is not a criminal case and the world according to Wittgenstein is not all that exists, but the world from the point of view of logic. However, what cannot be excluded and is even quite likely is the fact that both Doyle's detective story and the *Tractatus* are influenced by a *particular* zeitgeist of the late nineteenth century and early twentieth century, albeit in different ways.

The age of science and technology began in the middle of the nineteenth century. Especially in England, science became an inherent part of our thinking; there was a predominant 'rational positivist' outlook. In its wake followed endeavours to reach a consensual scientific worldview based on the natural sciences, with the expectation that there would be social and humanitarian progress as a result. The world expected greater insight and more justice from its scientists. As a doctor Doyle was deeply bound by the rational thinking of his day and age, despite his interest in spiritualism. In the case of Holmes he created a hero who, for the first time, triumphs time and again because of logic and scientific methods.

Wittgenstein corresponds with the spirit of the age insofar as he equates all of natural science with the sum of true propositions (*Tractatus*, 4.11), but he attempts to counter a naïve belief in science as we see in the foreword of *Tractatus*: 'Thus the aim of the book is to draw a limit to thought, or rather – not to thought, but to the expression of thoughts.' Towards the end of the book, its author admits that '[w]e feel that even when all *possible* scientific questions have been answered, the problems of life remain completely untouched.' Holmes and Watson would never agree with this sentence because they use scientific methods to solve urgent problems in their clients' lives, such as escaping arrest or even execution. Holmes rather matches Willard Van Quine's view according to which nothing in this world – not a wink, not even the flicker of a thought – happens without resulting in the redistribution of microphysical conditions. Such a shift leaves traces that a detective should recognise.

Siegfried Kracauer's *The Detective Novel: A Philosophical Treatise* is one of the most unusual and critical studies of crime literature. Kracauer completed it on 15 February 1925 at a time when he had not yet made a name for himself as film theorist and sociologist. The entire text was published posthumously. As early as the first page of the introduction, Kracauer refers primarily to Conan Doyle's Sherlock Holmes novels. In order to illustrate the elements of the philosophy of the classic detective novel and its exclusions and limitations, Kracauer chose an unexpected approach – Kierkegaard's existential philosophy. Taking this approach, and a critique of idealism after Kant, as his starting points, Kracauer defines the philosophy of the detective novel as a philosophy of immanence that contains traces of transcendence that are not easy to read, due to the distortion.

Humans are in an intermediate sphere between the lower sphere of nature and higher sphere of the supernatural. As a result, the individual finds himself in a state of suspense towards the sphere of God, from which he expects the release and reconciliation he is unable to receive in his own world. As a result, the reality of a devout person is characterised by a dramatic, paradoxical existence. In the immanent world of the detective novel, the reference to a higher sphere is missing entirely, and this has its price. The characters trust that worldly law and justice will be upheld and do not rely on divine justice. In the Sherlock Holmes detective stories and in others, the idea prevails with radical one-sidedness that civil society is rational through and through. According to Kracauer, civilisation is more concerned with the emphasis on reality's intellectual character rather than the realistic reproduction of reality. The image presented by these tales is frightening because it shows us a state of society in which unconditional intellect has won its final battle, a merely superficial disorder of characters and things that seems pale and confusing because it turns the eliminated reality into a caricature. It is a world without meaning in which there is no room for an existential society. For this reason, Holmes's reaction to Watson's intention to marry their client Morstan is anything but joyful: 'I feared as much... I really cannot congratulate you... love is an emotional thing, and whatever is emotional is opposed to that true, cold reason which I place above all things. I should never marry myself, lest I bias my judgement.' (*The Sign of Four*)

As a relaxed representative of reasoning, the detective moves within an empty space. As the representative of higher reasoning, he is the only god-like creature. He knows the secret of nature and society, 'The Book of Life', as Holmes refers to it, and can connect things that remain unnoticed by others. As a representative of higher reasoning rather than police legality, a reasoning that need not explain itself, he has an ironic relationship with the legal authority of the police. The master detective is superior not only because his knowledge of the secret does not follow the superficial differentiation between legal and illegal, but because of his confidence in overstepping the limits of legality. Thus, Holmes does not hide the fact that he uses illegal methods if they are necessary to solve a case. Due to his privileged position he is able to take on different roles: that of the investigator, of the agent of the law, of the witness or even the *agent provocateur*. It is this disguised proximity to being above the law that allows him to be assured and not to take any sides except that of the discerning glance. While Watson emphasises the benefit to justice and society from Holmes' work in stories such as 'The Final Problem' and 'The Empty House', justice is of minor interest to Holmes himself. He is more interested in the true artist's perfection ('The Dying Detective'). Whereas a doctor bases his diagnosis on given symptoms in order to heal the patient, the crime, 'the disease on the body of society' is merely a reason for deduction to the detective, a self-sufficient rational process that may save someone along the way.

Detectives like Holmes are characterised by an asceticism they share with priests and monks. As a secular priest he takes the criminal's confession, the content of which will never be revealed, and he thus becomes a confidant sharing their secrets (as in 'Silver Blaze'). The detective must restore the rational way of the world incorruptibly and dispassionately. He believes that the world is instrumental and rational, which determines the course against crime. According to Kracauer, the way that God created man according to his image is the way that reason creates itself in the detective's abstract schemes.

The detective's relation to his own body is marked by a similarly strict subordination to instrumental rationalism. Watson repeatedly describes his admiration of Holmes' physical fitness, his ability to work under pressure, his stamina, agility and discipline. These abilities, however, says Kracauer, are not the self-representation of enduring physicality that prevail in the world. Instead, it is reason's way of verifying its insights. If the physical abilities are used at all, they are not what help the detective in his victory. Rather, the plot consists of logical operations that serve to detect the culprit, and any sporting developments merely have the aesthetic purpose to prove the practical and evident value of these theoretical processes. Watson expresses Holmes' functional physical action very clearly in 'The Yellow Face': 'Sherlock Holmes was a man who seldom took exercise for exercise's sake. Few men were capable of greater muscular effort, and he was undoubtedly one of the finest boxers of his weight that I have ever seen; but he looked upon aimless bodily exertion as a waste of energy, and he seldom bestirred himself save when there was some professional object to be served. Then he was absolutely untiring and indefatigable. That he should have kept himself in training under such circumstances is remarkable, but his diet was usually of the sparest, and his habits were simple to the verge of austerity. Save for the occasional use of cocaine, he had no vices, and he only turned to the drug as a protest against the monotony of existence when cases were scanty and the papers uninteresting.'

Holmes' physical abilities are astonishing enough, but they are exceeded by his ability to disguise himself. Even his friend Watson does not recognise him on such occasions, as we see in *The Sign of Four* and 'The Empty House', for instance. Kracauer explains that 'the detective puts on a mask that turns him into someone else in order to prove his theory. Whereas everyone is different in reality, here the one stands for every man. This magic art that is not perceived as a miracle in the disenchanted world of the detective novel allows the detective to evaluate in reality the idea of totality, which he carries within him. As long as he does not simply mask himself in order to collect the rubbish that litters his path, but to find the missing links he needs to prove his theory, his disguise turns him into the conductor of a carefully led experiment… However he would be unable to conduct experiments that would lead him to conclusions regarding the validity of his theories if he were limited in the use of what is available to him. The ability to disguise oneself is the aesthetic expression of the detective's liberty and the absence of limitations of being… By turning into any given character, the detective confirms manifestly that he does not exist in the sphere in which unrepeatable beings exist. Instead, he exists in an environment whose characters can be randomly reproduced.' When reason emancipates itself, the developing person in its relation is ignored, and fixed single characteristics come together to form fragmented characters.

'Since reason, as the world-creating principle it understands itself to be in the end, should not be predetermined by anything, the detective novel therefore tries to begin the intellectual process at nothing. It takes its typical beginning from the "it" of illegal facts, an objectified result that is constructed in such a way from the start that it creates no difficulties for the intellectual handling of the mystery it presents. Whatever facts it encompasses – murder, burglary, a disappearance – it is always a selective incident that has been taken out of human contexts which reason cannot grasp in its entirety… It approaches intellect as a combination of scraps of facts and demands that our intellect makes the necessary connections to solve the problem. These connections can indeed be deducted rationally based on their intentions; the units whose connections are meant to be reconstructed are merely reductions of real events, alienated remaining features that represent atoms in the aesthetic medium… The distortion of results is expanded by restricting the facts to a minimum of factors. It is typical of the detective novel that reason finds material, the meagreness of which seems to offer no point of contact for the process it must pass through… This narrowed basis from which reason must set out coincides with the ambition inherent in every idealistic immanence philosophy to begin at nothing.' (Kracauer)

A reader who does not share Kracauer's shattered religious understanding of reality will think his critique of the specific reality as depicted in the world of Sherlock Holmes one-sided and exaggerated. One must remember that the Holmes stories are often much like adventure stories so that even the reader who does not follow every step of the investigation and its logical speculations can still follow the story and enjoy it. Some other classic detective stories are different in this respect. Some are constructed in a way that the reader will be unable to follow the story and enjoy it unless he pays close attention to every detail and every conclusion. Freeman Wills Crofts' story 'The Mystery of the Sleeping-Car Express' is an example of such a story that requires the reader's full attention. The story itself contains a diagram to make it easier to follow the fictional events. A line from Wittgenstein's *Tractatus*, 'The facts in logical space are the world', is particularly relevant with regard to such detective stories. The logical space is 'nothing other than the set of all logically possible worlds. The real world is one of many logically possible worlds. It is the only set of states of affairs in the logical space whose elements are facts without exception.'(Holm Tetens) To reconstruct this real world out of a multitude of logical possibilities based on the facts is the master detective's challenge. Still, the writer and reader of a detective story assume that the narrated facts and the given logical possibilities are fictional and selected and arranged in a way that they create suspense for pleasurable reading. Incidentally, Dr Watson's part is often underestimated due to the occasional naivety he displays. He is a defender of human emotions and common sense and is therefore an indispensable counterpart to the very logical Sherlock Holmes. Pure Holmes would be impossible to endure.

References and Further reading:

Arthur Conan Doyle
Doyle, Arthur Conan: *Memories and Adventures*, Boston 1924
Doyle, Arthur Conan: *Sherlock Holmes. The Complete Illustrated Novels* (A Study in Scarlet. The Sign of Four. The Hound of the Baskervilles. The Valley of Fear), London 2001
Doyle, Arthur Conan: *Sherlock Holmes. The Complete Stories*, Hertfordshire (1989) 2006

Other authors
Boileau-Narcejac: *Der Detektivroman*, Neuwied/Berlin 1964 (French edition: Boileau-Narcejac: *Le Roman policier*, Paris 1964)
Bowler, Peter J.: 'Herbert Spencers Idee der Evolution und ihre Rezeption', in: Engels, Eve-Marie (ed.): *Die Rezeption von Evolutionstheorien im 19. Jahrhundert*, Frankfurt am Main 1995, 309–325
Campbell, Mark: *Sherlock Holmes*, Harpenden 2007
Crofts, Freeman Wills: 'The Mystery of the Sleeping-Car Express', in: Sayers, Dorothy L. (ed.): *Tales of Detection*, London 1947, 225–249
Curtius, Ernst Robert: *Kritische Essays zur europäischen Literatur*, Frankfurt am Main 1984

Di Gregorio, Mario A.: 'The Importance of Being Ernst: Thomas Henry Huxley zwischen Karl Ernst von Baer und Ernst Haeckel', in: Engels, Eve-Marie (ed.): *Die Rezeption von Evolutionstheorien im 19. Jahrhundert*, Frankfurt am Main 1995, 182–213

Eco, Umberto/Sebeok, Thomas A. (ed.): *Der Zirkel oder Im Zeichen der Drei Dupin, Holmes, Peirce*, Munich 1985 (English edition: Eco, Umberto/Sebeok, Thomas A. (ed.): *The Sign of Three Dupin, Holmes, Peirce*, Bloomington 1983. Contributors: Thomas A. Sebeok/Jean Umiker-Sebeok, Marcello Truzzi, Massimo Bonfantini/Giampaolo Proni, Jaakko and Merrill B. Hintikka and others)

Engels, Eve-Marie: 'Biologische Ideen von Evolution im 19. Jahrhundert und ihre Leitfunktionen', in: Engels (ed.): *Die Rezeption von Evolutionstheorien im 19. Jahrhundert*, Frankfurt am Main 1995, 13–66

Hitchings, J. L.: 'Sherlock Holmes the Logician', in: The Baker Street Journal (1, 1946 (2) April, 113–117); www.bakerstreetjournal.com/

Hügli, Anton/Lübcke, Poul (ed.): *Philosophielexikon*, Reinbek bei Hamburg 1991

Hull, David L.: 'Die Rezeption von Darwins Evolutionstheorie bei britischen Wissenschaftsphilosophen des 19. Jahrhunderts', in: Engels, Eve-Marie (ed.): *Die Rezeption von Evolutionstheorien im 19. Jahrhundert*, Frankfurt am Main 1995, 67–104

Huxley, Thomas Henry: 'The Method of Scientific Investigation', in: Reilly, Joseph J. (ed.): *Masters of Nineteenth Century Prose*, Boston/New York, 1930, 634–641

Koch, Gertrud: *Kracauer zur Einführung*, Hamburg 1996

Kracauer, Siegfried: *Der Detektiv-Roman. Ein philosophischer Traktat*, Frankfurt am Main 1979 (English edition: Detective Novel, Cambridge 2006)

Kuenzle, Dominique/Schefczyk, Michael: *John Stuart Mill zur Einführung*, Hamburg 2009

Lycett, Andrew: *The Man Who Created Sherlock Holmes: The Life and Times of Sir Arthur Conan Doyle*, New York/London, 2007

Mill, John Stuart: *A System of Logic, Ratiocinative and Inductive, Being a Connected View of Principles of Evidence and the Methods of Scientific Investigation*, 1843, http://oll.libertyfund.org/

Mohr, Arno: 'Zur Einführung', in: Mill, John Stuart: *Zur Logik der Moralwissenschaften*, Frankfurt am Main 1997, 9–33

Pears, David/Kenny, Anthony: 'Von Mill bis Wittgenstein', in: Kenny, Anthony (ed.): *Illustrierte Geschichte der westlichen Philosophie*, Frankfurt am Main/New York 1995, 255–291

Peirce, Charles Sanders: *Lectures on Pragmatism. Vorlesungen über Pragmatismus*, Edited by Elisabeth Walther, Hamburg 1973

Peirce, Charles Sanders: *Chance, Love, and Logic. Philosophical Essays*, edited by Morris R. Cohen, Lincoln/London 1998

Pulte, Helmut: 'Darwin in der Physik und bei den Physikern des 19. Jahrhunderts', in: Engels, Eve-Marie (ed.): *Die Rezeption von Evolutionstheorien im 19. Jahrhundert*, Frankfurt am Main 1995, 105–146

Quine, Willard Van Orman: *Theories and Things*, Harvard, Cambridge 1981

Raatzsch, Richard: *Ludwig Wittgenstein zur Einführung*, Hamburg 2008

Schlick, Moritz: Foreword, in: Waismann, Friedrich: *Logik, Sprache, Philosophie*, Stuttgart 1976, 11–23

Schumacher, Ralph: *John Stuart Mill*, Frankfurt/New York 1994

Stashower, Daniel: *Sir Arthur Conan Doyle: Das Leben des Vaters von Sherlock Holmes*, Köln 2008 (English edition: Stashower, Daniel: *Teller of Tales: A Life of Sir Arthur Conan Doyle*, New York 1999)

Symons, Julian: *Bloody Murder. From the detective story to the crime novel: a history*, 3rd edition, London/Basingstoke 1992

Tetens, Holm: *Wittgensteins 'Tractatus'. Ein Kommentar*, Stuttgart 2009

Wittgenstein, Ludwig: *Philosophical Investigations*, 3rd edition Oxford 1995

Wittgenstein, Ludwig: *Tractatus Logico-Philosophicus*, London 1995

4

Gilbert Keith Chesterton's Christian Philosophy

What can one write about Chesterton that hasn't been written already? Almost nothing. Chesterton's most famous literary figure is Father Brown. The first Father Brown story, 'The Blue Cross', was published in September 1910 in 'Storyteller' magazine. Over fifty more followed. In these stories, the small, Catholic priest is a good detective not only because he is a competent minister and judge of character, but also because he is knowledgeable in philosophy. Unlike other experienced practitioners he doesn't scoff at the theory. 'People will tell you that theories don't matter and that logic and philosophy aren't practical. Don't you believe them. Reason is from God, and when things are unreasonable there is something the matter.' ('The Red Moon of Meru')

Chesterton is probably the most philosophical of the classic crime writers. After all, he wrote two unambiguously philosophical books, *Orthodoxy* and *Heretics*. Not surprisingly for a practising Christian, he embraces a philosophy that seamlessly crosses over into theology. This is not unlike many older philosophers, not least Thomas Aquinas. Both Father Brown and Chesterton, who wrote a biography of him, were great admirers of Aquinas. Chesterton sprinkles his crime stories with philosophical titbits. Particularly in his Father Brown stories, readers are presented with philosophical tenets, which in part can be found again in his theoretical works. Jorge Luis Borges wrote one of the most perceptive essays on Chesterton. Borges stresses how Chesterton time and again achieves the following twist in his crime stories: he depicts an inexplicable fact, a mystery, and provides at first supernatural explanations of a demonic or magical kind. In the end, however, worldly, reason-based arguments replace these and the riddle of the crime is solved. Chesterton's 'reason' is universal, rooted in Catholic belief and 'common sense'. According to Borges, what is dealt with here, philosophically and historically, is 'a complex of Hebraic ideas, which borrows from Plato or Aristotle'.

The religious anchoring of reason is already clearly apparent in the very first Father Brown story, 'The Blue Cross'. The master criminal Flambeau, disguised as a priest, has the following conversation with Father Brown: 'Ah, yes, these modern infidels appeal to their reason; but who can look at those millions of worlds and not feel that there may well be wonderful universes above us where reason is utterly unreasonable?' 'No', replies Father Brown: 'reason is always reasonable, even in the last limbo, in the lost borderland of things. I know that people charge the Church with lowering reason, but it is just the other way. Alone on earth, the Church makes reason really supreme. Alone on earth, the Church affirms that God himself is bound by reason.' Flambeau says: 'Yet who knows if in that infinite universe – ?', to which Father Brown replies: 'Only infinite physically… not infinite in the sense of escaping from the laws of truth… Reason and justice grip the remotest and the loneliest star.' After Father Brown unmasks Flambeau as the thief, he tells him what raised his suspicions against the fake priest, 'You attacked reason… It's bad theology.'

For Chesterton, the Christian faith is a kind of guarantee for preserving 'common sense'. In the story 'The Oracle of the Dog', Father Brown explains how he came to solve the riddle:

'The dog could almost have told you the story, if he could talk'… 'All I complain of is that because he couldn't talk you made up his story for him, and made him talk with the tongues of men and angels. It's part of something I've noticed more and more in the modern world… People readily swallow the untested claims of this, that, or the other. It's drowning all your old rationalism and scepticism, it's coming in like a sea; and the name of it is superstition… It's the first effect of not believing in God that you lose your common sense and can't see things as they are… And a dog is an omen, and a cat a mystery… calling up all the menagerie of polytheism from Egypt and old India… and all because you are frightened of four words: "He was made Man".'

God was made man; this for Chesterton provided the pledge that reason applied in heaven as much as it did on earth. It is not a great leap of faith from this perspective to Gianni Vattimo's historical-philosophical assumption that the creation of God as man, and Christ's crucifixion, set off the process of secularisation.

Especially as a priest Father Brown is intent on bringing the truth to light and condemns mystification and obfuscation: 'And I say to you, wherever you find men ruled merely by mystery, it is the mystery of iniquity. If the devil tells you something is too fearful to look at, look at it. If he says something is too terrible to hear, hear it. If you think some truth unbearable, bear it.' ('The Purple Wig'). Yet as a priest, Father Brown cannot get around acknowledging justification of the mystery, the miracle, which however must be arrived at exactly: 'The modern mind always mixes up two different ideas: mystery in the sense of what is marvellous, and mystery in the sense of what is complicated. That is half its difficulty about miracles. A miracle is startling; but it is simple. It is simple because it is a miracle. It is a power coming directly from God (or the devil) instead of indirectly through nature or human wills... Heaven and hell only know by what surrounding influences strange sins come into the lives of men. But for the present my point is this: if it was pure magic, as you think, then it is marvellous; but it is not mysterious – that is, it is not complicated. The quality of a miracle is mysterious, but its manner is simple. Now, the manner of this business has been the reverse of simple... I know the crooked track of a man.' ('The Wrong Shape'.)

The interplay of reason, scepticism, belief, empathy and a sense of justice presents a complicated dilemma for Chesterton and Father Brown, and emphasis should not be placed too hastily on one of these elements. Chesterton nurtures great scepticism and reserve for people who only argue according to the rules of the logic of reasoning. In his opinion, this is a sign of madness and institutions for the mentally impaired are full of people who follow formalised logical conclusions rather than healthy common sense. So, for example, you cannot logically prove that someone who suffers from the fear of persecution is not, in reality, being persecuted. Chesterton is equally sceptical of those who only consider scientifically proven facts as the truth. For Chesterton, the belief in facts remains too beholden to the surface of things. As someone who is ultimately committed to heavenly revelation, he counters with the view that truth is more than mere empirical facts. True science, according to Chesterton, is penetrated by the spirit of poetry. Often, criminologists and other scientifically trained crime solvers cannot recognise the actual act, because they are bound by false ideas of a determinism that must have caused the crime. Father Brown contradicts this with the conclusion, 'murder is of the will, which God made free.' ('The Doom of the Darnaways') The motive for a crime and the signature of the act are connected with a person's highly individual moral character, in whose soul Father Brown, an experienced pastor, can place himself to an astounding degree. An example of this can be found in the 'The Strange Crime of John Boulnois', where Father Brown explains why he does not suspect Boulnois of the murder:

'I attach a good deal of importance to vague ideas. All those things that "aren't evidence" are what convince me. I think a moral impossibility the biggest of all impossibilities. I know your husband only slightly, but I think this crime of his, as generally conceived, something very like a moral impossibility... Anybody can be wicked – as wicked as he chooses. We can direct our moral wills; but we can't generally change our instinctive tastes and ways of doing things. Boulnois might commit a murder, but not this murder... If Boulnois killed anyone he'd do it quietly and heavily, as he'd do any other doubtful thing – take a tenth glass of port, or read a loose Greek poet. No, the romantic setting is not like Boulnois.' Later Mrs. Boulnois confirms Father Brown's insight with the sentence, '...and there are some things the soul cannot do, as the body cannot fly.'

Chesterton is particularly sceptical of the belief in the advances of technology and the command of things through machines. Father Brown admits to the ex-detective Greywood Usher that machines don't lie, but they don't tell the truth either. Even when a lie detector is supposed to give reliable results, the man who operates the machine is fallible. Especially when measuring with machines, the basic problem of the right interpretation arises. 'There's a disadvantage in a stick pointing straight,' says Father Brown. 'What is it? Why, the other end of the stick always points the opposite way. It depends whether you get hold of the stick by the right end.' (The Mistake of the Machine).

Father Brown possesses a deep distrust of those who are not aware and humble of their weaknesses and sins, but are instead full of themselves and convinced of their strengths and have no need for a belief in a being higher than themselves. Once again Chesterton refers here to an institution for the mentally impaired. Many people are gathered here who instead of being self-critical are completely taken with themselves and succumb to crazy ideas, for example by thinking that they are Napoleon or another famous person, not doubting it for a moment, despite all reality to the contrary. A criminal nutter, who introduces himself as the founder of a new-fangled sun religion, meets Father Brown in 'The Eye of Apollo.' The sun priest of Apollo posits, 'if a man were really healthy he could stare at the sun.' Father Brown counters: 'If a man were really healthy (…) he would not bother to stare at it.' Because this new religion maintains it can heal all physical illnesses, Father Brown asks: 'Can it cure the one spiritual disease?' and elaborates with, 'Oh, thinking one is quite well.'

The evil characters in Chesterton's crime stories betray themselves by one characteristic: they do not blink. The murderers stare rigidly. Schopenhauer relates that the Hindus recognise gods by the fact that they do not blink. 'The unmoving eye is the image of oneness' (Michael Maar). Chesterton, however, is a dualist who hates monism, which is why he attacks the latter with drastic means. Immobility in people is also suspicious to him (Finn Riedel). Chesterton the Christian vehemently rejects the theology of an inner God. God must remain on the outside, just like the nature he created. It must not be possible to control him. Incidentally, Chesterton finds Nirvana boring compared to the more exciting existence as something foreign, as he highlights in his autobiography.

Chesterton's philosophical fighting spirit is directed in particular against followers of Nietzsche. He has only disdain for the idea of the 'Übermensch.' It becomes clear in 'The Actor and the Alibi' just how debilitating he finds Nietzsche's philosophy. In this story, Father Brown accuses an actress of murdering her husband. He says to one of her devastated followers: 'You talk about these highbrows having a higher art and a more philosophical drama. But remember what a lot of the philosophy is! Remember what sort of conduct those highbrows often present to the highest! All about the Will to Power and the Right to Live and the Right to Experience – damned nonsense and more than damned nonsense – nonsense that can damn.'

One of Chesterton's favourite words is 'paradox', one Father Brown also likes to use. The word 'paradox' brings together various meanings, which Chesterton allows to flourish in his work. Mostly, Chesterton follows the common interpretation of the paradox, as defined in the Encyclopaedia of the French Enlightenment, 'An absurd proposition, at least in appearance, because it runs counter to traditional views, which in fact is true, or at least contains a hint of truth.'

Chesterton's use of paradox frequently tends to the vulgar, the humorous. He identifies the paradox with the old adage of 'common sense' which he presents as his trump card. Chesterton develops paradoxes not only as an element of linguistic description, as rhetorical and explanatory-constructive paradoxes – as seen in the story collection *The Paradoxes of Mr. Pond* and in some Father Brown stories, – but rather he considers being itself as paradox. Hugh Kenner, author of a book on paradox in Chesterton, defines him as the metaphysician of the paradox. Chesterton posits, in contrast to George Bernard Shaw, a kind of paradox where two opposing strands of truth are bound in a knot, which cannot be untied, a knot that holds together the entire bundle of human life securely. Therefore, the daring contradictions, the insistence on opposition, are necessary for understanding the actual creation of an act, even including a crime (Norbert Miller). This is something that Father Brown commands masterfully.

Another of Chesterton's favourite words, which is closely connected to the paradox, is the adjective 'topsy-turvy' – in other words head over heels. Joachim Kalka points out that 'turning it on its head, in both senses, the fully celebrated metaphor and the actual act' constantly appears in Chesterton's works. In the Father Brown story, 'The Dagger with Wings', the adjective even becomes a noun. 'There must have been something in that topsy-turvydom to take the fancy of that darkly fanciful man. It was like some frightful fancy-dress ball to which the two mortal enemies were to go dressed up as each other.' The word topsy-turvy is used in the positive as well as negative sense. In a critical sense, topsy-turvy is applied when uncovering the reversal between purpose and means or cause and effect. On the other hand, a look at things from bottom to top – as in a headstand – is embraced as a new, unusual, enlightening viewpoint. The punch line in some Father Brown stories is constructed on the topsy-turvy principle. In 'The Arrow of Heaven' a man is killed by an arrow, which wasn't shot from a great distance, but rather used like a dagger from close proximity. In 'The Song of the Flying Fish' Father Brown explains his choice of perspective: 'There is one general truth to remember… A thing can sometimes be too close to be seen, as, for instance, a man cannot see himself. There was a man who had a fly in his eye when he looked through the telescope, and he discovered that there was a most incredible dragon in the moon. And I am told that if a man hears the exact reproduction of his own voice it sounds like the voice of a stranger. In the same way, if anything is right in the foreground of our life we hardly see it, and if we did we might think it quite odd. If the thing in the foreground got into the middle distance, we should probably think it had come from the remote distance. Just come outside the house again for a moment. I want to show you how it looks from another standpoint.'

Father Brown's and Chesterton's reason-based and perspective-flipping philosophy is not only for practising Christians, but also attractive to agnostics, and palatable even for Marxists like Bloch, Brecht and Gramsci. Today this attractiveness has the following primary reason: Kant warned with good reason against wanting to adopt the position of god. This is first a warning directed at philosophical thinkers. They should resist the temptation to construct a philosophical system or a 'Weltanschauung' which places themselves front and centre as the all-knowing subject. The warning however extends further. One should avoid placing any other authority as an all-knowing, omnipotent creator at the centre of a system, for example the party, the nation or society. Instead one must show modesty and be conscious of a lack of knowledge and ability. The point is that in the end it doesn't matter if there is an omnipotent and all-knowing creator. All that matters is not occupying this place in the universe with fantasies of omnipotence, but instead keeping it free or, as practising Christians do, leaving it to God. This is particularly true for the imposition of just punishment on sinners and criminals, in which the individual must not presume to be a god-like judge, who kills as the executor of the alleged will of God, like 'the Hammer of God' – as described in a Father Brown story.

Due to a large area that is not objectively or subjectively accessible in terms of knowledge, every man relies on assumptions, opinions, etc. – in brief, on faith, even the agnostic. Beliefs and principles can agree with reason, but must not necessarily so. According to a psychiatric view, madness is nothing other than a pathological special case of belief (Leo Navratil). Almost no man is completely free of delusionary, superstitious belief, as they are often confused with faith.

In Chesterton's works the personal delusion in the Catholic faith is preserved – and thus the belief in miracles like the virgin birth – and thus limited by the ecclesial community and practicably managed. Moreover, and closely connected with some religious principles, reason rules, as does a courageous, rational access to reality. This form of interplay of faith/lack of knowledge and reason/knowledge is also attractive to agnostics and perhaps even atheists, even if they lack the strong impetus for action that emanates from the religious message of redemption and God's commandment. Instead, a sceptical attitude often prevails among agnostics and atheists, causing them to hesitate, while a Father Brown jumps in.

A previous version of this text was published in CADS 59, December 2010, 17–20.

References and Further Reading

a) Gilbert Keith Chesterton

Chesterton, Gilbert Keith: *The Complete Father Brown Stories*, Ware 1992 (2006)
Chesterton, Gilbert Keith: *Orthodoxy*, London/Sydney/Auckland 1996
Chesterton, Gilbert Keith: *Heretics*, London 2001
Chesterton, Gilbert Keith: *The Paradoxes of Mr Pond*, London 2001

b) other authors

Borges, Jorge Luis, 'Über Chesterton', in: *Schreibheft Nr.50*, Essen November 1997, 67–68
Borges, Jorge Luis: 'The Labyrinths of the Detective Story and Chesterton', in: *Borges: On Writing*, London 2010, 115–118
Clark, Stephen R. L., *G. K. Chesterton: Thinking Backward, Looking Forward*, Philadelphia/London 2006
Davies, David Stuart: Introduction, in: Gilbert Keith Chesterton: The *Complete Father Brown Stories*, Ware 1992 (2006), 7–13
Kalka, Joachim, 'Achilles unterhält sich mit der Schildkröte', in: *Essen Schreibheft Nr.50*, November 1997, 104–108
Kenner, Hugh, *Paradox in Chesterton*, London 1948
Lacoue-Labarthe, Philippe, *L'imitation des modernes. Typographies II*, 1986 (German edition: *Die Nachahmung der Modernen. Typographien II*, Basel/Weil am Rhein/Wien 2003)
Maar, Michael: 'Men Alive', in: *Schreibheft. Zeitschrift für Literatur Nr. 50*, Essen November 1997, 13–17
Marx, Matthias: 'Einleitung: Chestertons Kampf mit dem Bösen', in: *Chesterton, Gilbert Keith, Die Unschuld des Kriminellen*, Bonn 2010, 3–7
Marx, Matthias: Anhang, in: *Chesterton, Gilbert Keith, Die Unschuld des Kriminellen, Bonn 2010*, 183–201
Miller, Norbert, 'Die Welt als Paradox und Wunderschachtel', in: *Gilbert Keith Chesterton, Detektivgeschichten*, Munich/Vienna 1975, 443–463

Navratil, Leo, *Schizophrenie und Religion*, Berlin 1992

Pearce, Joseph, *Wisdom and Innocence. A Life of G. K. Chesterton*, London 1996

Riedel, Finn: 'Mobility and Immobility in the Work of G. K. Chesterton, with Special Regard to the Winking of the Eye', in: *Inklings, Jahrbuch für Literatur und Ästhetik*, Bd. 14, 1996, 109–123

Sassoon, Anne Showstack: *Gramsci und das Geheimnis des Father Brown*, in: *Das Argument* 278/2008, 580–585

Schenkel, Elmar: 'Paradoxie als Denkfigur. Wiederzuentdecken: Gilbert Keith Chesterton', in: *Schreibheft. Zeitschrift für Literatur Nr. 50*, Essen November 1997, 69–71

Schenkel, Elmar: 'Durchkreuzter Kreis. Borges und Chesterton', in: *Schreibheft. Zeitschrift für Literatur Nr. 50*, Essen November 1997, 98–103

Vattimo, Gianni: *Jenseits des Christentums. Gibt es eine Welt ohne Gott?*, Munich/Vienna 2004 (English edition: Vattimo, Gianni: *After Christianity*, New York 2002)

Weber, Thomas: 'Samuel Kascher und Richter Lexer. Miniatur zu Bertold Brechts Initiativen', in: *Das Argument* 278/2008, 575–579

5

Hammett's Pragmatism

There are two ways in which philosophy works its way into an author's work: through the absorption of a philosophy by the author and through the author's own thinking. If the author is a philosophical thinker and expresses thoughts that are the same or similar to those representative of a certain philosophy, he will come to express this philosophy in his work. With Hammett both hold true. He absorbed the pragmatism and also thought in a similar vein.

Hammett, a pragmatist? Wasn't he a Marxist? Hammett professed his adherence to Marxism repeatedly and was a member of the Communist Party. However, Lillian Hellman, Hammett's partner in the second half of his life, describes how Hammett became politically radicalised only in the mid to late 1930s, when communism became chic in Hollywood. For Hammett, the newly attained political conviction was more than just fashion – it defined his later life. But there is much to suggest that he was not a Marxist before 1935, during the time he wrote crime stories. Upon the publication of *The Thin Man* in 1934 Alfred A. Knopf promoted the book and author: Hammett read everything but detective stories. His favourite book is Spengler's *The Decline of the West*, which is anything but a work of Marxism. Some assumed that Hammett's stories and novels were shaped by a Marxist worldview because of their radical and socially critical stance. The war of all against all (and not, in fact, a class war), which is depicted in *Red Harvest* and other stories, reminds Steven Marcus more of Thomas Hobbes than Marx. Hammett's literary depiction of American society and the violence, greed and dishonesty of its people could also have been influenced by his reading of Shakespeare. The most important experience, however, did not stem from books, but rather from his job as a Pinkerton agent. Hammett explained his success as an author by the fact that he had been a detective and wrote about detectives. In particular, the details of well-known Continental Op stories touched upon events which Hammett either experienced or learned about from other detectives.

Hammett's experience as a private detective taught him to adopt a philosophy of pragmatism. In some regards pragmatism corresponds to the company policy of a detective agency such as Pinkerton. The behavioural code of Pinkerton detectives that was instilled in Hammett was not geared towards the high ideals of justice etc., but rather towards finishing the job well and protecting yourself. His tendency towards pragmatism may have induced Hammett to give his protagonist in the famous Flitcraft parable (*The Maltese Falcon*) the name Charles Pierce, an allusion to the founder of pragmatism Charles S. Peirce. The Flitcraft parable owes much to essential aspects of Peirce's thoughts. Not only here, but also in other texts by Hammett are traces of a reception of pragmatism apparent. This will be clarified further.

Hammett was capable of reading publications by Peirce and other pragmatists and almost certainly did so. I have not found any evidence in biographical accounts of Hammett that he studied works of pragmatism. But Hammett's entire reading practice speaks in favour of it. In his lifetime, Hammett was an all-round reader, eclectic, interested, and endowed with a good memory. At the age of thirteen he had already read Kant's *Critique of Pure Reason* and retained a preference in the future for those books that tried to explain things clearly, even if in vain. David Goldway, a teacher at the Jefferson School for Social Science where Hammett began to teach 'mystery writing' in the 1940s, remembered that Hammett had a sound theoretical understanding, though this was something he denied.

In the 1920s Hammett read books on, among other subjects, criminology and mathematics. It would be remarkable if he didn't stumble across the works of Charles S. Peirce on logic or William James on psychology in his reading. He even drafted an unpublished philosophical paper with the title 'The Boundaries of Science and Philosophy'. According to this paper, philosophy needed the empirical proof of science so as to not lose itself in empty generalisations. Science needed the theoretical penetration of contexts by means of philosophy. Neither science nor philosophy can define and restrict itself. Both are dependent here on one another. Sean McCann alludes to most of Hammett's arguments at the beginning of the 1920s as being common knowledge in the intellectual discourse. However, what distinguished Hammett from the 'realists' and 'neo-progressives' of the time was that he defended the indispensability of philosophy in relation to science and even made metaphysical reflections. It is questionable, however, whether Hammett's argumentation is plausible in detail. This argumentation posits that science is based only on sense data, on that which is perceived (percepts), such as that 'white' occurs. Yet the act of perceiving (perception) is not a matter of science, but rather of philosophy. Einstein's hypothesis on the Theory of Relativity is a philosophical, not a scientific hypothesis. Hammett's extension of philosophy's reach to the detriment of science goes even further: in order to obtain a white thing, philosophy is required, since the 'thing' already belongs to philosophy.

It seems strange that philosophical considerations are necessary even to define an object as a white piece of chalk. Such a limitation of scientific activity is in some respects even more radical than Heidegger's view that science merely measures and calculates, but does not actually think. For with Hammett, not even the perceptive judgement of an object is a matter for science. Hammett's error lies in the schematic simplification of a complex matter by allocating percepts to science and perception to philosophy. It is, however, more plausible that both science and philosophy are concerned with percepts and perception, but that the formulation of questions and the methods of acquiring knowledge are different. Hammett's understanding of philosophy is not Marxist and is far removed from a philosophy of dialectic and historical materialism that sees itself as scientific. Rather, it has a certain proximity to the pragmatism of William James. In James' view, the bodies of knowledge from different scientific disciplines come together in philosophy. The critical metaphysical reflection of the presuppositions and findings of the sciences should dissipate contradictions and eliminate any knowledge that does not concur with reality. This should ensure that the greatest possible consistency is aspired to in science. As far as Hammett's crisp and striking style of argumentation and writing is concerned, his texts remind us less of James than of 'How to Make Our Ideas Clear,' by Peirce.

In Hammett's novel *The Dain Curse* (1929) the writer Fitzstephan criticises the 'Behaviourists' in a pronouncement on the state of psychology. Behaviourism, however, was defined essentially by the James student John B. Watson. In spite of grave differences, behaviourism is built demonstrably on the investigations of pragmatism. Aside from that, it is worth stating that pragmatism was the leading philosophical current in the first two decades of the twentieth century, at least in the USA. In

1923, Morris R. Cohen published the first collection of Peirce essays under the title *Chance, Love, and Logic* with a bibliography of his published works and an essay by John Dewey. This means that texts by Peirce were accessible to any reader interested in theory, including essays that formed a basis for pragmatism such as 'The Fixation of Belief' (1877) and 'How to Make our Ideas Clear' (1878). In his introduction to the reprint in 1998, Kenneth Laine Ketner assumes, with a view to the Flitcraft parable, that Hammett read the book *Chance, Love, and Logic*.

An influence of the reading of 'The Fixation of Belief' can be found in *The Dain Curse*. The Continental Op says to Gabrielle Collinson: 'Nobody thinks clearly, no matter what they pretend. Thinking's a dizzy business, a matter of catching as many of those foggy glimpses as you can and fitting them together the best you can. That's why people hang on so tight to their beliefs and opinions; because, compared to the haphazard way in which they arrived at, even the goofiest opinion seems wonderfully clear, sane, and self-evident. And if you let it get away from you, then you've got to dive back into that foggy muddle to wangle yourself out another to take its place.' Continental Op's pronouncements should be seen against the backdrop of a cult deception, which Gabrielle Collinson fell for in a way that endangered her.

Hammett's text presents a version of the 'belief-doubt-belief' theory from 'The Fixation of Belief'; it hones in dramatically on the individual. Peirce writes at the beginning of his essay: 'We come to the full possession of our power of drawing inferences the last of all our faculties, for it is not so much a natural gift as a long and difficult art.' Later he emphasises: '…that conceptions which are really products of logical reflections, without being readily seen to be so, mingle with our ordinary thoughts, and are frequently the causes of great confusion.' So much for the difficulty of clear thinking. Let us turn to the 'belief-doubt-belief' theory: 'Our beliefs guide our desires and shape our actions… Doubt is an uneasy and dissatisfied state from which we struggle to free ourselves and pass into the state of belief; while the latter is a calm and satisfactory state which we do not wish to avoid, or to change to a belief in anything else. On the contrary, we cling tenaciously, not merely to believing, but to believing just what we do believe… The irritation of doubt is the only immediate motive for the struggle to attain belief… With the doubt, therefore, the struggle begins, and with the cessation of doubt it ends. Hence, the sole object of inquiry is the settlement of opinion. We may fancy that this is not enough for us, and that we seek not merely an opinion, but a true opinion. But put this fancy to the test, and it proves groundless; for as soon as a firm belief is reached we are entirely satisfied, whether the belief be false or true.'

Peirce addresses four methods by which someone arrives at a conviction and consolidates it. The first method is one of tenacity. Here a person becomes accustomed to repeatedly answering a question with a certain reply and refuses to pay even the smallest attention to anything confusing. The second is the method of authority, through which an institution (state, religious body) determines and upholds teachings by deploying instruments of power. Peirce sees this method being used wherever there is priesthood. Hammett depicts an especially devious example of this method: the way in which the temple of the Holy Grail functions in *The Dain Curse*. The third method is the a priori method, for which the history of metaphysics offers the most complete example. According to this, a conviction is accepted because it seems to be the most reasonable. The fourth method is, in Peirce's opinion, the only acceptable one; it is the scientific method. It leads to the result that 'opinions… coincide with fact.' The scientific method, applied by every person to many things in Peirce's view, was also preferred by Hammett. The Continental Op says the following to Fitzstephan about his investigative methods: 'You've got a flighty mind. That's no good in this business. You don't catch murderers by amusing yourself with interesting thoughts. You've got to sit down to all the facts you can get and turn them over and over till they click.'

The scientific method, however, requires more than the observation of facts. According to Peirce and other pragmatists, it also requires logic and experimentation. The significance of logic for Peirce's thinking is already clarified in the first part of *Chance, Love, and Logic*, which is entitled 'Chance and Logic (Illustrations of the Logic of Science)' and which shapes his entire work. As presented above, Peirce knows three forms of conclusion: deduction, induction, and abduction. Deduction is the derivation of a result from a general rule and a case, in other words from premises. In contrast, induction infers the general rule from the case and the result; it concerns an empirical examination of prognoses, which are constructed on the basis of hypotheses. The original contribution by Peirce is the form of conclusion of abduction, a guessed construction of a hypothesis. From an invented general rule, introduced as a test, and from fact ('result') that is the cause of the deliberations and requires explanation, it is concluded that the fact (i.e. the occurrence) is a case of the (experimentally assumed) rule. The process of abduction, which is carried out largely unconsciously and playfully, requires intuition, creative inspiration, a kind of guessing instinct so that it, as the Continental Op says, 'clicks'. Abduction does not only play a role in the investigative process, but also in day-to-day perception. The perception of reality is subject to a process of interpreting signs, a continuous formation of hypotheses. Every perception that is articulated consciously is pervaded by abduction.

Abduction and deduction do not suffice for the scientific solution of a riddle; the hypothesis reached and the related prognoses require verification by experiment, induction. For Peirce and other pragmatists the experiment, the practical proof in experience, is an indispensable process in investigating reality. In the foundation stone of pragmatism, 'How to Make Our Ideas Clear', Peirce writes: 'Thus, we come down to what is tangible and practical, as the root of every real distinction of thought, no matter how subtle it may be,' which he illustrates with the example of 'hardness' by means of a scratch test on diamonds, commenting further: 'The whole conception of this quality [to be hard – author's note], as of every other, lies in its conceived effects.' The novel *The Dain Curse* begins with the words: 'It was a diamond all right...' That is no coincidence. It is usually interpreted as a reminiscence of Hammett's job as an ad writer for the jeweller and diamond trader Albert S. Samuels, to whom the novel is dedicated. At the same time, however, it could also be seen as an allusion to the 'foundation stone of pragmatism'.

Hammett and his detective figures appreciate both logic and the experiment. The story of how Hammett, as a Pinkerton detective, found a stolen Ferris wheel is well known. He searched all the funfairs in the region that might have a Ferris wheel until he found one where the owner could not prove his ownership. For Hammett this was pure logic. A thief could not have stolen something so big for his backyard. Therefore, it must be at some other funfair. Hammett's protagonists also rely on the power of logical conclusions in order to solve a case. Sam Spade in 'A Man called Spade', for example, reconstructs the crime primarily through a series of logical conclusions and declares, 'Understand, I'm just putting together what the evidence says, and what we got out of his wife, and the not much that we got out of him.' In 'Death on Pine Street' the attention of the Continental Op is drawn to the policeman Kelly ('the logical suspect'), after he makes logical conclusions from a variety of witness statements. According to William F. Nolan, the Continental Op stories follow strict rules, as in a game of chess. In spite of all their innovation, despite the fact that they are enhanced by social realism and action, Hammett's stories are clearly in the tradition of the detective story of puzzle solving. The detective's repertoire in Hammett's stories includes abduction, namely the use of guessing when following leads and intelligent inspiration, which was also the case with Sherlock Holmes.

But frequently this is not enough; experimental action is necessary. In *Red Harvest* the Op explains his methods to Dinah Brand: 'The closest I've got to an idea is to dig up any and all the dirty work I can that might implicate others, and run it out...' 'Is that what you were up to when you uncooked the fight?' 'That was only an experiment – just to see what would happen.' 'So that's the way you scientific detectives work', remarks Dinah Brand. Sam Spade describes his methodology as follows: 'My way of learning is to heave a wild and unpredictable monkey-wrench into the machinery.' Such behaviour does not correspond to the layout and progression of scientific experiments, but it makes clear that Hammett's detectives are not content with thought acrobatics that have no relation to reality, but they instead place value on experiments and their consequences when investigating a case and tracking down a criminal. In this respect they resemble the pragmatists.

The private detective in Hammett's stories has an utterly pragmatic approach to truth and its investigation. William James in particular worked out a pragmatic conception of truth. He was the one who originated the provocative question of the 'cash-value' of truth. 'Cash-Value' directs and limits the Continental Op's search for truth. This is especially noticeable in the different stages of the investigative work in *The Dain Curse*, each of which is introduced with a new contract to investigate in return for cash. At the end of the second part of the case Fitzstephan says to the Op: 'But if, as you say, you aren't satisfied that you've learned the whole truth of the affair, I should think you –' To which the Op responds that it has nothing to do with him, and that it was the client who terminated the business deal. Admittedly, William James' concept of truth is not founded so commercially. But there are other similarities between the relationship to truth in James' work and in the detective stories by Hammett. James stresses the usefulness of truth.

Hammett provides a cynical version of this view in the conclusion to the *The Maltese Falcon*. At the point where Sam Spade must decide whether or not to expose his lover Brigid O'Shaughnessy as a murderer and hand her over to the police, he argues neither with the necessity of clarifying the truth nor with just punishment. Instead he counts off seven reasons why for him, particularly as private detective, it is more convenient to hand her over to the law. Nick Charles in *The Thin Man* also has a pragmatic relationship to the truth. At the end of the novel Nick explains to his wife Nora how the story of the crime must have played out, based on the facts at hand, and why Macaulay the lawyer is accused. Nick asks Nora: 'Now are you satisfied with what we've got on him?' 'Yes, in a way. There seems to be enough of it, but it's not very neat.' 'It's neat enough to send him to the chair', responds Nick, 'and that's all that counts. It takes care of all the angles and I can't think of any other theory that would...' 'Have it your own way', she says, 'but I always thought detectives waited until they had every little detail fixed in –' 'And then wonder why the suspect's had time to get to the farthest country that has no extradition treaty.'

It would, of course, be a typical misinterpretation to reduce the pragmatic concept of truth to practical or even material benefits. The pragmatic concept of truth is much more complex and is oriented more towards an intellectual use. A well-known statement by James is: '"The true", to put it very briefly, is only the expedient in the way of our thinking, just as "the right" is only the expedient in the way of our behaving.' The orientation is effected by the result, ultimately by the test of the verification process, which can also be subject to error. An example for a related understanding of truth can be found in Hammett's story 'A Man Called Spade.' A policeman has found the necktie of the murder victim in a rubbish bin. It reveals three small, irregular stains. Spade assumes it is blood, while the police detective objects that it could possibly be dirt. They agree that it is better for the progress of the investigation to assume that it is blood, and they confront the suspect with this 'fact'. By these means they succeed in capturing the criminal, and it does turn out that it really was his blood. The detectives assumed something to be true, which brought them further in their thinking and was then confirmed in the verification process.

William James is convinced that, with regard to all of life's important tasks, we must all dare to jump into darkness. He thus characterises a stance that also marks Hammett's detective figures. Private detectives hope that from time to time they will be helped by chance. Allan Pinkerton even spoke of 'Detective Chance'. Hammett was familiar with the factor of chance from his detective work and his passion for gambling. Chance plays a dominant role in the Flitcraft parable. Sam Spade explains that he was looking for a missing man from Tacoma named Charles Flitcraft. He found him again five years after his disappearance in Spokane, under the name Charles Pierce. There he had assumed similar living habits to those he had in Tacoma. Flitcraft explains to Spade his hasty abandonment of his earlier family and life in the following manner: When he went to lunch, a beam fell down from the eighth or tenth floor, brushed very closely past him and slammed onto the sidewalk. He got a shock. 'He felt like somebody had taken the lid off life and let him look at the works… He knew then that men died at haphazard like that, and lived only while blind chance spared them… What disturbed him was the discovery that in sensibly ordering his affairs he had got out of step, and not into step, with life… Life could be ended for him at random by a falling beam: he would change his life at random by simply going away.' For two years he moved around and then settled down in Spokane. There he fell into the same old pattern that he had so abruptly left in Tacoma. Spade summarises: 'He adjusted himself to beams falling, and then no more of them fell, and he adjusted himself to them not falling.' In the end the tendency of people to adapt to certain life circumstances and to develop corresponding behavioural habits prevails, irrespective of the emphatic degree to which chance can determine life.

This thinking noticeably resembles the thoughts of Charles S. Peirce in *Chance, Love, and Logic*. Peirce, however, relates his teachings less to the individual life of man than to nature as a whole. On the one hand he assumes a moment of spontaneity or absolute chance in nature, while on the other hand he stresses the tendency for nature to develop behavioural habits. For Peirce this is not an unsolvable contradiction, but rather both elements belong to evolution: 'In biology, the idea of arbitrary sporting is First, heredity is Second, the process whereby the accidental characters become fixed is Third. Chance is First, Law is Second, the tendency to take habits is Third.' He summarises elsewhere: 'I make use of chance chiefly to make room for a principle of generalisation, or tendency to form habits, which I hold has produced all regularities.' Both the developing of behavioural habits and the breaking out from them is influenced decisively by the adaptation of organisms to their environment. People's convictions when generally approaching the truth are also subject to this process of adaptation. Even logical thinking, which is directed at practical things, could have emerged from the process of natural selection. For Peirce the process of evolution amounts to a development of concrete reason and even universal love; a relatively idealised view of the world that will have remained alien to Hammett. Whereas a tendency for love, good, and optimism dominates with Peirce and other pragmatists, Hammett's pragmatism is coloured by 'noir': violence, passions and conflicts are added to chance and behavioural habits as fundamental elements of life.

This is especially apparent in Hammett's novel *The Glass Key* (1931). The hero of the story, Ned Beaumont, is not a private detective but investigates a murder case on his own initiative out of loyalty to his friend Paul Madvig and his family, as well as out of antipathy towards Senator Henry. As such, Beaumont is not subject to the pragmatic restrictions that normally apply in the profession of the private detective. All the same, there are traces of pragmatism in *The Glass Key*. Just as Charles S. Peirce attempts in 'Man's Glassy Essence' to illuminate the physical nature of man, Hammett tries in *The Glass Key* to provide an insight into the social nature of people. He tries to portray the manner in which political power, money, social standing and feelings (friendship, love, antipathy) are woven together. The word 'glass' should be understood metaphorically in both texts. Human nature does not consist of glass with Peirce, nor is there any glass key in the reality of the novel. If, ultimately, the Maltese Falcon is a non-tangible object or, as it says in John Huston's film, the stuff of which dreams are made, similarly the glass key is the object of a dream told by the senator's daughter Janet Henry, to the hero of the novel. 'Glass' represents both transparency and fragility. In Janet's dream she and Ned Beaumont get lost in the woods. They come across a house, through whose barred windows she sees a richly laid table. Under the doormat she finds a glass key. It breaks just as they open the door, because the door got stuck and they had to use force. On the floor of the house they see hundreds of swarming snakes, which come out and attack them.

The dream leaves itself open to Freudian interpretation. The house represents woman, mother. The food in the house is motherly love and sexuality. The keyhole of the house represents the vagina, the key the phallus. The snakes are the sexual drive of the intruder, which is no longer controllable, and the fears of being overcome by this drive. But an argument against this dream interpretation is the fact that it is an Oedipal, masculine dream, not the dream of a woman. It should also be considered that the dream has an elevated place in the aesthetic construction of the novel, and the interpretation should therefore be taken from the aesthetic context. In the course of the novel Ned Beaumont infiltrates the secrets of the social relationships of the city, at the centre of which is the unsolved murder of Janet's brother Taylor. Beaumont does not do this as a cool observer, but rather as an active intruder, who puts himself into existential danger. Janet helps him with his investigations and ultimately leaves her home, as her father, the Senator, is the murderer. The dream story is a mixture of the 'Hansel and Gretel' fairytale, the biblical story of the fall from grace after eating from the tree of knowledge, and William James' example of the house in the forest as a symbol of usefulness in the search for truth. The house in the dream is the place of awareness and experience. But awareness and experience have a price, the loss of innocence of the unknowing/inexperienced: the door to the house can no longer be closed. The key breaks, and the process of awareness, or the experience of doing and suffering, as a process of change, is irreversible; it can neither be undone nor used to hold off unwanted awareness or knowledge. A dangerous knowledge can result from awareness, experience, and its publication, which may have uncontrollable consequences, especially for those with awareness. This is symbolised by the snakes that attack both intruders. In Hammett's dream story an existential, action-oriented attitude to the search for truth shines through, which is typical for pragmatism.

Another influence of pragmatism in *The Glass Key* is displayed in the critical view of social Darwinism in practice. Peirce wrote: 'The *Origin of Species* of Darwin merely extends the politico-economical views of progress to the entire realm of animal and vegetable life... As Darwin puts it on his title-page, it is the struggle for existence; and he should have added for his motto: Every individual for himself, and the Devil take the hind-most! ... On the other side, the conviction of the nineteenth century is that progress takes place by virtue of every individual's striving for himself with all his might and trampling his neighbor under foot whenever he gets a chance to do so. This may accurately be called the Gospel of Greed.' Hammett already staged such a gospel of greed in *Red Harvest*; but a merciless, political, and economic conflict also rages between competitors in the city in *The Glass Key*. Paul Madvig, head of the political camp currently in power is tricked and used shamelessly by Senator Henry and his daughter. Ned Beaumont explains to Janet Henry: 'I tried to tell him [Paul Madvig – author's note] you both considered him a lower form of animal life and fair game for any kind of treatment. I tried to tell him your father was a man all his life used to winning without much trouble and that in a hole he'd either lose his head or turn wolf.' Hammett does not write about class status and consciousness, although it would have required just a small step, but instead exposes the prevailing social Darwinism by means of an animal metaphor. He sees as decisive the habits that shape a social group of people and their perception and behaviour towards people of another class.

Peirce also attaches considerable meaning to thought and behavioural habits. He does not refer to the individual alone but rather stresses the real existence of an *esprit de corps*. According to his assumption: 'there should be something like personal consciousness in bodies of men who are in intimate and intensely sympathetic communion.' The *esprit de corps* of such a collective personality can be expressed both in simultaneous crimes and equally in virtuous dealings. While Peirce sees reason for hope in the development of a 'mind of corporations', Hammett describes the damaging influence of people on each other. His favourite word is 'poison'. The corrupt city in *Red Harvest* is named 'Poisonvillle.' In *The Glass Key* Senator Henry and his daughter are 'poison' for Paul Madvig. In *The Dain Curse* the Continental Op rejects a curse on the Dain family as a reason for Gabrielle Collinson's confusion. He does not believe in a curse, be it God-given or an effect of inheritance. He explains Gabrielle's thinking and behaviour as being the bad influence of the step mother: 'You got a hell of a start in life. You got into bad hands at the very beginning. Your step-mother was plain poison, and did her best to ruin you, and in the end succeeded in convincing you that you were smeared with a very special family curse.' The badness of the world does not spring from a mysterious force, but rather results from the thoughts, habits, passions, and interests of certain people. Other people can successfully counter this if they are supported by a well-functioning, incorrupt organisation, as in the case of the Op's Continental Agency; yet the fight never seems to end. Thoughts like this are not far removed from the view, and in particular the understanding of democracy of a pragmatist like Dewey, who, however, places his faith in a comprehensive process of education to overcome the historical inheritance burden of class differences. Hammett's view of politics and society, which is shaped by his experiences as a Pinkerton agent dealing with crime and the underbelly of society, is presented as somewhat more pessimistic, sinister, and bitter.

It is highlighted repeatedly in literature on Hammett that the detective heroes are tough through and through, that they act without expressing emotions, and that they rely only on their cool reason; their pragmatism is characterised as being cynical. This could be countered, however, by the argument that the heroes in Hammett's novels clearly are guided by feelings. In *Red Harvest* the Continental Op takes on the task of cleaning the city of crime and corruption with a perilous dedication that goes well beyond the paid contract; this dedication might well be connected with a desire for intrigue and violence, but is also borne of a disgust for crime and corruption. The Op demonstrates empathy to both Dinah Brand and Gabrielle Collinson, which allows him to form a relationship of trust with the women, albeit one-sided. For the most part Ned Beaumont's approach can only be explained by his friendship with Paul Madvig and his daughter, and is determined by an antipathy for Senator Henry, as a so called aristocrat of society, and his unmistakable feeling for justice. In their investigations Hammett's detective figures often follow the right lead precisely by utilising their knowledge of human nature to further a process of intertwining actions by the people involved, which ultimately leads to the unmasking of the criminal; such knowledge of human nature is hardly possible to attain without sensitivity, empathy or social feelings.

The importance of feelings for reflective dealing is not alien to pragmatism. Peirce praises 'the natural judgements of the sensible heart' and places them in the same context as the French Revolution and future social revolutionary upheavals. Emotion in no way stops at logic. The hypothetical conclusion, the abduction, is accompanied by a specific emotional movement; the hypothesis generates the 'sensuous element of thought', the induction the 'habitual', while deduction is the 'volitional element' of thinking. With Peirce, logic is based on ethics, on the social impulse of people. Hammett's descriptions in his detective stories are also characterised by a critical reflective social impulse.

Dashiell Hammett's mindset as a writer and his view of the function of literature correspond with the views of pragmatism. According to Peirce, artists have a particular ability to perceive reality unadulterated, without the filter of generally usual interpretations. The work of the artist consists of reproducing what he sees or hears, which is a highly complicated matter in every form of art. Dewey's stipulations for literature and art go further. Because portrayal is a matter for art, it is the obligation of art to convey to the greater public new objects and the results of investigations by the manner of its presentation, and thus to break through the crust of conventional, routine consciousness. The effect of literature is decisive.

What is Hammett's view? He commented on the work of a writer in a speech at the Third Writers Congress in June 1937. According to him the job of a contemporary writer is to take parts of life and to arrange them on paper. The more direct the path from the street to paper, the more real to life it will be. The writer must make what he writes down appear believably contemporary; the things must give the impression that they are happening here and now; the reader should have a feeling of immediacy. For that reason the writer must know how things happen, not how one remembers them later, and in this way he must write them down. Hammett chose the crime story as a form of communication and aesthetic expression, a popular genre that is appreciated for its exciting drama and its effect on the reader. He first published his texts in *Black Mask* and other magazines, which reached a mass public. Hammett was a pragmatic writer in his entire manner of production.

In the fragment 'Tulip' Hammett describes a writer who, like himself, had not written for many years in his later life. He has him pronounce some ideas about writing a novel and sees the problem in the proper organisation of the material. James Naremore comments: 'In the long view, and given the particular historical context of Hammett's work, this emphasis on the problem of form has important political implications. It suggests that Hammett had become philosophical about the relation between language and ideology.'

My theory, in contrast, is that Hammett's position on language and writing *had always been philosophical*. The difference between the earlier and later Hammett consists of the fact that the philosophy changed. Marxism replaced pragmatism. It may be that Hammett's support of Hellman's writing career, his piecework for Hollywood and the many years of alcohol abuse were contributing factors in his writer's block. But the main reason is that he could not meet the high demands of Marxism on literature. He did not succeed in revolutionising the novel and thus make his contribution to the social revolution as a Marxist writer. As a writer, pragmatism gave him wings, while Marxism paralysed him. His works are the fruits of his own, independent pragmatism.

Previous versions of this text were published in CADS 50, October 2006, 29–35 and online: http://www.thrillingdetective.com

References and Further Reading

a) Dashiell Hammett
Hammett, Dashiell: *The Dain Curse*, New York 1972
Hammett, Dashiell: 'Tulip', in: *The Big Knockover and Other Stories*, ed. Lillian Hellman, Harmondsworth 1984, 283–323
Hammett, Dashiell: *Red Harvest*, New York 1992
Hammett, Dashiell: *The Glass Key*, New York 1992
Hammett, Dashiell: *The Maltese Falcon*, New York 1992
Hammett, Dashiell: *The Thin Man*, New York 1992
Hammett, Dashiell: 'A Man Called Spade', in: *Nightmare Town: Stories*, New York 1999, 277–304
Hammett, Dashiell: 'Death on Pine Street', in: *Nightmare Town: Stories*, New York 1999, 189–213
Hammett, Dashiell: 'The Boundaries of Science and Philosophy', in: Richard Layman (ed.): *Discovering The Maltese Falcon and Sam Spade*, revised edition San Francisco 2005, 120–122

b) on Hammett
Hellman, Lillian: Introduction, in: Dashiell Hammett, *The Big Knockover and Other Stories*, Harmondsworth 1984 (1969), 7–23
Hellman, Lillian: *Scoundrel Time*, Boston, Toronto, 1976
Johnson, Diane: *The Life of Dashiell Hammett*, London, 1985
Layman, Richard: *Shadow Man: The Life of Dashiell Hammett*, N. Y., London, 1981
Layman, Richard (ed.): *Discovering the Maltese Falcon and Sam Spade*, revised edition San Francisco 2005
Marcus, Steven: Introduction, in: Dashiell Hammett, *The Continental Op*, London 1984 (1977), 7–23
McCann, Sean: *Gumshoe America*, Durham, London 2000
Mellen, Joan: *Hellman and Hammett*, N. Y. 1996
Naremore, James: '*Dashiell Hammett and the Poetics of Hard-Boiled Detection*', in: *Essays on Detective Fiction*, ed. by Bernard Benstock, London, Basingstoke 1983, 49–72

Nolan, William F.: Introduction, in: Dashiell Hammett, *Nightmare Town: Stories*, N. Y. 1999, vii-xvii

Nolan, William F.: *Hammett – A Life at the Edge*, London 1983

Symons, Julian: *Bloody Murder. From the Detective Story to the Crime Novel: A History*, 3rd edition London, Basingstoke, 1992

Walther, Hanns: *Die Schule der Detektive. Die abenteuerliche Laufbahn der ersten Detektive*, Würzburg 1961

Zumoff, Jacob A.: 'The Politics of Dashiell Hammett's Red Harvest', Mosaic 40, December 1, 2007, 119–131 (*http://www.highbeam.com*)

Zumoff, Jacob A.: 'Politics and the 1920s Writings of Dashiell Hammett', 2009 (script)

c) on philosophy, especially pragmatism and logic

Cohen, Morris R.: Introduction, in: Charles Sanders Peirce: *Chance, Love, and Logic: Philosophical Essays*, ed. and introduced by Morris R. Cohen, Lincoln, London 1998 (1923), xix-xlv

Dewey, John: *Democracy and Education*, New York 1955 (1916)

Dewey, John: *The Public and Its Problems*, Athens 1991 (1927)

Dewey, John: 'The Pragmatism of Peirce', in: Charles Sanders Peirce: *Chance, Love, and Logic: Philosophical Essays*, ed. and introduced by Morris R. Cohen, Lincoln, London 1998 (1923), 301–308

Diaz-Bone, Rainer/Schubert, Klaus: *William James zur Einführung*, Hamburg 1996

Eco, Umberto: 'Die Abduktion in Uqbar', in: Jorge Luis Borges/Adolfo Bioy Casares: *Sechs Aufgaben für Don Isidro Parodi. Zwei denkwürdige Phantasien. Ein Modell für den Tod*, Munich/Vienna 1983: 271–286

Heidegger, Martin: *Was heißt Denken?*, Stuttgart 1992

James, William: *Pragmatism*, Cambridge, London, 1975

James, William: *The Meaning of Truth*, New York, 1968

James, William: *The Will to Believe and Other Essays, in: Popular Philosophy*, Cambridge, London 1979

Kelkel, Arion L.: 'Zum Verhältnis von Dichtung und Denken bei Heidegger. Skizze eines Problems', in: Volker Bohn (ed.): *Romantik Literatur und Philosophie*, Frankfurt am Main 1987, 279–287

Ketner, Kenneth Laine: Introduction to the Bison Books Edition, in: Charles Sanders Peirce: *Chance, Love, and Logic: Philosophical Essays*, ed. and introduced by Morris R. Cohen, Lincoln, London 1998 (1923), v-xiii

Klein, Kathleen Gregory/Keller, Joseph: 'Der deduktive Detektivroman: Ein Genre, das sich selbst zerstört', in: Jochen Vogt (ed.): *Der Kriminalroman: Poetik – Theorie – Geschichte*, Munich 1998, 428–443

Martens, Ekkehard: Einleitung, in: Martens (ed.): *Pragmatismus*, Stuttgart 1975, 3–59

Nagel, Thomas: *What Does It All Mean? A Very Short Introduction to Philosophy*, New York, Oxford 1987

Nagl, Ludwig: *Charles Sanders Peirce*, Frankfurt/M., New York 1992

Nagl, Ludwig: *Pragmatismus*, Frankfurt/M., New York 1998

Oehler, Klaus: *Charles Sanders Peirce*, Munich 1993

Peirce, Charles Sanders: *Chance, Love, and Logic: Philosophical Essays*, ed. and introduced by Morris R. Cohen, Lincoln, London 1998 (1923)

Peirce, Charles Sanders: *Lectures on pragmatism – Vorlesungen über Pragmatismus*, Hamburg 1973

Russell, Bertrand: *A History of Western Philosophy*, London 1945

Sebeok, Thomas A./Umiker-Sebeok, Jean: 'Du kennst meine Methode.' Charles S. Peirce und Sherlock Holmes, Frankfurt am Main 1982 (English edition: 'You Know My Method: A Juxtaposition of Charles S. Peirce and Sherlock Holmes.', in: *Semiotica*, 26 (2/3), 203–250)

Shusterman, Richard: 'Pragmatismus und Liberalismus', in: Christoph Demmerling/Thomas Rentsch (ed.): *Die Gegenwart der Gerechtigkeit*, Berlin 1995, 155–180

Suhr, Martin: *John Dewey zur Einführung*, Hamburg 1994

Walther, Elisabeth: Einleitung, in: Charles Sanders Peirce: *Die Festigung der Überzeugung und andere Schriften*, Frankfurt am Main/Berlin/ Wien, 1985, 9–41

6

Wittgenstein, PI, and the Mystery of the Missing Link

a) Wittgenstein – reader of detective stories

When Ludwig Wittgenstein returned to Cambridge in 1929, he entered an academic milieu that eagerly and devotedly read crime fiction. It is not known when exactly Wittgenstein began to read detective stories regularly. At any rate, in his lecture on 'Sense Data and Private Experience' in the autumn of 1935, Wittgenstein quoted from a story in Street & Smith's *Detective Story Magazine*, as recorded in notes by Rush Rhees: The detective is standing alone at night on the deck of a ship. It is quiet except for the ticking of the ship's clock. 'A clock is a bewildering instrument at best,' he thinks, 'measuring a fragment of infinity: measuring something which does not exist perhaps'. Wittgenstein commented that this confusion in a supposedly 'silly detective story' can set off more thought processes than the chatter of a 'silly philosopher'. One could object 'obviously a clock is not a bewildering instrument at all'. If someone thinks a clock bewildering yet then says it is not bewildering, then 'this is a way to solve a philosophical problem'. In the detective story the clock is something strange, because it measures, according to the detective, something endless, 'something which does not exist perhaps'. Because it is invisible, it seems like a ghost to the detective. What connection is there to sense data? 'What is bewildering is the introduction of something we might call "intangible". It seems as though there is nothing intangible about the chair or the table, but there is about the fleeting personal experience'. ('The Language of Sense Data and Private Experience – I, Notes taken by Rush Rhees of Wittgenstein's Lectures, 1936', in: *Philosophical Investigations*, VII, no. 1 (January 1984), 1–45; quoted from Monk 1991: 355, 618–619).

Street & Smith's *Detective Story Magazine* was a monthly publication, a pulp magazine, which Wittgenstein read more or less regularly until his death. In letters to his student Norman Malcolm, a philosopher in the US, he often expressed how important the magazine was for him and far more important than the leading philosophy magazine of the time, *Mind*. He wrote to Malcolm on 8 September, 1945, referring to the paper rationing in England: 'Thanks a lot for the mags... The one way in which the ending of Lend-Lease really hits me is by producing a shortage of detective mags in this country. I can only hope Lord Keynes will make this quite clear in Washington. For I say: if the U.S.A. won't give us detective mags we can't give them philosophy...'

A letter dated 15 March, 1948 contains the following lines: 'Your mags are wonderful. How people can read *Mind* when they could read *Street & Smith* beats me. If philosophy has anything to do with wisdom there's certainly not a grain of that in *Mind*, and quite often a grain in the detective stories.'

Mind came off even more negatively in another comparison made in his letter of 30 October, 1945: 'If I read your mags I often wonder how anyone can read *Mind* with all its impotence and bankruptcy when they could read Street & Smith mags. Well, everyone to his taste'.

The Street & Smith's *Detective Story Magazine* in those days differed little from the more prestigious pulp magazine *Black Mask*. In the 1930s and 40s it published stories by *Black Mask* authors like Raymond Chandler, Carroll John Daly, Erle Stanley Gardner, Cornell Woolrich and Norbert Davis. Wittgenstein was a loyal reader of Street & Smith's *Detective Story Magazine*. When Norman Malcolm sent him other magazines, he complained and warned him not to get creative as long as there is the 'good, old, tried out stuff'. Because Wittgenstein constantly spoke of *detective* stories, it can perhaps be presumed that other sub-genres of crime fiction like gangster stories, action novels or psychological thrillers appealed to him less. The majority of detective stories from the hard-boiled school still had supporting elements in common with the classic whodunit, so that the shift in reading tastes from the classic to the hard-boiled could gradually take place.

Wittgenstein also had private discussions about detective stories with students and peers. M. O'C. Drury, a student and close friend of Wittgenstein's, recalled a conversation he once had about crime fiction with Wittgenstein in 1936, during which Wittgenstein praised Agatha Christie, claiming that it required a specifically English talent to be able to write such books. For Wittgenstein, Christie's crime stories were a pure delight. Not only were the plots cleverly worked out, the characters too, were portrayed so well that they seemed like real people. On once being recommended to read Chesterton's Father Brown stories, Wittgenstein turned up his nose: 'Oh no, I couldn't stand the idea of a Roman Catholic priest playing the part of a detective. I don't want that'. In light of that conversation with Drury in the mid-1930s, it can be safely assumed that Wittgenstein's taste complied with that of his time, and that he therefore followed all the developments in crime fiction. At Cambridge he particularly enjoyed talking with the political economist Piero Sraffa. When Sraffa was interned in a camp as an Italian citizen during the Second World War for a few months, Wittgenstein sent him *The Thin Man* by Dashiell Hammett, which he had told him about previously.

Wittgenstein particularly admired the American crime novelist Norbert Davis, which becomes clear in a letter to Norman Malcolm from June 4, 1948:

'Dear Norman,

Thanks a lot for the detective mags. I had, before they arrived, been reading a detective story by Dorothy Sayers, and it was so bl… foul that it depressed me. Then when I opened one of your mags it was like getting out of a stuffy room into the fresh air. And, talking of detective fiction, I'd like you to make an enquiry for me when once you've got nothing better to do. A couple of years ago I read with great pleasure a detective story called 'Rendezvous with Fear' by a man Norbert Davis. I enjoyed it so much that I gave it not only to Smythies but also to Moore to read and both shared my high opinion of it. For, though, as you know, I've read hundreds of stories that amused me and that I liked reading, I think I've only read two perhaps that I'd call good stuff, and Davis's is one of them. Some weeks ago I found it again by a queer coincidence in a village in Ireland, it has appeared in an edition called 'Cherry Tree books', something like 'Penguin'. Now I'd like you to ask at a bookshop if Norbert Davis has written other books, and what kind. (He's an American) It may sound crazy, but when I recently re-read the story I liked it again so much that I thought I'd really like to write to the author and thank him. If this is nuts don't be surprised, for so am I. – I shouldn't be surprised if he had written quite a lot and only this one story were really good'.

Wittgenstein's enthusiasm for *The Mouse in the Mountain*, the American edition's original title for Norbert Davis's novel, is explained by his feeling that he had encountered a soul mate in Davis. What connects the two is a sarcastic humour, which Ray Monk correctly emphasises. This is expressed most strongly in Davis's dialogue. *In The Mouse in the Mountain* is a scene where the bandit García lies lifelessly on the floor after a shoot-out with the private detective Doan. After a Mexican officer examines García, the following dialogue ensues:

'Dead,' said the tall man. 'That is unfortunate'.

'For him,' Doan agreed.

The humour of this verbal and situation comedy is often achieved by the suppression of customary forms of communication, and especially by obstinately taking what people say (but not necessarily mean) literally – like a *reductio ad absurdum*. As a result, Davis's humour takes on anarchic and bizarre features, similar to those of Marx Brothers films. Here is a sample from *The Mouse in the Mountain*:

'Friend,' said Henshaw, '...I'm in the plumbing business – "Better Bathrooms for a Better America". What's your line'?

'Crime,' Doan told him.

'You mean you're a public enemy?' Henshaw asked, interested.

'There have been rumours to that effect,' Doan said. 'But I claim I'm a private detective'.

This clever and laconic narrative style is probably a further reason why Davis's novel appealed to Wittgenstein so much.

Almost nothing is sacred to the hard-boiled private detectives. Their impertinence and unscrupulousness overwhelm not only their opponents and competitors but even their clients. In Davis's short stories, the detective figures play a particularly cunning game with the people they encounter. The following statement by Wittgenstein could also have been made by a trickster such as Detective Doan: 'Someone says to me: "Show the children a game." I teach them gaming with dice, and the other says 'I didn't mean that sort of game." (PI, note added to §70)

The relationship between life and death has always been a fundamental preoccupation in philosophy, as in crime fiction. Davis's novel *The Mouse in the Mountain* could well have inspired Wittgenstein to the following statement: 'And so, too, a corpse seems to us quite inaccessible to pain. – Our attitude to what is alive and to what is dead, is not the same. All our reactions are different'. (PI §284)

Davis's story contains a piece of dialogue that humorously illustrates Wittgenstein's claim. After private detective Doan shoots gangster Bautiste

Bonofile in a struggle, Doan's companion Janet asks, worried: 'Is he – hurt?' 'Not a bit,' said Doan. 'He's just dead'.

A few pages later, Doan puts forward a variation on a logical problem contained in the proposition, 'A Cretan says, 'All Cretans are liars''

'Yes, I lied to him'... 'Well, aren't you ashamed? You involved me, too'.

'You shouldn't have believed me,' Doan said...

'Why not'? Janet demanded indignantly.

'Because I'm a detective,' Doan said... 'Detectives never tell the truth if they can help it. They lie all the time. It's just business'.

'Not all detectives!'

Doan nodded, seriously now. 'Yes. Every detective ever born, and every one who ever will be. Honest'.

The same unsentimental, self-mocking humour with regard to his own profession can be found, expressed in equally mordant tones, in Wittgenstein's statements on the philosopher: 'I am sitting with a philosopher in the garden; he says again and again "I know that that's a tree", pointing to a tree that is near us. Someone else arrives and hears this, and I tell him: "This fellow isn't insane. We are only doing philosophy."' (On Certainty § 467)

It is a shame that Norman Malcolm did not take Wittgenstein's request more seriously and did not find more novels by Davis or find out his address. In 1948 he could have got his hands on some short stories and books by Norbert Davis without much difficulty. After years of writing for the pulp magazines, Davis had managed in the 1940s to have his detective stories published in book form. Between 1943 and 1947 four such books appeared: *The Mouse in the Mountain* (1943; the paperback issues were called *Rendezvous with Fear* and *Dead Little Rich Girl*); *Sally's in the Alley* (1943); *Oh Murderer Mine* (1946); (in co-operation with W. T. Ballard) *Murder Picks the Jury* (1947). No more books were to come. In 1949 Norbert Davis, forty years old, killed himself.

b) Traces and affinities of crime fiction in Wittgenstein's way of thinking and writing

After Wittgenstein's return to Cambridge, excerpts of texts which recall detective work and crime fiction can be found time and again in his works or other statements.

In December 1929 Wittgenstein reported a dream about a man called Vertsag: 'He opens fire with a machine-gun at a cyclist behind him who writhes with pain and is mercilessly gunned to the ground with several shots. Vertsag has driven past, and now comes to a young, poor-looking girl on a cycle and she too is shot at by Vertsag as he drives on. And these shots, when they hit her breast make a bubbling sound like an almost empty kettle over a flame'.

In the early 1930s Wittgenstein compared verification with police investigative work. To the question by philosopher and psychologist G. F. Stout on his view of verification he replied with a parable: 'Imagine that there is a town in which the policemen are required to obtain information from each inhabitant, e. g. his age, where he came from, and what work he does. A record is kept of this information and some use is made of it. Occasionally when a policeman questions an inhabitant he discovers that the latter does not do any work. The policeman enters this fact on the record, because this too is a useful piece of information about the man!'

In the course of the Michaelmas term in 1930, Wittgenstein mentions the process of 'reading minds', a process which Poe's Dupin and Conan Doyle's Sherlock Holmes demonstrate and then rationally explain to their amazed sidekicks. Not unlike the two detectives, Wittgenstein traces the reading of minds back to perfectly natural processes.

He answers the question – what do we mean by reading minds – with the explanation that reading minds can only occur through the interpretation of symbols and this is therefore on the same level as language. Language is not an indirect method of communicating that is juxtaposed to the 'direct' reading of minds. One cannot simply get rid of the symbolic process. There is no more direct way of mind reading than by means of language. Thinking is not a hidden process; it is out in the open for all to see. The two master detectives would be in full agreement with this last sentence in particular.

In his philosophy lectures of 1932/33, recorded by Alice Ambrose, Wittgenstein spoke of the fact that a gentleman always wears a brown suit. This is most likely a reference to Agatha Christie's detective novel *The Man in the Brown Suit* from 1924.

As in both the traditional and the more modern detective stories, Wittgenstein's main concern in his work is with transparency, with arriving at certainty about facts, at a correct view and elucidation of the real connections by means of eliminating deceptions and sham constructs. Wittgenstein's wish was to expose pretence, hypocrisy, puffiness, slovenliness and obscuration, which are as widespread in the realms of philosophy and science as they are in the avaricious world of commerce. He compared many contemporary philosophers to cheats and businessmen who capitalised on poor districts, and saw it as his task to put a stop to such activities by his colleagues. In one of his earliest conversations with Drury he told him: 'Philosophy is like trying to open a safe with a combination lock: each little adjustment of the dials seems to achieve nothing; only when everything is in place does the door open.'

In some of Wittgenstein's remarks on the task of philosophy, all that is necessary is to substitute a few words like philosophy, philosopher, etc with **detective work, detective** – those marked in bold type in the following – in order to illustrate their affinity to crime fiction:

'What we find out in **detective work** is trivial; it does not teach us new facts, only science does that. But the proper synopsis of these trivialities is enormously difficult, and has immense importance. **Detective work** is in fact the synopsis of trivialities'. (Lecture 1930) 'A **detective's** problem has the form: 'I don't know my way about'. (PI §123) 'The work of the **detective** consists in assembling reminders for a particular purpose'. (PI §127) 'What is your aim working as a **detective**? – To show the fly the way out of the fly-bottle'. (PI §309)

In his remarks on this statement, Wittgenstein expert Joachim Schulte further underlines its similarity, in form and content, to the attitude of a private detective à la Philip Marlowe towards a female client, the threatened 'fly', as it were. In Schulte's view, the fact that the fly has fallen into the trap means it is in considerable danger, not just because of a total lack of orientation, but because it has become so completely entangled that it cannot free itself. The man who comes to the aid of such an 'imprisoned' client is indeed a veritable saviour in her hour of need.

Not only did Wittgenstein distrust abstruse, mysterious-sounding waffling in philosophy, he also regarded the equation of mathematical logic and science as a misconception. In this sense Ray Monk may be correct in assuming that Wittgenstein was better able to identify with the approach of the hardened American private detective than with the methods of a Sherlock Holmes or Hercule Poirot. And just as the new-style, down-to-earth private eye was opposed to the old-style detective and his apparently logical deductions, Wittgenstein too was keen to distance himself from the representatives of a mathematisation of philosophy and science. For him, the fundamentals of mathematical logic were based on mere agreements, that is to say, human inventions, and were thus totally different from the laws of nature.

Given that Wittgenstein's philosophical work, like the typical detective story, dealt with the exposure of deception, he naturally approached facts in a way that was reminiscent of a detective's approach to solving problems. § 129 of his *Philosophical Investigations* reads like a summary of Poe's 'The Purloined Letter', a story in which a stolen letter remains concealed from the eyes of the investigators simply by being placed openly on a card-rack, visible to all at any time. Wittgenstein writes: 'The aspects of things that are most important for us are hidden because of their simplicity and familiarity. (One is unable to notice something – because it is always before one's eyes.)'

Individual sentences in § 99 of his *Philosophical Investigations* may even contain an allusion to a typical element of crime fiction, namely, 'the locked room mystery': '… if I say "I have locked the man up fast in the room – there is only one door left open" – I simply haven't locked him in at all; his being locked in is a sham… An enclosure with a hole in it is as good as none'.

Are the following lines from § 293 of 'Philosophical Investigations' not almost a parody-like portrayal of the typical scene in which the master detective recapitulates the events of the crime before a confounded audience, eliminating a 'red herring' that had misled the investigations? 'Suppose everyone had a box with something in it: we call it a "beetle". No one can look into anyone else's box, and everyone says he knows what a beetle is only by looking at his beetle. – Here it would be quite possible for everyone to have something different in his box. One might even imagine such a thing constantly changing. – But suppose the word "beetle" had a use in these people's language? – If so it would not be used as the name of a thing. The thing in the box has no place in the language-game at all; not even as a something: for the box might even be empty. – No, one can "divide through" by the thing in the box; it cancels out, whatever it is'.

§ 115 PU points in a similar direction: 'A picture held us captive.'

Wittgenstein's remarks on the work of philosophers like the fly bottle metaphor quoted above reveal a disillusioned, bitter but also tough, dogged approach to his profession which recalls the private detective's professional attitude and special worldly knowledge – 'street wisdom'. Wittgenstein, as founder of the so-called 'ordinary language philosophy,' could display sympathy for detectives who speak the language of the average guy on the street, who wrangle with everyday problems and real opponents and have the scars to show for it, rather than for the classic detective who gets his criminals because of his brilliant powers of deduction or even his clairvoyant abilities.

Wittgenstein's preference for the working methods of hard-boiled detectives can also be easily demonstrated by the use of slightly modified quotations from his *Philosophical Investigations*: 'In the detective's work we do not draw conclusions.' (§599) 'Here it is difficult as it were to keep our heads up, – to see that we must stick to the subjects of our every-day thinking, and not go astray and imagine that we have to reconstruct extreme subtleties, which in turn we are after all quite unable to reconstruct with the means at our disposal. We feel as if we had to repair a torn spider's web with our fingers'. (§ 106)

'We have got on to slippery ice where there is no friction and… we are unable to walk. We want to walk: so we need friction. Back to the rough ground!' (§ 107) 'I can look for him when he is not there, but not hang him when he is not there'. (§ 462) 'The results of a detective's work are the uncovering of one or another piece of plain nonsense and of bumps that he has got by running its head up against the limits prescribed. These bumps make us see the value of the discovery'. (§ 119)

Could such terms not also be used to describe the 'philosophy' of the 'tough private eye'? In 'You Can Die Any Day', Norbert Davis puts it somewhat more bluntly and briefly: '…so I went right ahead anyway. I couldn't wait to investigate. I had to poke my neck out'.

It is quite possible that some of Wittgenstein's remarks on the theme of the rules of the game, on 'being guided', and on reading might well have been inspired by the narrative technique of crime fiction, by that subtle tactic of keeping the reader on tenterhooks until the finale. For example, in § 652 of *Philosophical Investigations* we read: "He measured him with a hostile glance and said …." The reader of the narrative understands this; he has no doubt in his mind… But it is possible that the hostile glance and the words later prove to have been pretence, or that the reader is kept in doubt whether they are so or not, and so that he really does guess at a possible interpretation. – But then the main thing he guesses at is a context. He says to himself for example: The two men who are here so hostile to one another are in reality friends, etc. etc.'

The following passages could stem from crime fiction:

'I see someone pointing a gun and say "I expect a report". The shot is fired'. (PI § 442)

'I watch a slow match burning, in high excitement follow the progress of the burning and its approach to the explosive'. (PI § 576)

The hard-boiled crime stories of the 1940s frequently contain accounts of torture scenes and pain endurance rites. A favourite plot element is the state of complete uncertainty in which the detective or the victim of the crime find themselves. In his way of examining philosophical problems, Wittgenstein succeeded in blending these two elements:

'…several people standing in a ring, and me among them. One of us, sometimes this one, sometimes that, is connected to the poles of an electrical machine without our being able to see this. I observe the faces of the others and try to see which of us has just been electrified – Then I say: "Now I know who it is; for it's myself"'. (PI § 409)

The following German sentence '*Dass mich das Feuer brennen wird, wenn ich die Hand hineinstecke: das ist Sicherheit.*' is rendered as follows in the English version: 'I shall get burnt if I put my hand in the fire: that is certainty.' (PI § 474) Were the German to have been translated literally, it would read: 'That fire will burn me if I put my hand into it: that is certainty'.

Wittgenstein's German text makes a particularly sharp point due to the fact that the German word *Sicherheit* means both certainty and security. The second connotation is absent from the English word 'certainty'. The syntactical alteration also diminishes the harshness of the expression.

Wittgenstein's linguistic style has in some respects a kinship with the prose of the Black Mask School, in particular with that of Norbert Davis. Wittgenstein detested 'long-windedness'. He was practically obsessed with a short, precise, logical form of expression and tormented those around him with a relentless correction of erroneous sentences. Not only in private texts like conversations, journal entries and letters but also in philosophical discourses did he tend to crass, hard-nosed statements and sarcastic humour. Wittgenstein preferred laconic formulations, which 'in a flash' could bring a thought to life. The word 'wisecrack' could aptly describe his writing style if it wasn't already taken for the sharp tongued, humorous cracks used by Philip Marlowe and his colleagues. But one cannot describe it with Eagleton's misleading exaggerations, comparing the *Philosophical Investigations* with a mesh of 'jokes, images and anecdotes'.

c) The 'fair play rule' discourse among crime fiction writers and Wittgenstein's concept of the language-game

Since Wittgenstein liked to chat with colleagues and students about detective stories, he cannot have avoided a discussion about the rule of fair play in whodunits. An occasion for the debate on rules of fair play in detective stories was provided by the publication of Agatha Christie's novel *The Murder of Roger Ackroyd* in 1926, in which it is commonly known that the narrator and detective Poirot's assistant is revealed as the murderer. In 1928 Monsignor Ronald Knox, crime writer and chaplain at Oxford University, created a Decalogue for telling detective stories: 'Ten Commandments of Detection'. The first commandment said: 'The criminal must be mentioned in the early part of the story, but must not be anyone whose thoughts the reader has been allowed to follow'. The seventh commandment ordered: 'The detective himself must not commit the crime'. The ninth commandment called for: 'The stupid friend of the detective, the Watson, must not conceal from the reader any thoughts which pass through his mind; his intelligence must be slightly, but very slightly, below that of the average reader'. If a writer takes these commandments to heart, deceiving the reader as in *The Murder of Roger Ackroyd* is ruled out. For Knox, as for most members of his generation, detective stories were not only a riddle but also a game. His friend and fellow believer G. K. Chesterton described in his essay 'How to Write a Detective Story' how the detective story was a game between writer and reader 'playing hide-and-seek'. Knox called the same process of communication 'a great battle of wits between the writer and reader'. Such a game needs rules, just as philosophy and cricket need rules and what is needed above all is the spirit of fair play.

The discourse about the 'Rules of the Detective Story' extended further to other circles. In the US the crime writer S.S. Van Dine published 'Twenty Rules for Writing Detective Stories' in the September 1928 issue of *The American Magazine*. He also stressed the characteristic of an intellectual game, a sports-like event with firm rules that ensure fair play. After its founding in 1930, the British Detection Club required its members to abide by certain rules. Dorothy Sayers, a graduate of Oxford, gave a lecture on 5 March, 1935 at Oxford entitled 'Aristotle on Detective Fiction'. Mainly it dealt with the actuality of Aristotle's *Poetics* in relation to crime literature. In this context Sayers also addressed the topic of the rules of fair play. She took up this aspect once again in the introduction to the anthology she also edited called *Tales of Detection* (1936). Here she stressed that the establishment of the 'fair-play rule' coincided with the growing knowledge about crime technology, such as fingerprints, bloodstain analysis and so forth. The 'clues' must be presented and the solution must be reached through rational conclusions, whereby the author assumes that the reader is familiar with any established or reported facts regardless how obscure or novel they may be.

If we summarise the discussion on fair play in detective stories, we have the following elements: it involves a linguistic-communicative process that is regarded as a game. In order to enjoy the game with pleasure, certain rules are required which guarantee the author's fair handling of the reader of his text. Wittgenstein occupied himself during his time in Cambridge with the following questions among others: How does language work? What thoughts can be expressed by language? What rules does language follow? What does it mean to follow a rule? How does the meaning of a word come about? What relationships exist between language and the world? How do people who communicate with each other, understand each other? Wittgenstein's well-known response can mainly be found in his concept of the language-game. The basic elements in the concept of the language-game already exist in the 'fair-play rule' discussion, ready to be taken up and conceptually transformed by a philosophical thinker such as Wittgenstein.

Wittgenstein experts have always asked what triggered Wittgenstein's switch from the *Tractatus* to later philosophy. A number of factors and reasons have been given. One reason among others was probably the impetus that the 'fair-play rule' discussion among crime writers gave to Wittgenstein's ideas. This stimulation of thought is a missing link in the reconstruction from early to late Wittgenstein. Even if this cannot be proved, it shows in any event how clever and advanced the theories of crime writers were in practice, even before Wittgenstein's findings on language.

d) Detective stories and the language-game
Let us return to the concept of the language-game and detective stories. In § 23 of *Philosophical Investigations* he clarifies the term 'language-game': 'Here the word "language-game" is meant to bring into prominence the fact that the speaking of language is part of an activity, or of a form of life.' There are many diverse language-games, for example:

'Giving orders, and obeying them-
Describing the appearance of an object, or giving its measurements-
Constructing an object from a description (a drawing)-
Reporting an event-
Speculating about an event-
Forming and testing a hypothesis- …
Making up a story; and reading it- …
Guessing riddles-
Making a joke; telling it- …
Translating from one language into another-.'

It will be apparent to crime fiction readers that many of the given examples for language-games are familiar from crime stories. Detective stories prove to be a veritable treasure trove of language-games. In this manner, police officers receive their investigative orders and carry them out. The crime weapon and location are described exactly. If the crime weapon is smashed or has been misplaced, it is reconstructed with, for example, witness statements or from the victim's wounds etc. The crime sequence is reported by witnesses. If the crime sequence isn't clear, speculations are made. A hypothesis for a possible suspect's motive is put forth. Translations are specially prepared for witness statements and other important announcements made in a foreign language. Other, relatively orderly forms of text can be named, which can obviously be characterised as language games: being interrogated by a detective, the witness statements, the alternating examination of a witness at a court trial etc. But what is more important is that detective stories do not just contain language-games, they are themselves language-games. We can combine Wittgenstein's 'making up a story; and reading it' with 'guessing riddles'. Telling a joke is also a similar language-game to telling a detective story. Both depend on a punch line (i.e. who's the culprit?), which must be placed correctly in the course of the telling so that the heightened suspense and drama remain intact.

The question of fair play in a crime story poses the question of obligatory rules and when they have been broken; a question which Wittgenstein also asked. 'One learns the game by watching how others play. But we say that it is played according to such-and-such rules because an observer can read these rules off from the practice of the game – like a natural law governing the play. But how does the observer distinguish in this case between players' mistakes and correct play? – There are characteristic signs of it in the players' behaviour'. (*Philosophical Investigations*, § 54)

This also holds true of the fair-play rule. Because there is neither a natural or state law on how to construct and tell a detective story, it depends considerably on the behaviour of the authors and readers. If a reader feels duped by the way a case is solved and is annoyed, for example when the narrator turns out to be the culprit, then one can view this as behaviour that suggests a breaking of the rules. But this is not necessarily the case. The reader can also view this as a bending of the rules and a particularly clever usage of the rules of detective stories. Wittgenstein is aware of this problem when he writes: 'And is there not also the case where we play and – make up the rules as we go along? And there is even one where we alter them – as we go along'. (*Philosophical Investigations*, §83) What makes good crime literature so attractive is precisely this following of the storytelling rules of a genre, only to then take a surprising turn after all – when it's done right. Nothing is drearier than a schematic crime story written down without any fantasy, nothing harder to stomach than crime stories which are totally overdone or without any planned design at all.

e) The final clue

There is another connection between detective stories and language-games, namely the investigation of the meaning of words. Often the progress of the investigation depends on the exact meaning of a text, for example, what bits of conversation were overheard by witnesses during a fight that preceded the murder. Often there is a word with multiple meanings, for example a name which is also an object, like 'Jewel' in the Miss Marple story 'Sanctuary'. Or one finds an incomprehensible succession of words in a foreign language, for example in Poe's 'The Murders in the Rue Morgue'. The memory, playback and interpretation of words in a criminal context show in particular 'the danger of words'. Wittgenstein wanted to draw attention to this, just as his student M. O'C. Drury announced. Drury emphasised the importance of this aspect by titling his own book on Wittgenstein's main influence on his own thinking with these words. The danger that one word can emit can be seen in the example 'national character'. When the German government accused the British of planning to assassinate Hitler, Norman Malcolm, unlike Wittgenstein, thought this impossible, because such an act would be contrary to the 'British national character'. Wittgenstein was angry about this 'primitive' expression and doubted the benefits of studying philosophy if it didn't allow for one to conscientiously handle the use of such dangerous terms.

Particularly favoured in detective stories is the fragmented language-game: the last, broken, mysterious words of the dying. This is not necessarily about an esteemed person's solemn last words and inner last wishes on their deathbed, but rather a very practical clue regarding the motive or sequence of the crime provided by the victim's last fragmented sentence. In decrypting the fragmented text the detectives follow Wittgenstein's view: The meaning of a word is a result of its use within a language-game and the customs observed by people when verbally expressing themselves. Because this language-game is interrupted by death and the fragmented text cannot be understood on its own, it is necessary to reconstruct the language-game to be able to make assumptions on the missing text and its meaning. The detectives try to reconstruct crime situations and sequences based on existing clues and witness statements. The overheard verbal expression represents only one building block of an entire building of thoughts, at the end of which the culprit should be turned over.

Wittgenstein's main work *Philosophical Investigations* remains a fragment. He chose the title for the planned publication of the book himself: *Philosophische Untersuchungen* in German and *Philosophical Investigations* in English. He did not choose the term 'enquiry', one well known in the history of philosophy, particularly from David Hume, and which corresponds to the German 'Untersuchung'. 'Investigate' is defined in Webster's College Dictionary thus: 'to examine the particulars of so as to learn about something hidden, unique, or complex, esp. in an attempt to find a motive, cause, or culprit: to investigate a murder.' So it seems that Wittgenstein's preference for detective stories is to blame for choosing the word 'investigation'. However, the punch line is something else all together. Looking ahead, Wittgenstein saw that his book in German would have the academic abbreviation 'PU', and in English, 'PI.' 'PI' is also the abbreviation for private investigator. Wittgenstein conducted his philosophical investigations throughout most of his life in private solitude. He fled, as soon as possible, the public life of Cambridge and retreated to a hut in Norway, a house on the Irish coast, or wherever, to pursue his ideas further. Wittgenstein was both a 'philosophical

131

investigator' and a 'private investigator', to be precise P.I. Wittgenstein.

Note: This chapter is based for the most part on two former texts on Wittgenstein:

Hoffmann, Josef: 'Hard-boiled Wit: Ludwig Wittgenstein und Norbert Davis', in: Martin Compart (Hg.): *Noir 2000. Ein Reader*, Köln 2000, 121–150; abridged and corrected English Version in: CADS 44, Oct. 2003, 11–18; also in: Mystery File Online

Hoffmann,Josef: 'PI Wittgenstein and Language-games from Detective Stories', in: *CADS 48*, Oct. 2005, 17–19

References and Further Reading:

Adrian, Jack/Pronzini, Bill (Hg.): *Hard-Boiled: An Anthology of American Crime Stories*, Oxford/New York 1995, 189–190

Cavell, Stanley: 'The Uncanniness of the Ordinary', in: *In Quest of the Ordinary*, Chicago/London 1988/1994, 153–178

Chesterton, Gilbert Keith: 'How to Write a Detective Story', in: Michael Dibdin (Hg.): *The Picador Book of Crime Writing*, London/ Basingstoke, 1994, 199

Drury, M. O' C.: 'Conversations with Wittgenstein', in: *The Danger of Words and Writings on Wittgenstein*, hg. v. David Berman/Michael Fitzgerald/John Hayes, Bristol 1996, 97–171

Drury, M. O' C.: 'The Danger of Words', in: *The Danger of Words and Writings on Wittgenstein*, hg. v. David Berman/Michael Fitzgerald/ John Hayes, Bristol 1996, v–141

Drury, M. O' C.: 'Some Notes on Conversations with Wittgenstein', in: *The Danger of Words and Writings on Wittgenstein*, hg. v. David Berman/Michael Fitzgerald/John Hayes, Bristol 1996, 76–96

Eagleton, Terry: 'Ludwig Wittgenstein', in: *Figures of Dissent*, London/New York 2005, 109–112

Hintikka, Merrill B./Hintikka, Jaakko: *Untersuchungen zu Wittgenstein*, Frankfurt am Main 1996 (English edition: *Investigating Wittgenstein*, Oxford 1986)

Holman, C. Hugh: 'Van Dine, S. S.', in: John M. Reilly (ed.): *Twentieth-Century Crime and Mystery Writers*, 2nd edition London 1985, 866–868

Kienzler, Wolfgang: *Wittgensteins Wende zu seiner Spätphilosophie 1930–1932*, Frankfurt am Main 1997

Leavis, F. R.: 'Wittgenstein – einige Erinnerungsbilder', in: Rush Rhees (Hg.): *Ludwig Wittgenstein: Porträts und Gespräche*, Frankfurt am Main 1992, 84–106 (English edition: Rush Rhees (ed.): *Recollections of Wittgenstein*, Oxford 1984)

Malcolm, Norman: *Ludwig Wittgenstein: a memoir*, 2nd edition Oxford 1984

McGuinness, Brian (ed.): *Wittgenstein in Cambridge: Letters and Documents 1911–1951*, 4th edition Oxford u. a. 2008

Monk, Ray: *Ludwig Wittgenstein. The Duty of Genius*, London 1991

Monk, Ray: *Wittgenstein. Das Handwerk des Genies*, 3rd edition Stuttgart 1993

Ousby, Ian: *The Crime and Mystery Book. A Reader's Companion*, London, 1997

Raatzsch, Richard: *Ludwig Wittgenstein zur Einführung*, Hamburg 2008

Rhees, Rush: Nachwort, in: Rhees (ed.): *Ludwig Wittgenstein: Porträts und Gespräche*, Frankfurt am Main 1992, 236–275 (English edition: Rush Rhees (ed.): Recollections of Wittgenstein, Oxford 1984)

Sayers, Dorothy: Introduction, in: Sayers (ed.): *Tales of Detection*, London 1947, vii-xiv

Sayers, Dorothy: 'Aristoteles über Detektivliteratur', in: Jochen Vogt (ed.), *Der Kriminalroman I. Zur Theorie und Geschichte einer Gattung*, 1971, 123–138 (English edition:

Sayers, Dorothy: 'Aristotle on Detective Fiction', in: *Unpopular Opinions*, 2nd edition. London 1951, 178–190)

Schulte, Joachim: *Wittgenstein. Eine Einführung*, Stuttgart 1989

Symons, Julian: *Bloody Murder. From the Detective Story to the Crime Novel: a History*, 3rd edition London/Basingstoke 1992

Van Dine, S. S.: 'Zwanzig Regeln für das Schreiben von Detektivgeschichten', in: Jochen Vogt (Hg.): *Der Kriminalroman I*, Munich 1971, 143–147 (English edition: Van Dine, S. S.: 'Twenty Rules for Writing Detective Stories', in: Howard Haycraft (ed.): *The Art of the Mystery Story*, New York 1946, 189–193)

Wittgenstein, Ludwig: *On Certainty*, ed. G. E. M. Anscombe, G. H. von Wright, Oxford 1969

Wittgenstein's Lectures: Cambridge, 1930–1932, ed. Desmond Lee, Oxford 1980

Wittgenstein's Lectures: Cambridge, 1932–1935, ed. Alice Ambrose, Oxford 1979

Wittgenstein, Ludwig: *Vorlesungen 1930 – 1935*, Frankfurt am Main 1984

Wittgenstein, Ludwig: *Philosophische Untersuchungen*, Werkausgabe Band 1, 7th edition Frankfurt am Main 1990, 225–580

Wittgenstein, Ludwig: *Über Gewissheit*, Werkausgabe Band 8., 4th edition Frankfurt am Main 1990, 113–257

Wright, Georg Henrik von: *Wittgenstein*, Frankfurt am Main 1990 (English edition: *Wittgenstein*, Oxford 1982)

7

Albert Camus and the
Philosophy of Crime

What is Albert Camus doing in a book on crime fiction and philosophy? Is it not the case that some do not take Camus seriously as a philosopher, and others not as a crime writer? Professional philosophers do not take Camus seriously because of his laconic style of thinking and writing. They find that Camus lacks an academic system for the presentation of an idea and a detailed analysis of thesis and antithesis. Crime experts probably do not see Camus as a crime writer, because he has only written one fairly short crime novel, at the centre of which is a murder and the prosecution of the perpetrator, yet its suspense does not stem from the crime itself, as in a typical crime novel, or the subsequent investigation of the crime and punishment of the offender, but rather from psychological and philosophical questions. Camus' crime story does not fit into any of the usual classifications: it is not a detective or a gangster novel, a psycho thriller or courtroom drama, or another kind of other subgenres of crime fiction. At most it might be considered to be 'noir.' And yet there are many books on crime fiction that take note of Camus. He is represented in the secondary literature with two works, the novel *The Stranger* (*L'Étranger*, 1942), and – less often – the philosophical essay *The Rebel* (L'Homme Révolté, 1951).

It is variously suggested or claimed that James M. Cain's classic *The Postman Always Rings Twice* influenced the first-person narration in *The Stranger*, which centres on a murder. No explicit reference shows up in Camus' diaries and interviews, but the comparison of the two novels suggests a stylistic influence that Camus probably would not have liked to concede for fear of minimising the originality of his work. The leading publishing house Gallimard released the French translation of Cain's crime novel in 1936, and also went on to publish Camus' works. At that time, the hard American novels of Faulkner, Steinbeck, Caldwell and Cain were in fashion among French writers such as Andre Malraux and his peers. Malraux wrote a preface in 1933 for the French edition of

Faulkner's gangster novel *Sanctuary*. And it was none other than Malraux who sent the manuscript of *The Stranger* with a recommendation to Gaston Gallimard, which led to its publication. After the huge success of his novel, Camus, in an interview in 1945 after the war, confessed that he had used American writing techniques. He had done so simply because the techniques served to characterise a person 'without an obvious consciousness.' He rejected a generalised application of these techniques. It would lead to 'a world of robots and engines,' which would be detrimental to the richness of the genre of the novel.

Camus touched on the hard American novels of the thirties in a similar manner in the chapter 'Rebellion and the Novel' in his book *The Rebel. An Essay on Man in Revolt*. According to Camus, a basic need of every human being is the desire for a unity of life, for unity with himself and his surroundings. This is also the underlying premise of the novel: 'Life… is without style. It is only an impulse that endlessly pursues its form without ever finding it. Man, tortured by this, tries in vain to find the form that will impose certain limits between which he can be king…This passion which lifts the mind above the commonplaces of a dispersed world, from which it nevertheless cannot free itself, is the passion for unity. It does not result in mediocre efforts to escape, however, but in the most obstinate demands. Religion or crime, every human endeavour in fact, finally obeys this unreasonable desire and claims to give life a form it does not have… What, in fact, is a novel but a universe in which action is endowed with form, where final words are pronounced, where people possess one another completely, and where life assumes the aspect of destiny? The world of the novel is only a rectification of the world we live in, in pursuance of man's deepest wishes… Here we have an imaginary world, therefore, which is created by the rectification of the actual world … Man is finally able to give himself the alleviating form and limits which he pursues in vain in his own life. The novel creates destiny to suit any eventuality. In this way it competes with creation and, provisionally, conquers death… Far from being moral or even purely formal, this alteration aims, primarily, at unity and thereby expresses a metaphysical need. The novel, on this level, is primarily an exercise of the intelligence in the service of nostalgic or rebellious sensibilities.'

Camus also exemplifies his thesis on the novel in the 'hard' American novel of the thirties and forties: 'The American Novel claims to find its unity in reducing man either to elementals or to his external reactions and to his behaviour... It rejects analysis and the search for a fundamental psychological motive that could explain and recapitulate the behaviour of a character. This is why the unity of this novel form is only the unity of the flash of recognition. Its technique consists in describing men by their outside appearances, in their most casual actions, of reproducing, without comment, everything they say down to their repetitions, and finally by acting as if men were entirely defined by their daily automatisms... This technique is called realistic only owing to a misapprehension. In addition ... it is perfectly obvious that this fictitious world is not attempting a reproduction, pure and simple, of reality, but the most arbitrary form of stylisation. It is born of a mutilation, and of a voluntary mutilation, performed on reality. The unity thus obtained is a degraded unity, a levelling off of human beings and of the world... This type of novel, purged of interior life, in which men seem to be observed behind a pane of glass, logically ends, with its emphasis on the pathological, by giving itself as its unique subject the supposedly average man. In this way it is possible to explain the extraordinary number of "innocents" who appear in this universe. The simpleton is the ideal subject for such an enterprise since he can only be defined – and completely defined – by his behaviour. He is the symbol of the despairing world in which wretched automatons live in a machine-ridden universe, which American novelists have presented as a heart-rending but sterile protest.' Against a novel world of 'people without memory', Camus emphasises that the revolt that forms the basis for the art of the novel creates the unity from the inner reality and does not deny or hide this reality.

Camus recognised William Faulkner as the best writer of this generation of American novelists. When Faulkner was awarded the Nobel Prize for Literature in 1950, a magazine asked Camus to write a eulogy on him. He did not fulfil the request, but confirmed his opinion that Faulkner was America's greatest writer, who like Melville, Dostoevsky and Proust created a separate universe. Camus named *The Sanctuary* as one of Faulkner's outstanding masterpieces, in other words his crime novel. In light of this appreciation and his extensive critical reading of the 'hard' American novels, it is extremely unlikely that Camus did not know Cain's *The Postman Always Rings Twice*, especially since the novel was filmed in 1939 by the French director Pierre Chenal. What does Cain's novel have in common with *The Stranger*? In both texts there is a first-person narrative by a man sentenced to execution. The narrator tells the events that led up to the circumstances of his death sentence. There is a story before the murder and one after, although in Camus' novel the subsequent judicial investigation takes up greater room. In both stories the murderer expresses no sympathy for the victim, who is depersonalised and referred to only ethnically – 'the Greek', 'the Arab.' The killer allows himself to be determined primarily by the circumstances and his own impulses. He does not attempt to exert his conscience and reasoning powers to twist the narrative outcome of the disastrous events. The much praised narrative tone of Camus, which takes in the reader immediately, is different, but similar to the narrative of Cain, which is somewhat colder, at times almost brash. Camus' style is characterised by laconic brevity, by narrow, almost brusque terms, such as prevails in hard-boiled detective stories. Of course, there are also enough differences to distinguish Camus' novel from its template and give it its own identity.

In the preface to the American edition of his novel, Camus assesses the actions of his hero Meursault in a rather positive light. Even with the first-person narrative the author's clear sympathies for his protagonist come across. In the preface, Camus emphasises that Meursault refuses to lie, even refusing to say more than what is there. The hero refuses to disguise his feelings, which makes those around him feel threatened. He is a stranger to the society in which he lives. Without adopting heroic gestures, he is willing to die for the truth. This is a euphemistic description for Meursault's actions and a short-sighted view of truth. On the other hand, it seems Meursault is a prime example of the banality of evil as defined by Hannah Arendt. He is not a monstrous mass murderer like Eichmann, but meets the key criteria that exemplify the banality of evil.

How little Meursault is concerned with the truth in the sense of a genuine representation of reality is shown in his support of his neighbour Raymond Sintès. Sintès has the reputation of being a pimp, but he describes himself as a warehouse manager. It doesn't matter to Meursault what he really is. He writes a letter for him to a 'Moor' woman, which serves as a lure to enable Sintès to wreak revenge on her. He tolerates Sintès hitting her hard until a policeman ends the physical abuse. He promises Sintès that he will testify to the police as a witness in his favour because he does not care. After Meursault testifies to the Commissioner that the girl had injured Sintès' honour, without knowing what had really happened, Sintès gets away with it with just a warning. Meursault's entire behaviour does not speak for a special love of truth, but for a conformist act, depending on whatever issue his friends and acquaintances approach him with. The framework for this conformism stems from the cultural dominance of the colonial power of France over Algeria. In the face of the social unrest that broke out in the thirties and the Algerian people's emancipation efforts, the European settlers, despite many differences and almost without exception, stuck together to preserve the status quo. They had a common enemy, the colonised, the 'Arabs.' In this colonial situation, Meursault allows himself to become 'entangled in an affair' by his neighbour, 'in which the latter deploys both his male and his colonial dominance in a calculated manner – in such a cleverly demanding manner that the counter-violence of the other side rises up against them both' (Sändig). First Sintès, then Meursault are observed and tracked later by a number of 'Arabs.'

During a trip to the ocean there is finally a confrontation with two Arabs, who have apparently followed them. Sintès, Meursault and a friend both outnumber them and are more powerful. In order to keep the French at bay, an Arab takes out a knife and injures Sintès on the mouth and arm, after which the Algerians run away. After attending to Sintès' wounds, he and Meursault go back along the beach until they come across the two Arabs, lying perfectly quietly at a small spring behind a large rock. This time Sintès has a gun with him and asks Meursault if he should 'finish off' the Arab who had hurt him. Meursault tries to calm him down and bring him to reason. He suggests they fight man to man and to give him, Meursault, the revolver so that if necessary he can shoot the knifing bandits. But after the revolver has been handed over, the Arabs suddenly disappear behind the rocks and the two Frenchmen go away.

By now the sun is beating down mercilessly from the sky. Meursault can hardly stand the heat and starts longing for that spot with a shady spring. He returns to the spot alone, with the revolver in hand. To his surprise, he sees the Arab, who has the knife, lying alone in the shadow of the rocks. Meursault harbours no feelings of revenge, for him the matter is settled. Despite a situation full of conflict and danger, he does not turn around. Instead he rejects the path back through the heat, and approaches, hand on the weapon, closer and closer to the place where the Arab lies. At a distance of a few metres the Algerian pulls out a knife and shows it to Meursault threateningly. The sweat accumulating on his brow pours into Meursault's eyes, so that he is practically blind. The sun causes him extreme anxiety and fantasies and Meursault suffers what is colloquially called a blackout. He pulls the trigger of the revolver and shoots the Algerian, then he fires four more times at the lifeless body.

Since the Arab did not attack Meursault and was a few feet away, it cannot be said that he acted in self-defence. At best he had acted incorrectly in an emergency, due to his sun-addled and confused mind. It was certainly not a murder in revenge for the previous injuries incurred by Sintès. Meursault did not kill intentionally and in cold blood in support of the dealings of a pimp, as the prosecutor maintained later in order to sustain a murder charge without extenuating circumstances. If Meursault were to be granted extenuating circumstances, he would not be executed. According to the details of the exact sequence of the deadly outcome, extenuating circumstances should have been granted, or even an acquittal by reason of insanity because of the effects of the sunlight at the time of the act. Yet the end result was the death penalty – as requested by the prosecutor. The jurors did not believe the submissions by Meursault and his defender. Why not?

Meursault could have pleaded in his defence that the Arab had attacked him with the knife, whereupon he shot him in self-defence. Since no witness saw the crime, he would have had a good chance of success with this false representation. But Meursault – and here Camus states this correctly – refuses to lie. Not only that, he makes hardly any effort to present an effective defence, which is foolhardy, considering that the charge was murder. He simply reports to the examining magistrate the events as he saw them. The court appoints him a public defender, who is not particularly good and who pursues the wrong strategy. Meursault finds him ridiculous, but does not try to get a better lawyer. The judiciary body is primarily concerned with determining the motive of the act, since according to Meursault's representation the killing seems unmotivated. They therefore address Meursault's mental impulses. First the examining magistrate, then the prosecutor, and finally the chaplain are all horrified to find in Meursault no sign of a Christian soul, no remorse, guilt, appeals to God or requests for forgiveness, etc. Instead, they see in the defendant an 'emptiness of heart.' What finally dooms Meursault is his refusal to at least respect the Christian conventions and pretend as if Christian values were important to him, for example, observing the mourning rituals on the death of his mother. He is not a hypocrite. But the reader does not gain the impression that Meursault acts out of duty to the truth, but out of loyalty to his feelings, to which he clings in an almost naive, narrow-minded way, laying them bare. If he were interested in a more accurate representation of the real crime, he would have to do more than simply respond to the questions from the judiciary that it was the sun's fault or that the killing was accidental. He would have to try to recall the event in embarrassing detail and describe his blackout as precisely and comprehensibly as possible to the jury; how he felt everything swaying and that he did not know what else to do but to shoot. He would have to apply for a psychiatric evaluation of his reactions to extreme sunlight or have his lawyer do so. But now we know the protagonist well and how deeply repugnant this would have been for Meursault. For him, the court represents only an 'annoyance.' He does not want to change in any way whatsoever, but to continue to live as he has up until this point.

To return to the thesis that Meursault is an example of the banality of evil: Arendt applies its criteria not only to monstrous criminals like Eichmann but to all Nazi perpetrators and the simple hangers-on. In these people she found a lack of reflection, the internal dialogue of reflection, including a lack of imagination and creativity. Critical and moral discernment is impaired. What is striking is a fundamental indifference, also with regard to the choice of people with which to commune. Such an attitude is displayed without hypocrisy. All of these features are present in Meursault. The most noticeable is his indifference, which is emphasised in various scenes in the novel. Meursault's guiding principle is: 'I do not care.' Instead of *L'Etranger* the title of the novel was originally intended to be *L'Indifferent*. Meursault does not care whether a pimp is his 'buddy' or whether he is sent to Paris or remains in Algiers on behalf of his company, whether he marries his lover, Marie, whether the Arab girl is injured in the 'punishment' by the pimp, etc. He thinks with little foresight and admits: 'I have never had any real imagination.' As Meursault's behaviour in support of his pimp friend shows, he is not interested in distinguishing between right and wrong, but instead he adapts to the demands and circumstances. When he returned to the spring on the day of the murder, he must have reckoned with the fact that the Arabs were still there. He must have expected an armed conflict and that he would kill a man, whether in self-defence or otherwise. Someone who judges morally and thinks with foresight would not, under these circumstances, have returned to the spring. It is better to suffer injustice than to exercise it – although it is questionable whether he would have suffered any injustice if he hadn't sought out the shady spot. At no point in Meursault's whole first-person narrative is the murdered Algerian perceived as a person. He is not interested in the victim's name, if the man leaves behind his wife and children, etc. He is just an Arab. In view of the escalating conflict between Algerians and French at the time, Meursault should have had to form an opinion regarding his position on the Arab population. Yet he neither criticises nor affirms the structures of colonial society. He is indifferent to them, almost in a sense distanced from them. According to Brigitte Sändig, even this results in 'silent complicity.' 'Meursault's truth is – and only in the face of death is he entirely conscious of this – a large indifference to external goals to the benefit of the beauty of the natural world and the physical joy in it.' In addition one must keep in mind not just his indifference to external goals, but also to moral issues and distinctions.

It is astonishing that a writer like Camus, a critic of colonialism and political activist – albeit not a radical or uncompromising one – finds his hero Meursault likeable. This is due to two circumstances. The first is that the judicial machinery in French Algeria is not religiously neutral, but is oiled by aggressive Christian beliefs. Camus' experiences as a court reporter helped him in his impressive description of the biased judicial system. The battle for the soul of the criminal has a long tradition in French justice. Already in the Age of Enlightenment, the principle was formulated that the punishment is to be applied to the soul rather than the body. It is to shape the thinking and the will of the delinquents. The soul is the 'prison of the body' (Michel Foucault). Such a grasp at the soul of the accused is particularly distressing when the soul is comprehended in the Christian sense, or at least theologically and not primarily psychologically, and when the accused is not a Christian and is characterised by an emptiness of heart. The prosecutor follows an insidious strategy to reveal Meursault as having the soul of a criminal capable of deliberate murder, because of his indifferent attitude during and after the funeral of his mother. The absurdity of the trial is that Meursault is ultimately sentenced to death because he has shed no tears at his mother's grave. Here the sincerity of the hero, as far as his feelings are concerned, seems positive, especially if, like Camus, one prefers the Hellenistic view of man and the world to that of the Christians.

The second factor is related to Camus' belief that every person strives to achieve unity in life. Thinking and moral judgments presuppose an inner dialogue and therefore a duality of the person. Meursault, however and according to Camus, is a man with no apparent consciousness. Tellingly, the French word for consciousness is (and also means) 'conscience'. Meursault now almost reaches the desired unity of life by means of an unconditional devotion to the natural world and its earthly joys, while emotional and mental efforts and progress remain for the most part suppressed. He openly confesses to his mistress Marie that he is indeed bound to her sexually and as a friend, but despite their intense closeness and good understanding he does not love her. When asked by the prison chaplain in light of his imminent death: 'Do you love this earth so much?' Meursault is silent. The answer would have to be 'yes.' This achievement of unity of life through the emptiness of heart, while at the same time turning to earthly things – an ideal in some Asian religions – impressed Camus, who observed a similar mentality in a friend and an artist and sometimes in himself. Camus' preference for a pre-Christian vision of man and the world also reveals itself here. Despite the loathsomeness of the aggressive introduction of Christian-conventional assessments by the judiciary in the prosecution, Meursault's denial of Judeo-Christian heritage seems questionable. As much as the earthly things are essential and valuable for people's lives, priority is given in the Judeo-Christian culture to turning to the other and the ethically sound relationship with other people, rather than turning to the earthly things. Meursault accepts that his mistress no longer comes to visit him in prison after his death sentence and probably offers her pretty lips to kiss another man. He consoles himself with the stars, the country sounds, the night smells, earth and salt. Before death, he opens up 'in the face of a night full of signs and stars for the first time to the gentle indifference of the world.' An indifference to the cares of the world was the basic attitude of the early Camus, in which he rediscovered himself in his later years.

There might be a third reason why Camus does not judge Meursault's action as a crime. It does not meet the metaphysical logic of crime, which is developed in *The Rebel*. Camus separates the crime or the murder from the revolt. A person who revolts is a man who says no. He says: 'Up to this point yes, beyond it no' or 'There is a limit beyond which you shall not go.' At the same time, the one revolting says yes to his rights, yes to a part of himself. Even if only one individual revolts, he refers to all other people in the community and thinks and acts in solidarity, 'I rebel, therefore we exist.' In this way we can see that an act of rebellion is not, essentially, an egoistic act. Solidarity is based on the movement of revolt and this is justified by sticking together. But the flip side of the revolt is the crime: 'We have, then, the right to say that any rebellion which claims the right to deny or destroy this solidarity loses simultaneously its right to be called rebellion and becomes in reality an acquiescence in murder.'

Camus presumably refers to the 'Cold War', the colonial wars of liberation and nuclear deterrence, when he put it pointedly: 'In that every action today leads to murder, direct or indirect, we can not act until we know whether or why we have the right to kill.' Even if one does not act, it is tantamount to accepting the murder of others. Camus distinguishes between crimes of passion and crimes of consideration, which today search for their causes in reason. The latter are for him the problem and the object of investigation. Camus asks the question 'whether all rebellion must end in the justification of universal murder.' This would contradict the recognition of life as the only necessary good, as revolt is a basic state of human life. It is connected with the absurdity of life. It is absurd, simply because it is not infinite, because the death sentence is imposed on it. The absurd is evident in 'the desperate encounter between human inquiry and the silence of the universe.' The alternative, however, is not suicide, but rather 'allowing the absurd to live' which means 'looking it in the eye.' Man should acknowledge the disjointed, nonsensical, but also rebel against it. The rebellion is 'a permanent confrontation of man with his own darkness... This revolt gives life its value' (*The Myth of Sisyphus*). Camus draws the conclusion: 'I proclaim that I believe in nothing and that everything is absurd, but I can not doubt the validity of my proclamation and I must at least believe in my protest. The first and only evidence that is supplied me, within the terms of the absurdist experience, is rebellion.' Revolt can lead to murder, but it does not have to. A tendency to crime is inherent in a certain kind of revolt, the metaphysical revolt.

In the chapter 'Metaphysical Rebellion' Camus develops a logic of justification for the crime of murder. He derives it from works of writers like de Sade, Dostoevsky, Lautréamont and philosophers such as Nietzsche and Stirner. 'Metaphysical rebellion is the movement by which Man protests against his condition and against the whole of creation.' If we were to attempt to simplify the different approaches and arguments of metaphysical revolt and bring them into line, it would result in approximately the following sequence: life and creation are unjust and evil. Therefore, the Creator, God, must be morally condemned or declared to be non-existent. There is no divine justice, no divine punishment for sins and crimes. Every man is mortal, including the soul. The belief in the difference between true and false, good and evil, right and wrong is pointless. Consequently, everything is permitted. Even murder is allowed. It is not only allowed, but it is a reasonable, rational option to use this instrument for pursuing individual interests and purposes, if it promises success. Therefore, in line with Sändig, the impulse for a metaphysical revolt can be characterised as an individual selfish urge for self-realisation. This kind of crime logic is not the premise of Meursault's actions. The murder is more a product of indifference together with the circumstances of an unfortunate accident than a metaphysical revolt. Meursault does not revolt against his life circumstances, but feels at home with them. Had not the extreme exposure to the sun addled his senses and clouded his mind, he may never have shot and killed a man. His act of killing was precisely not deliberate, not for supposedly rational reasons. And he admits this too.

Camus sees the deliberate murder that seeks to be rationally justified primarily in state-political contexts and the terrorism of a 'historical rebellion'. Crime stories, on the other hand, deal more with individual crimes, in particular murders. This raises the question, therefore, whether the criminal logic of metaphysical revolt plays a role in crime stories, especially those of the American hard-boiled novels of the Thirties, which Camus studied. Two novels above all come into question here, both of which Camus would have known. One is a gangster novel, *Little Caesar* (1929) by W.R. Burnett, which was filmed successfully and established its own subgenre of literature and film. The other is Horace McCoy's novel *They Shoot Horses, Don't They* (1935), which was greatly appreciated by Sartre and other existentialists. In *Little Caesar* the gangster Rico kills every man, without a thought, who endangers his gangster career or could harm his interests. No indications of a metaphysical revolt, on which the crime is based, can be recognised. It is presented as self-evident that there are alternative options for a career – the legal way and illegal way. If someone chooses the illegal way, ultimately he cannot shy away from any crime if he wants to be successful and does not want to be caught. The fact that Rico failed to 'liquidate' a potential traitor in his gang in due time has fatal consequences for him. God, or the workings of divine justice, are not mentioned in the entire novel, while Camus' metaphysical rebellion is fixated negatively on it. Camus never propounded a completely secular theory of individual crimes, governed by the naked material interests; it probably didn't interest him at all.

The thinking and actions of the two protagonists in McCoy's crime novel have some relation to metaphysical revolt. It tells the story of a crime from the perspective of a person sentenced to death. A young man, Robert Syverten, befriends a young woman, Gloria Beatty. They both came to Hollywood to make a career in film, but so far have failed miserably. In order to get some accommodation and food for a while, and perhaps even to win the first prize and be 'discovered,' they take part in a dance marathon. As they undergo the humiliating rituals and rigours of this event, it becomes clear how desperate and embittered Gloria is. In contrast to Robert she no longer has any hope. She would prefer for God to end her life prematurely. Yet she lacks the courage to commit suicide. At the end of the dance marathon she asks Robert in a state of total exhaustion and denial of life to shoot her with her gun. He does this in order to deliver her from a life that is no longer good for anything. Then he is arrested by the police and sentenced to death at the trial for premeditated murder.

The revolt of the two protagonists is directed less against God, as Robert in Gloria's view acts as a representative of God, at the same time relieving him of his work, but instead against the world with its mechanisms and laws. Actually, it is only Gloria who revolts and decides to go so far and no further. She revolts in a defeatist manner against her destiny, so that suicide would be the logical consequence. Yet she does not commit suicide, but imposes the responsibility of killing on Robert, thereby destroying his future and bringing about his death. In a way, Robert becomes an accomplice of Gloria's revolt. Robert does not murder but rather kills her on request out of compassion. This fact does not follow the logic of the crime, in the sense of the metaphysical revolt. The telling of the story in crime novels, especially when the whole range is taken into account, is too diverse to be able to lead back to a single logic of the crime or the revolt.

References and Further Reading

a) Albert Camus
Camus, Albert: *The Rebel. An Essay on Man in Revolt*, New York 1956 (L'Homme révolté, 1951)
Camus, Albert: *Der Mythos von Sisyphos. Ein Versuch über das Absurde,*

Hamburg 1960 (*Le Mythe des Sisyphe. Essai sur l'absurde*, 1942; English edition: *The Myth of Sisyphus*, 1955)

Camus, Albert: *Lyrical and Critical Essays*, New York 1970

Camus, Albert: *Tagebücher 1935–1951*, Reinbek bei Hamburg 1997 (*Carnets, mai 1935 – février 1942*, 1962; *Carnets, janvier 1942 – mars 1951*, 1964)

Camus, Albert: *Der Fremde*, Reinbek bei Hamburg 2010 (*L'Étranger*, 1942; English edition: *The Stranger*, New York 1989)

b) other authors

Arendt, Hannah: *Über das Böse*, 3rd edition Munich 2009

Augstein, Franziska: 'Taten und Täter', in: Hannah Arendt: *Über das Böse*, 3rd edition Munich 2009, 177–195

Buchloh, Paul G./Becker, Jens P.: *Der Detektivroman*, 4th edition Darmstadt 1990

Burnett, W. R.: *Little Caesar*, New York 1951

DeAndrea, William L.: *Encyclopedia Mysteriosa*, New York/London 1994

Duncan, Paul: *Noir Fiction*, Harpenden 2000

Edenbaum, Robert I., *The Poetics of the Private-Eye: The Novels of Dashiell Hammett*, in: David Madden (ed.): *Tough Guy Writers of the Thirties*, 3rd edition Carbondale/London 1977, 80–103

Foucault, Michel: *Überwachen und Strafen. Die Geburt des Gefängnisses*, 3rd edition Frankfurt am Main 1979 (English edition: *Discipline and Punish*, London 1977)

Gorman, Ed/Collins, Max Allan: 'McCoy; Horace. They Shoot Horses, Don't They?', in: Bill Pronzini/Marcia Muller (ed.): *1001 Midnights. The Aficionado's Guide to Mystery and Detective Fiction*, New York 1986, 512–513

Han, Byung-Chul: *Philosophie des Zen-Buddhismus*, Stuttgart 2006

Haut, Woody: *Pulp Culture: Hardboiled Fiction and the Cold War*, London 1995

Haut, Woody: *Neon Noir: Contemporary American Crime Fiction*, London 1999

Hengelbrock, Jürgen: *Albert Camus. Ursprünglichkeit der Empfindung und Krisis des Denkens*, Freiburg/München 1982

Horsley, Lee: *The Noir Thriller*, Basingstoke/New York 2001

Knight, Stephen: *Crime Fiction 1800 – 2000: Detection, Death, Diversity*, Basingstoke/New York 2004

Lao-Tse: *Tao Te King*, Zürich 1959

Lebesque, Morvan: *Albert Camus in Selbstzeugnissen und Bilddokumenten*, Reinbek bei Hamburg 1961

Lottman, Herbert R.: *Camus. Eine Biographie*, Hamburg 1986 (Albert Camus – a biography, 1979)

Marsch, Edgar: *Die Kriminalerzählung. Theorie – Geschichte – Analyse*, 2nd edition Munich 1983

McCoy, Horace: *They Shoot Horses, Don't They*, New York 1948

Mesplède, Claude (ed.): *Dictionnaire des littératures policières*, 2 vol., 2007

Mosès, Stéphane: 'Gerechtigkeit und Gemeinschaft bei Emmanuel Lévinas', in: Micha Brumlik/Hauke Brunkhorst (ed.), *Gemeinschaft und Gerechtigkeit*, Frankfurt am Main 1993, 364–384

Oates, Joyce Carol: 'Man Under Sentence of Death: The Novels of James M. Cain', in: David Madden (ed.): *Tough Guy Writers of the Thirties*, 3rd edition Carbondale/London 1977, 110–128

Pieper, Annemarie: *Albert Camus*, Munich 1984

Sändig, Brigitte: *Albert Camus*, Reinbek bei Hamburg 2000

Sherman, David: *Camus*, Malden/Oxford 2009

Sturak, Thomas: 'Horace McCoy's Objective Lyricism', in: David Madden (Hg.): *Tough Guy Writers of the Thirties*, 3rd edition Carbondale/London 1977, 137–162

Symons, Julian: *Bloody Murder. From the detective story to the crime novel: a history*, London/Basingstoke 1992

Taureck, Bernhard: *Französische Philosophie im 20. Jahrhundert: Analysen, Texte, Kommentare*, Reinbek bei Hamburg 1988

Todd, Olivier: *Albert Camus. Ein Leben*, Reinbek bei Hamburg 2001

Voss, Dietmar: 'Heldenkonstruktionen', in: *KulturPoetik* 2011, 181–202

8

Jorge Luis Borges'
Logic of Staging

Jorge Luis Borges' far-reaching and diverse body of work relates in one way or another to almost everything that has rank and name in the world of books and thinking. So it is no surprise that several philosophers and their theories are represented in his work. Furthermore, it comes as no surprise that Borges was active in the crime fiction genre, which he loved and whose reputation he spread and fostered in his home country through reviews and editions. He valued crime stories because, in an era tending to chaos, they uphold the classical virtues in the very fact that they must have a beginning, middle and end. They retain 'a form of order in an era of disorder.' The classic detective story, as invented by Poe, includes the discovery of a mystery and the solution to a riddle by the intellectual power of an abstract thinker. In crime stories, logic is satisfied, not the sense of justice, because according to Borges, 'even the desire for justice… is an excess.'

Borges' detective and crime stories can be divided into three sub-genres: detective, espionage and crime stories, although in some of the latter the typical suspense drama of the crime story is missing, thereby excluding them from the genre of crime fiction in the strictest sense. The detective stories include: 'Death and the Compass,' 'Ibn Hakkan al-Bokhari, Dead in his Labyrinth,' and the stories written together with Bioy Casares about Don Isidro Parodi. His spy stories include 'The Garden of Forking Paths' and 'Theme of the Traitor and the Hero.' The crime stories include 'Emma Zunz,' 'The South' and 'Man of Esquina Rosada,' to list just the better known. Most of these stories have one thing in common: a staged sequence of events that leads to a crime and its concealment. In reality things are not as they might first appear and what people know through hearsay, since the logic of events has been invented by another mind setting into motion and feigning a certain reality. The detective Don Isidro Parodi discovered in his prison cell, 'that his clients were already in the context of a story and acting according to the narrative laws in which they are the unconscious *dramatis personae* of an already written drama. Don Isidro discovers the "truth", because both he, with his fertile mind, and the subjects of his investigation act according to the same laws of fiction.' (Umberto Eco) The successful detective is someone who reads the story correctly, because reading is, according to Borges, 'thinking with a different brain.'

Umberto Eco recognises in the mechanism of the Don Isidro stories and many other stories by Borges the 'mechanism of conjecture in a sick world of Spinoza.' I doubt whether the tales of Borges or even the crime stories can be boiled down to a – distorted – version of Spinoza's philosophy. Certainly Spinoza plays an important role in the texts of Borges. He wrote a short and very beautiful poem about him, and 'Death and the Compass' mentions the name Baruch Spinoza and his geometric method. But does this suffice for such a generalised verdict?

Eco refers less to explicit answers and references from Spinoza's philosophy and argues more fundamentally for a recognition of reality. This can be found in Spinoza's central proposition 7 of Part II of the *Ethics* – 'Ordo et connexio idearum idem est ac ordo et connexio rerum' (The order and connection of ideas is the same as the order and connection of things). This also applies the other way around, as Spinoza stressed in the axioms in the fifth part of the *Ethics*. This has the following consequences for solving a criminal case: if the detective thinks correctly he must think in accordance with the same laws that govern the relationship of things. The detective not only understands what the murderer did, but also what he will do next, since there is just one logic for both the mind and things. He only needs to put himself in the mind of the murderer. The problem is that this also applies the other way around. The murderer can predict the detective's sequence of actions and then act accordingly, as the gangster Red Scarlet does in 'Death and the Compass.' In any event, detective and murderer must meet in the end if they follow the given logic. At least in Eco's view.

Yet neither the world of Spinoza nor that of Borges is so simple and mechanical. The problem in the first place is that it is by no means guaranteed, according to Spinoza, that someone thinks 'correctly.' He must have – literally – 'true ideas', which he comprehends by means of intellectual activity. The facts are thus correctly recognised when recognised from the real cause. Spinoza does not exclude a faulty, erroneous thinking. Inadequate, confused knowledge arises in particular from the imagination, 'because of affections of the body it only contains images (*imagines*) of things affected by the body that don't reflect what these things really are...' (Bartuschat). In particular, fictions hinder an adequate knowledge of things. With Borges a special twist is now added to the method of cognition, because the logic of his criminal stories does not follow the nature of things, or the laws of nature, which can be researched and identified, but rather results from the staged pseudo-logic of an inventive, criminal brain. His 'fictions,' the constructed 'labyrinths' and 'spider webs', which are fatal to the victim, must be penetrated by the detective. However, if he has mentally reconstructed them, there is no need for empirical proof or any verification of the conjecture. The detective, the decipherer of the staged logic, is sure of his footing. Here there is – to this extent Eco is right – an echo of Spinoza's philosophy that accepts an intuitive certainty when having a true idea: 'Whoever has a true idea, simultaneously knows that he has a true idea and cannot doubt the truth of the matter.'

What leads Eco to talk about a sick Spinozan world is the 'illogicality' of the staged chain of events, the one people follow. Since it is a staged drama, it would be surprising if it followed the rules of rational logic. But Eco is wrong when he suggests the passionate librarian Borges is always beholden in his detective stories to the 'illogicality' or order of a library. In the story 'The Library of Babel,' Borges creates the universe as an infinite library. This, however, does not mean that he understands the laws that govern the universe to be on equal standing with the logic of the library and sees this as a unified scheme on which to base his detective stories. The so-called 'illogicality' of a library arranges books by subject and alphabetical sequence. In contrast, Borges' staged logic follows a plan devised by a criminal that in each story is designed quite differently with different effects. Also, this varying logic does not necessarily mean that detective and criminal follow it inevitably and always meet each other at the end of the 'labyrinth', as is the case in 'Death and the Compass.' Emma Zunz fakes a rape and an emergency situation to cover up the murder, caused by a family feud, of the alleged rapist. The arrival of the police investigator is not expected until later, after the conclusion of the story. In 'The Garden of Forking Paths,' shortly before his arrest, a spy in enemy territory commits the seemingly motive-less murder of a famous Sinologist named Albert, thereby launching a newspaper report that sends a message to the spy chief to bomb the town of Albert. The investigator who arrested the spy does not see through the staged logic nor follow it; instead the arrest is carried out because of previous acts of espionage. That is the reason, the murder is secondary. In the crime story 'Ibn Hakkan al-Bokhari, Dead in his Labyrinth,' two British gentlemen modelled after Holmes and Watson debate the murder of the exiled King Ibn Hakkan in his stone labyrinth a quarter of a century after the crime.

A lion and a slave with fractured skulls were also found in the labyrinth. The reconstruction of the case indicates that not the king, but his vizier Said, posing as Ibn Hakkan, had a maze built in Cornwall within sight of the sea in order to ensnare the real Ibn Hakkan. The latter came and walked through the maze where Said killed him in an ambush. To portray the murder as a serial murder, the slave and the lion were also killed. The faces were crushed to prevent the identification of the real murdered King Ibn Hakkan and to fake a series of crimes. The fake Ibn Hakkan, the vizier Said, could escape undetected. The staging of his logic cost the king, who fell for it, his life. The residents and the police were also deceived. Only the two intellectuals can – for the sheer pleasure of solving a puzzle – reconstruct the apparent logic. In the first case of Don Isidro Parodi, 'The Twelve Zodiac Signs', an inauguration rite based on the zodiac is staged in a Druze community, which is a farce and only serves to make fun of the candidate. This staging takes advantage of a crooked accountant in the community to murder the chairman undetected and set fire to the building in order to destroy the falsified account books. The candidate, informed by Parodi of the true facts, does not see through this. What we have here are two separate productions that interlock. The staged logic is followed by the candidate, not by the murderer or the detective. These examples should suffice to show that Umberto Eco is indeed correct when he identifies staging as the core idea of Borgesian detective stories, but is wrong when he claims a certain kind of 'illogicality' which the parties, especially criminal and detective, must follow.

In so far as a detective or narrator reconstructs the staged logic that leads to crimes, this does not usually occur according to Spinoza's recognition method. Because the matter at hand is the apparent logic of fiction, not only the intellect, but above all the imagination is required to follow the criminal fantasy production until a clear picture of the facts arises. Usually there is no investigation of cause in the empirical or logical sense. Furthermore, the point is not the intuitive extraction of the true ideas of the (natural) things in the sense of Spinoza, but rather seeing through bogus ideas. Even the detective story 'Death and the Compass,' which mentions the name Spinoza, is not based on his philosophy. The starting point of the story is a series of three murders committed on the third day of each month. The next murder is due on the third of March. On March 1, the investigating Commissioner receives a letter signed with the name of Baruch Spinoza, along with a detailed map. The letter predicts that a fourth murder will not take place because the recent crime scenes form the exact vertices of an 'equilateral mystical triangle', as shown by a drawing on the map. This is an argumentation *more geometrico*, according to Spinoza. The assistant to the Commissioner, Lönnrot, who has the main responsibility for the case, interprets the information differently. Following the geometric method, he turns the triangle on the map into a tetragon to calculate the location of the upcoming fourth murder. This is an empty villa. Lönnrot looks for it before the 3rd of the following month in order to gain a picture of the purported crime scene. But criminals are already waiting there to seek revenge on him. The murders were especially orchestrated to lure him into a trap. The crime boss was aware of Lönnrot's philosophical inclinations and took advantage of this to get hold of him and then to shoot him. The police detective's investigation, therefore, went astray. This has nothing to do with Spinoza's method, because the real cause of the crime series is not investigated. In reality, by referring to the geometric method, it aims to seduce the headstrong detective to incorrectly apply his philosophical training in order to derail him. By no means is the crime story based on Spinoza's logic. Rather, it is a satire of such a supposed logic. The connection of ideas in Lönnrot's head did not match the actual connection of things. So he failed with the geometric method.

Although Borges recognised Spinoza as an important philosopher, he distanced himself clearly from his space and time concept in the essay 'The Penultimate Version of Reality.' The philosopher George Berkeley and his work were important to him. In the essay 'On the Classic,' he names him next to Schopenhauer as the only philosopher who will survive and be read by generations. The influence of Berkeley's thinking is also evident in Borges' detective stories. Berkeley's central tenet is *esse est percipi*. By claiming the dependency of being on perception, matter as an independent, unified and stable condition is denied. The fact that things unperceived by people do not disappear is explained by assuming that the omniscient God always perceives all things. With Hume, Borges radicalises Berkeley's philosophy and goes a step further; ultimately, he not only denies the continuity of space, matter and spirit, but also time in 'New Refutation of Time.' It is known that metaphysics for Borges is a branch of fantasy literature. For him it should not serve to acquire knowledge, but to astonish the reader. The interest in philosophy – and science, too – is, as Borges admits, primarily aesthetic. But this does not mean that his philosophical thoughts enter his stories uninterrupted. Crime stories that are not based on the everyday understanding of space and time simply wouldn't work.

My theory is that Borges' detective stories are influenced more by Berkeley than by Spinoza, since he exploits the idea *esse est percipi* for the plot. The point is not what is real, but what is perceivable. It is, therefore, important to produce something perceptible, a staged logic, which draws the people in. If – as in Berkeley – material as a consistent, solid substance does not exist, but everything is instead spirit, and objects exist only in perception, they can be manipulated much more easily and installed in a feigned drama. With Spinoza, in contrast, things as elements of nature possess a degree of inertia and resist any manipulation by a criminal imagination. The staging of an unreal perception relationship and its replacement by an alternative, real model through the detective is easier with Berkeley than Spinoza. The 'illogicality' that Borges usually follows is not that of the library, but the referenced reading. Thus the reader, for example, comes to a passage in a book, where another is named, then again another, etc., etc. The avidly seeking reader jumps from one text to another and on and on. The world is, as Derrida wrote, either a text, or it is not. Basically this is a never-ending process that builds a network of referrals, which only occasionally have something to do with a limited and intended solution for practical problems. It is no wonder that, for some, Borges is the spiritual father of the Internet. The perception of the staged logic of criminal operations also follows the method of reading in the sense of thinking with a different mindset, whereby the decoding of the staged event as such represents a deeper reading, yet its consistency with reality is not backed by any empirical evidence. To conclude, a remark by Borges on an appreciation of reading, 'Sometimes I tend to believe that good readers are even more mysterious and rare birds than good writers… Reading is certainly an activity which allows the writing to go first: it is more austere, more courteous and more intellectual.'

References and Further Reading:

a) Jorge Luis Borges

Borges, Jorge Luis: 'Die Kriminalgeschichte', in: ders., *Essays 1952–1979*, München/Wien 1981, 262–274 (English edition: 'The Detective Story', in: Jorge Luis Borges: *On Writing*, London 2010, 125–134)

Borges, Jorge Luis: *Die zwei Labyrinthe*. Lesebuch, München 1986

Borges, Jorge Luis: *Inquisitionen. Essays 1941 – 1952*, Frankfurt am Main 1992 (u. a. Neue Widerlegung der Zeit, Über die Klassiker) (English edition: *Other Inquisitions*, 1937–1952, New York 1965)

Borges, Jorge Luis: *Fiktionen. Erzählungen 1939 – 1944*, Frankfurt am Main 1994 (u. a. Der Garten der Pfade, die sich verzweigen; Tlön, Uqbar, Orbis Tertius; Die Bibliothek von Babel; Thema vom Verräter und vom Helden; Der Tod und der Kompass; Der Süden) (English edition: *Ficciones*, New York 1962)

Borges, Jorge Luis: Niedertracht und Ewigkeit. Erzählungen und Essays 1935 – 1936, 2. Aufl. Frankfurt am Main 2003

Borges, Jorge Luis: *Kabbala und Tango. Essays 1930 – 1932*, 3. Aufl. Frankfurt am Main 2008 (u. a. Die vorletzte Fassung der Wirklichkeit)

Borges, Jorge Luis: *Das Aleph (El Aleph). Erzählungen 1944 – 1952*, 8. Aufl. Frankfurt am Main 2009 (u. a. Emma Zunz, Ibn Hakkan al-Bokhari, gestorben in seinem Labyrinth) (English edition: *The Aleph and Other Stories, 1933–1969*, New York 1978)

Borges, Jorge Luis/Casares, Adolfo Bioy: *Gemeinsame Werke Band 1: Sechs Aufgaben für Don Isidro Parodi. Zwei denkwürdige Phantasien. Ein Modell für den Tod*, München, Wien 1983 (English edition: Six Problems for Don Isidro Parodi, New York 1981)

Borges, Jorge Luis/Ferrari, Osvaldo: *Lesen ist denken mit fremdem Gehirn. Gespräche über Bücher & Borges*, Zürich 1990

b) Other Authors

Bartuschat, Wolfgang: *Baruch de Spinoza*, 2. Aufl. München 2006

Berkeley, George: *Eine Abhandlung über die Prinzipien der menschlichen Erkenntnis*, Stuttgart 2005 (English edition: *A Treatise Concerning the Principles of Human Knowledge*, ed. by J. Dancy, Oxford/New York 1998; wikisource: A Treatise Concerning the Principles of Human Knowledge)

Bothe, Alexander H. D.: *Ästhetische Transzendenz und spekulative*

Metaphysik des Jorge Luis Borges, Saarbrücken 2007

Eco, Umberto: 'Die Abduktion in Uqbar', in: Borges, Jorge Luis/Casares, Adolfo Bioy: *Gemeinsame Werke Band 1: Sechs Aufgaben für Don Isidro Parodi. Zwei denkwürdige Phantasien. Ein Modell für den Tod*, München, Wien 1983, 271–286

Engelmann, Peter: 'Einführung: Postmoderne und Dekonstruktion', in: *Postmoderne und Dekonstruktion. Texte französischer Philosophen der Gegenwart*, hg. v. Peter Engelmann, Stuttgart 1990, 5–32

Gawlick, Günter/Kreimendahl, Lothar: Nachwort, in: Berkeley, George: *Eine Abhandlung über die Prinzipien der menschlichen Erkenntnis*, Stuttgart 2005, 155–191

Seidel, Helmut: *Baruch de Spinoza zur Einführung*, 2. Aufl. Hamburg 2007

Spinoza, Baruch de: *Abhandlung über die Verbesserung des Verstandes*, 2. Aufl. Hamburg 2003

Spinoza, Baruch de: *Ethik in geometrischer Ordnung dargestellt*. Lateinisch-Deutsch, Hamburg 2007

9

Death in Crime Fiction
and Philosophy

As a rule, death is the starting point of a crime story – the unnatural death of a person, the murder. Death is also central to philosophy, as testified by the ancient Greek opinion that to philosophise means to learn to die. As this statement suggests, philosophers address death as such to a lesser degree than its effects in advance and thereafter. Death itself is referred to as the end of life. It is also understood as the separation of body and soul; the rotting corpse is soulless. None of this, however, explains the nature of the soul, whether it lives on after death and, if so, in what condition. Contemporary philosophy concerns itself less with life after death but instead with human mortality, of which we are aware, and with the right attitude to life in the face of certain, and perhaps even imminent, death.

In crime fiction, death plays a significant role in the work of Agatha Christie, the most widely read crime author. In the British television series 'J'accuse her fellow novelist Michael Dibdin compared the role of death in Christie's crime novels with the role of the sexual act in pornography. Just as people in pornographic novels engage repeatedly in sex without any special reason or personal relationship between people, the protagonists in Christie's novels simply die. Dibdin's criticism may be exaggerated, but it cannot be denied that people drop like flies in some of Christie's crime novels. Just as in pornography the sexual act is spectacular and often conducted in unusual circumstances, beyond normal human capacity, death in Christie's books is staged also spectacularly: the murder may be excessive, or simply inexplicable, or committed in the wrong place, as illustrated impressively by *The Body in the Library* (the title of which verges on parody), or there may be a different reason altogether. The most famous – or perhaps infamous – example of death as a spectacle is *And Then There Were None* (original title: *Ten Little Niggers*). Ten very different characters, two of them servants, are invited by an unknown host to spend the weekend on a small island named 'Nigger Island'. The guests come to the island and realise that the host is not present in the house and that no

157

one knows who he is. A copy of the nursery rhyme 'Ten Little Niggers' hangs in every room, in the rhyme the characters die one by one. During dinner, a record is played that, to the guests' surprise, contains an accusation against each one of them. Each guest is accused of causing the death of one or more people in one way or another, be it murder, manslaughter, or incentive to suicide, though somehow the law has been unable to trace them. Once the first guest dies the reader then, at the latest, suspects what will happen next. According to the rhyme's chain of events, all guests on this otherwise deserted island will die a violent death. They cannot escape because a storm separates the island from the mainland. The guests are killed mercilessly in murderous acts of revenge. Exciting questions are thrown up: Who will be the next to die? Who is the murderer? How can he execute his murderous plans without being discovered? How do the individual characters handle the threat? Unlike in more cheerful detective stories, death cannot be ignored here because it remains in everyone's consciousness as a threat and an inescapable event.

Once the surviving guests realise that the murderer must be among them, the situation of mutual distrust and fear perfectly represents Jean-Paul Sartre's famous phrase 'hell is other people'. The line is taken from the play *Huis Clos* (*No Exit*) in which hell is imagined as a gathering of deceased persons in a room with locked doors. In eternal death, these people are unable to escape the impositions and intrusiveness of others. Each is the source of the other's anguish and agony, in other words hell. The play was written several years after Christie's crime novel. As Sartre was an avid reader of crime stories, it can be assumed that he was inspired by the 'closed society' that is common in the setting of crime stories. It is likely that he knew Christie's novel from 1939 and may have been influenced by it.

Christie's crime novel has a philosophical touch due to each character's individual attitude towards their remaining life and their expected demise. Also, since everyone is accused of having taken lives, a further point of interest discussed by philosophers is the question of adequate retribution for murder. As usual in crime fiction, everything that happens is rational. None of the protagonists is superstitious or believes in an evil spirit. No one asks God for forgiveness or thinks about their life after death, not even Bible-reader Emily Brent, who is absolutely convinced of her innocence. Still, it appears as though the guests' deadly punishment by the absent host is a kind of secular Last Judgement. Because they escaped earthly justice, they now face punishment by a higher power, a godlike, unknown person who seems to be omniscient and almighty and appears to even influence the weather. None of the victims is described sympathetically enough for the reader to feel much pity for their plight. It may be murder because there is no proper trial under law, but their death seems justified to a certain extent. General Macarthur even views death as a farewell to a world that has disappointed him, a deliverance from a guilt that burdens him and taints his relationships, an opportunity to find peace. Others, in contrast, cling to life and are completely impervious to their own guilt. Christie managed to depict the inexorability of the host's revenge so convincingly because she was a passionate advocate of the death penalty. This is not only clear from the dialogues in Christie's novels, but is also stated explicitly in her autobiography. In Agatha Christie's view a murderer no longer had any right to live. She shares this opinion with a number of illustrious philosophers including Hobbes, Locke, Rousseau, Kant, Hegel and Schopenhauer. Contemporary philosophy, however, has presented enough arguments to prove that the death penalty cannot be justified rationally. Banning of the death penalty, though, also cannot be justified rationally. The murderous vigilantism on the island is a monstrous crime in any case. Christie makes this clear in the novel, making it a very ambivalent story.

The novel *And Then There Were None* was published in 1939, the year when the Second World War began. Agatha Christie's autobiography contains two extensive chapters regarding both World Wars in which she describes the shock of the outbreak and the course of the First World War, which no humanely-minded person had expected. As Christie worked in a military hospital, she experienced the suffering of injured and dying soldiers at first hand. The Second World War, in contrast, did not come as a surprise. No one expected the Munich Agreement to secure lasting peace and this new World War cast its shadow on Christie's novel. It is not a detective story, but it describes frenzied and merciless murder. The first sentence already contains the name of the (as revealed in the final chapter) murderer, Justice Wargrave. This represents not only the name of the judge, but also a keyword for a murderous agenda: Justice, War, Grave. Germany started the war to remove the so-called injustices of the Treaty of Versailles. It led to mass death, to the grave. Wargrave is also the term for a soldier's grave. I am not certain whether Christie planned this kind of foreshadowing, but like most artists she could sense the concerns of her day and age, especially in view of a war as merciless as this. The whole story takes on a particularly visionary hue if we replace the racist, derogatory word 'nigger' with the equally derogatory and racist word 'Jew', as depicted in Nazi ideology. Christie knew what German Nazis thought about Jews since meeting Dr Julius Jordan in Baghdad in 1933. He had invited Agatha and her husband to tea in his house and his manners were exceptionally polite. Yet when their conversation casually turned to Jews, his facial expression changed suddenly in a frightening manner. Jordan was fanatical in his conviction that Jews must be exterminated. Agatha Christie was stunned. To return to Justice Wargrave's extermination plan: In a letter claiming responsibility, he explains that he wanted to commit murder on a grand scale, and had chosen the rhyme 'Ten Little Niggers' as a template in order to give his plans an artistic touch. Hitler, who as 'Führer' of the German Reich ruled as highest war lord and judge, was a failed would-be artist and planned the Final Solution as his murder on a grand scale. Like Wargrave, he committed suicide. To a certain extent, Wargrave's murders are also a final solution, albeit aimed at a smaller group: 'And then there were none'.

As we know, everyone is mortal, be they rich or poor, old or young, beautiful or ugly and so on. Death does not differentiate. This is a matter of course. It is noticeable in Agatha Christie's crime stories that the murder victims come from all classes, all age groups, and all walks of life, and this is by no means a matter of course. Christie radicalises the idea that death can come to anyone and turns it into a literary idea that a violent unnatural death can come to anyone. Modern warfare is the best example for such an idea in our reality. Christie views everyone as a potential victim of violence, not only for narrative reasons so as to add an unexpected twist to the story, but also against the background of her experience of both World Wars. Anyone can be hit by a bomb. In the so-called material slaughter of the wars, millions of people were used as cannon fodder. In her autobiography, Christie very clearly speaks out against war and describes it as a catastrophic, pointless pursuit of interests in our time.

The historical experience of mass death in the First World War also left traces in philosophy. Agatha Christie would not have read this philosophy, but she shares the dramatic experience and thus comes to similar conclusions regarding life and death. Death as the end of life was already an important subject in the philosophy of life from 1900. After the experiences of the First World War, death gained a more prominent role in the new German philosophy. Martin Heidegger is arguably the most significant philosopher here, who published his fundamental work *Being and Time* in 1927. In it, he explains that human existence, because it is mortal, is inevitably geared towards death. Unlike animals, humans are aware of this. Death concludes life which would otherwise be incomplete. Heidegger speaks of being-toward-death. This causes fear. Mortality is not some later event, due to come at some stage; it is in the here and now. The condition of existence ('being there') dies as long as it exists. Our simple everyday view ('we must all die someday') treats death as a simple incident and tends to disguise and repress that being-toward-death of oneself. In contrast, the actual issue is to have the courage to be afraid and confront one's own death. This is the only way to gain a new, strong type of 'Eigentlichkeit', an authenticity of existence from death. Heidegger postulates a 'freedom-towards-death'. It means an extension of the range of possibilities for action in view of inescapable death, the determination to lead one's life in a way that seems existentially significant. Yet Heidegger's philosophy of death is not as new as it certainly appeared at the time. Montaigne previously said that the continuous work of our life is to build death. He claimed that death is equally near to us all and quotes Seneca: '*Nemo altero fragilior est, nemo in crastinum sui certior*' ('No man is more fragile than another: no man more certain than another of tomorrow.') Therefore we must be aware of it all the time and act accordingly. This corresponds – in R. A. York's view – with the famous cliché in Christie's work that '[i]n the midst of life we are in death.'

In Agatha Christie's *And Then There Were None* the protagonists do not seize the liberty of death unless it is in the case of a perverted, megalomaniac form of murder. Vera Claythorne's suicide is not a free act, as she was forced into it. As a rule, characters tend not to have the chance to choose death because part of the crime novel's plot is that the victim is surprised by death, which creates variety and suspense for the reader. Yet even the protagonists who expect to die (kidnapped victims, for instance) are usually subject to fear and the hope of survival and do not confront death. While we might recognise in the striking focus on death in crime novels an implicit philosophical view of life as being-towards-death, as a rule any positive turn towards a freedom-towards-death is absent. The frequency of death in many crime novels is simply the consequence of a particular observation of modern everyday life, as Walter Benjamin states: 'There is only one radical novelty for people today – and it is always the same: death.'

Raymond Chandler's crime novels also demonstrate a significant reference to death. Two of his books use newfangled colloquial metaphors for death in their titles: *The Big Sleep* and *The Long Goodbye*. The American literary scholar Fredric Jameson emphasises that Chandler's specific writing and narrative technique focuses the reader's attention on death and presents it in an unusual manner. Chandler does not design a great model of the American experience, but instead sketches fragmented images of situations and locations, describes impressions: corroding mail boxes, sand-filled spittoons, carpet stains, glass doors that won't close, dusty offices, monotonous waiting rooms, shabby bus stops – seen through the fleeting eyes of a passenger on a passing bus while his conscience is busy with other matters. This type of perception depends on chance and anonymity to bring out the true significance of such objects – which is insignificance. Similar to the things we see only from the corner of our eye, there are certain moments in life that can only be perceived due to a certain lack of conscious attention. Time is an undefined sequence from which specific, explosive and unrepeatable moments stand out. The unique time structure in the best crime novels, including those by Chandler, forms an organising frame for isolated observations.

Even in those days Marlowe's Los Angeles was a kind of microcosm and an anticipation of social reality in the US: a city with no centre in which social groups live in areas isolated from each other in their own local districts, so that they have lost touch with one another. Instead of a visible vertical and hierarchical composition of living quarters we find a horizontally spread city in which social structures dissolve. The detective becomes a character whose routine and personal life serve to put together the separate, isolated parts of society. He does not actually do this from a position of privileged, lived experience, but as a collector of knowledge, an involuntary researcher. The honest detective equals a sensitive sensory organ that, when touched, is able to register the nature of things in its surroundings; it can sense the resistance of things and consciously process what it experiences. Similarly it becomes conscious of mortality, dying, emptiness and death. The seemingly insignificant details cause a sensation and remain in our memory. Precisely those things and circumstances whose description seems superfluous against the backdrop of the story's progress generate the impression of an awkward, bleak, authentic reality, because they are not misappropriated by the aesthetic functionality or sense of the narrative. On this point, Chandler wrote a letter to Frederick Lewis Allen regarding the readers of crime stories: '…the things they remembered, that haunted them, were not for example that a man got killed, but that in the moment of his death he was trying to pick a paper clip up off the polished surface of a desk, and it kept slipping away from him, so that there was a look of strain on his face and his mouth was half open in a kind of tormented grin, and the last thing in the world he thought about was death. He didn't even hear death knock on the door. That damn little paper clip kept slipping away from his fingers and he just wouldn't push it to the edge of the desk and catch it as it fell.'

Chandler loves depicting the morbid transience of decaying cityscapes and interiors that were once full of life. Facades crumble and office furniture is dusty and worn. The description of empty places, rooms and objects is a recurring theme. Death in Chandler's writing is, in a way, a spatial concept. In *The Long Goodbye*, Marlowe goes to a dilapidated, deserted holiday camp: 'The place seemed to be as dead as Pharaoh'. A few lines earlier we find the often quoted line, 'Off to my left there was an empty swimming pool, and nothing ever looks emptier than an empty swimming pool.' The emptiness in this sentence is made visible in the frequent use of the letter O, an empty circle. Like the philosopher Martin Seel, we may see this line as an expression of the 'metaphysical emptiness' of the pool, an emptiness that is characteristic of Marlowe stories. Then again, we might also see this emptiness as a symbol of death, which some philosophers understand as the presence of the absent. Death as such is not actually visible. It becomes particularly palpable for friends and relatives who have lost a loved one because the person is missing, is no longer there, and will be forever absent. The experience of absence is felt in such a forceful manner that it is like a punch from a fist. It is the experience of an oppressive emptiness that was once filled with life.

Death is essential to Chandler's crime plots as a violent death, as murder, but in a way that differs from the classic whodunit. The latter allocates a purpose to the murder as a central element of the story, in which all other elements converge and give meaning to the entire plot. For this reason, murder itself is always intended and deliberate. Chandler's stories, however, are different. Here, murder often seems to be purposeless and coincidental, the useless end of a thread. This effect is created by guiding the reader's attention back and forth between the murder and the investigation in a complex pattern so that there is never just one single focus for the attention of the reader. If the reader follows the motive of the murder, the investigation attains a threatening and oppressive inevitability, like an ever-narrowing spiral. If attention is focused, however, on the search as an organising centre of the events of the story, the murder, as mentioned, is reduced to a pointless coincidence, the interruption of a trail. This effect is enhanced by the coincidental violence that gets in the way of the sub-plot and contaminates the murder. Once the reader finally arrives at an explanation of the events at the end of the story, all violence appears in the same light and the murder seems just as shabby, brutal and contemptible as everyday violence. The name of the murderer is now known, but it might just as well be anybody else. The murder and the murderer are demystified in Chandler's narrative and have lost their symbolic quality. While the common detective story depicts murder as an almost non-physical result of intellectual planning, similar to the solving of a mathematical puzzle, Chandler's stories describe a gap between intention and implementation. The event of the murderous act, the turn towards physical action, always happens suddenly and abruptly without having been justified previously in the real world by logic. In expectation of an intellectual mystery, the reader's reasoning leads him nowhere. Instead, he is gripped by the sudden hunch, a sensation of death in all its physicality, which he cannot escape, at whose mercy he is.

The crime underlying Chandler's story is always old and buried in the past. Usually, it has taken place before the story begins. The reader, on the other hand, assumes that the central crime is part of the present, of the events being played out directly before him. In the end, however, all events appear in a new and depressing light. All effort was in vain. The person that was sought is long since dead. The present is unimportant to him, the corpse rots in the earth. In view of the resolution of the case and the physical decomposition and soullessness of the central person, who had had a name for so long, the sham that is life and the immediate present becomes transparent and we feel the transience of everything that is destined to die. Chandler's narrative has the effect that, with the revelation of the identity of the murderer, who then mutates into something other, a confrontation takes place with the reality of death, stale death that tries to seize the living. The past that seemed forgotten and dead still has power over the present and the living. Marlowe contemplates the power of death: 'What did it matter where you lay once you were dead? In a dirty sump or in a marble tower on top of a high hill? You were dead, you were sleeping the big sleep, you were not bothered by things like that... You just slept the big sleep, not caring about the nastiness of how you died or where you fell. Me, I was part of the nastiness now.' (*The Big Sleep*) This is, in short, Jameson's theory of death in Chandler's work.

Chandler's hero Philip Marlowe wants to be a master, or more precisely his own master. How does one become a master? The German philosopher Hegel answered this question with his well-known theory of authority and servitude in *The Phenomenology of Mind*, one of the most influential philosophical books of the nineteenth and twentieth centuries. According to this book, the difference between masters and servants originally resulted from a struggle of life and death. What made the struggle's victor the master was that he risked his life. The loser, on the other hand, submitted to servitude and recognised the other as master because his will to survive was greater than it was to accept a possible death. The master also proved himself to be superior to the servant by risking his life for an ideal goal (to become master) for which he first had to overcome his biological need to live. Servitude, on the other hand, means to serve the master who gives orders and enjoys the benefits of the servant's labours. The dialectics of authority and servitude constitute the development of work and thus the history of humanity; this, according to Alexandre Kojève's interpretation of Hegel.

Marlowe's American society is a highly differentiated one based on a division of labour. The master is characterised by his independence, as someone who does not earn his living as a dependent worker. He is in charge of his own workforce, be they employees, labourers or servants. Marlowe wants to be a master. He wants to be independent and 'not to get pushed around', as he makes clear repeatedly. But he does not want to be the kind of master who has servants. He despises the rich who give orders to servants and let themselves be served by them instead of going about their lives independently. Hegel also realised that the master is also dependent on the work and appreciation of the servant even though he is superior. Because Marlowe wants to avoid such dependence and be master nonetheless, his only option is to be a loner in the independent freelance profession as private eye. As such, he often gets into situations in which he must display the original characteristics of a master: the risk of bodily harm and the engagement of his life in violent struggle. Normally, a master need not prove himself in such an archaic manner. Contracts of employment, monitored by the justice system, regulate the extent of his authority and his status as boss. In the depths of Chandler's society, however, there lurks the original violent conflict that may spread like a virus at any moment, especially in areas in which crime and illegal actions are concerned. Marlowe does not only want to be his own master as a private eye in a social niche. Rather, he wants people such as the police, clients, gangsters, witnesses and others to recognise this. His insistence on this recognition demands on the one hand his personal code of honour and, on the other, his prestige as private eye on whose energy, discretion and loyalty his clients must be able to rely, even when threatened with death.

In the classic crime novel we differentiate between two worlds: the world of the legal and the world of the illegal. It is the same in Chandler's novels. He realises that we step into a different world when we pass beyond the green lights of the police station and enter a place beyond the law. A second invisible line also seems to separate the society of men in Marlowe's universe: those who are willing to risk their lives in the struggle, and those men who are not. Marlowe's contempt for the wealthy also stems from the fact that they generally did not attain their privileged status by means of a struggle, but simply by inheritance or economic good fortune. For this reason, Marlowe is able to accept the odd gangster who has a heart rather than the rich man because the gangster is a man who can look death straight in the eye. As for women, Marlowe admires them if they display womanly qualities, but as a rule he does not let them get close to him. Dependent jobholders and the poor are mostly blanked out of Marlowe's world, or at least not particularly appreciated. Marlowe even tries to avoid working dependently for another when taking on a client. According to Knight, an expert on Chandler, Marlowe actually investigates very little for the actual assignment. Usually, he follows his own aims and interests in his investigation of a crime and completes his client's assignment along the way. In short, he does not submit to dependent work. Marlowe always remains his own master, even if the price is social isolation.

It is commonly understood that Philip Marlowe is Chandler idealised, a man he would have liked to have been himself, as James Ellroy said at a reading in Frankfurt. Raymond Chandler, this hypersensitive, vulnerable man subject to poetic reveries certainly proved that he can also face the struggle of life and death in his own personal situation. Although his poor eyesight prevented him from joining the US Army, he volunteered to become a soldier in the Canadian Army in order to take part in the First World War. As a platoon leader, he and his men were attacked by barrage fire, which cost everyone's lives but his. The experience shook him greatly. Despite a concussion, he remained a soldier after his recovery though he was never sent into battle again. Even as a writer he risked his health, perhaps even his life in an emergency. While a script writer in Hollywood, he was forced to finish a script as soon as possible due to an unexpected lack of time. Despite the risk for his health, Chandler was charged with this task and only accepted it under the condition that he, a recovered alcoholic, would be allowed to drink as much alcohol as he required to hasten his output, under the supervision of a doctor. Chandler managed to finish the script in time for the deadline, but was physically and mentally exhausted. He could have ruined his health. Even though writing scripts secured a good income, Chandler increasingly hated such wage labour and preferred making a living as a freelance writer instead. Like Marlowe, Chandler wanted to be his own master.

The bank robber Earl Drake in Dan J. Marlowe's extraordinary crime novel *The Name of the Game is Death* (1962) also wants to be his own master. Death is used as a trump card in a professional game of death. Earl Drake has decided not to conform to the norms and values of society. To remain undetected, he sometimes works as a tree surgeon, but lives from the spoils of his bank robberies. He changes his name several times, lives alone and finds suitable new partners for every coup only to go his own separate way again afterwards. Anyone who becomes a threat to him, be they enemy or traitor, crosses an invisible line that can only mean death for him. Drake considers it his professional duty to kill such a person. The price of being independent, his own master, is a life in mortal danger and the constant willingness to kill if necessary. It is a cold life without scruples. This, too, is the life of a master without servants.

It remains a matter of contention among philosophers as to whether there is life after death. It is an unarguable fact, however, that there is a life in the memory of others after death. Mildred Davis' crime novel *They Buried a Man* (1953) deals with this subject. In the small town of Little Forks, Selwyn Buoman dies in a tragic car crash. Buoman was a pharmacist and well-liked in his town. During his research for the obituary, a journalist comes across an old message that makes him very suspicious. He systematically questions those who were close to the deceased about their memories of him, and compares their statements. His probing not only leads to suspicions among some of those questioned, and dramatic events that cause commotion in the community; new light is also shed on the deceased and other esteemed members of the community of Little Forks, bringing the grim reality to light. Mildred Davis' novel demonstrates how the past can gain control over the present and how the memories of a deceased person can influence the existence and social memory of the living.

To conclude this chapter, one book should not be forgotten, which is one of the best crime novels about death: *Ted Lewis*' novel *Jack's Return Home* (1970) begins with the unique line 'The rain rained'. Right after the title and this first sentence the experienced, language-aware reader knows that Jack Carter's return will end in death. He returns to the place whence he originated and on which the rain falls: to the earth. The rain falls relentlessly, without aim or intention because it is inorganic matter. Death is ultimately the change from a living organism to inorganic matter. 'You are dust and shall turn to dust,' said the German philosopher Kant, quoting the Bible. Death is as inevitable and pointless as the fact that the rain rains.

Jack Carter's home town is an industrial town of average size in the north of England. The last time he returned was years ago, for his father's funeral. This time he is back for Frank's funeral, the brother with whom he feels connected by their happy childhood. When Jack arrives, Frank's body is displayed in an open coffin at home. The next day, the body is buried with a church ceremony. Lewis describes how different people who were close to Frank react to his death. The circumstances of his death are strange. Frank's body was found in his car away from the road and at the foot of a steep slope. Frank was full of whisky and some of his clothes were drenched with it too. The official version, therefore, was that he died while driving under the influence of alcohol. The strange thing is that Frank was a very cautious person who would never have driven while drunk. Besides which, he never drank whisky. Jack Carter suspects that the accident was staged and thus murder. He therefore starts to ask questions and causes a stir. He knows that he is endangering himself, but Frank's name deserves to be cleared and the truth about his death must be brought to light. Jack owes it to his brother, and also to himself. In London he works as executor and killer for a gangster syndicate, a fact that is known in the criminal circles of his home town. Nobody like Jack Carter can accept such an underhanded murder of his brother; it must be avenged.

In this novel, the hero is also a master in the Hegelian sense due to his readiness to fight to the death in order to gain respect. Furthermore, the novel is about a dead person's life after death in the memory of living people. The staging of the fatal accident of a hopelessly drunk driver creates the wrong impression of Frank, an impression he himself would have abhorred. Philosophers have differing opinions regarding what the living owe to the dead, in Jack's case, his closest family member. Some derive such obligations from the existence of the dead person as a physical unit that has not yet decomposed or been cremated, allowing for identification and criminal investigation. But this does not apply to Jack Carter: 'Death didn't really make much difference at all; the face just reassembled the particles of memory. And as usual when you see someone dead who you've seen alive it was impossible to imagine the corpse as being related to its former occupant.' Other philosophers, and this seems more self-evident, refer to a person's right of self-determination with regard to the period after death, similar to a final will and testament. A person's dignity must also be respected after death. There is also a construct in terms of social contract theory: while living, the people of a community conclude a (fictional) contract defining what should be done with their corpse, memory and goods once they die. The influence a deceased person has or may have on the living, and vice versa, is regulated, so to speak, in advance.

What about these duties in the novel? Jack Carter first fulfils his duty to arrange a dignified funeral. At this point, his concern is his brother's memory and how people will remember him. Frank's defamation as a drunkard diminishes not only the deceased's own image and therefore his right to self-determination and self-portrayal while alive; it also casts a shadow on his living relatives and friends. The defamation hurts them, probably makes them angry, and damages their relationship with the deceased because this false image does not do him justice. After a murder, the bereaved usually feel the strong need to avenge the dead, to punish the killer. Moreover, it is generally considered to be the obligation of a community to expose the killer in its midst, arrest him and bring him to justice. The community owes it to the victim as well as itself. But what if the community, including the police, does not react adequately, and a murder is presented and covered up as an accident?

In some respects Jack Carter's situation and actions resemble those of Antigone in Sophocles' play of the same name, which has been dealt with in philosophy in different ways. In both cases the brother has been killed, in Antigone's case in a battle with Creon, the ruler of Thebes. Creon decrees that the body of the fallen brother should not be buried, a high-handed break with tradition. Antigone opposes this edict, buries Polynices' body and publicly admits the deed. Creon then condemns her to death by immurement; Antigone hangs herself.

Antigone's ethical conflict consists of the question whether she should comply with the king's rules, or honour the traditional obligations of the living toward the dead, express her love for her brother, and in doing so accept the possibility of her own death. Jack Carter is in a conflict between his gangster bosses and their criminal business partners who want to hush up the murder. He is also in conflict with the police and judicial authorities that are part of the conspiracy. Because of this, he additionally gets into trouble with the law since he is more or less forced to use illegal methods to re-establish his brother's honour, reveal the truth about his death and bring the murderer to justice. Since the authorities ought to be the ones to legally prosecute the murderer, Jack's aims are in line with the law, even though his methods are not.

As a hard-boiled gangster, Jack Carter does not think about whether his illegal actions, especially vigilante justice, are an inappropriate means of retaliation. And he also does not think about whether he may lose his own life in the process, as predicted by his enemies. Towards the end of the story it becomes clear just how important it is for him to reveal the facts of his brother's murder. When Jack's death begins to seem more and more likely, he gets in touch with a journalist and sends him a film that contains evidence of the true reason for Frank's death. Since his brother's daughter (who is possibly his own) is indirectly involved in the matter, Jack Carter also disregards her interests. As expected the story ends with Carter's violent death, and the impressions of the dying man end the story. His final words are, 'Then there is silence for a long time until I hear the car door slam again and the engine start up and I listen to the sound until it dies away and then there is nothing, nothing at all.' Jack has returned home.

While the ethical conflicts of both Antigone and Jack Carter are similar, they also demonstrate clear differences. Their situations are alike in their decision to put their obligations towards their dead brothers above any governmental law, even if the price is their own death. Both Antigone and Carter publicly admit their deed. Both manifest familial relations as a form of action. In both cases, the legitimacy of the actions of the authorities is questionable. However, the difference and partial opposition between male and female status, gender roles, and the sense of justice in Antigone's tragedy are not central to Carter's story, but are instead marginal. In its place the crime novel is enhanced by a second level in addition to that of the state, the level of the criminal underworld, which is far more important to a criminal like Carter than governmental authority. Even though Carter often explains that he only wants to bring order to his home town so he can leave it again, this re-establishment of legal order is a mere side effect. What must be corrected above all is the memory and public image of his deceased brother, Frank Carter, but also the violent and secretly maintained order of the underworld, a sense of authority that is unstable and hard-fought. Frank must die because he goes after a criminal porn ring that has recruited his 15-year-old daughter Doreen as an actress in a porn film. Unlike in his youth, when Frank was too frightened to confront criminal gangs, he now has the courage to protect his beloved daughter and defend his family ties. Jack Carter now continues the fight, the exact cause of which he does not know at the beginning, but wants to find out. He is motivated not only by his obligation towards Frank, who as an upstanding civilian hated his brother's life of crime. It concerns primarily Jack Carter's obligation to himself. The fact that he disregards and challenges the government's monopoly on authority in his pursuit to kill his brother's murderer is not unusual for him since, as a gangster, he does not recognise this authority anyway. Besides, he plans to leave the country for South Africa along with his lover once he has completed his mission. The arrogance he displays by challenging the underworld's hierarchy is a far graver situation, which in view of the increased peril to his own life is like an act of unconditional sovereignty. The motive for such a reckless endeavour is not only the battle for the status as 'master' and the reputation of the dangerous gangster who demands respect, but also the memory of happy childhood moments he shared with Frank. Now these memories are painful and increase Jack's hatred towards the murderer. His personal happiness, honour and appreciation of his loss are more important to Jack than any law, any demands of society, whether those of the state or the underworld.

In that respect he copies Frank's deed, his brother's challenge of the underworld, in a radicalised form.

The more Jack's enemies harry him and threaten him with death, the more tough-minded he becomes, as though he wants to reveal the suppressed truth and seal it with his death in an almost Socratic gesture of provocation to the community. Similar to Antigone, Jack is already half dead in the eyes of others. His subsequent killer, Eric, says to him, 'You're dead now Jack, only you don't know it.' Since Jack, destined to death, still lives, fights and kills though he is bound to die, he publicly confirms death as the limitation of life. Carter's tragedy certainly differs from that of Antigone and Socrates in that his death is not imposed by the powers of the state (the king, the court of Athens), but by his criminal enemies. Unlike Socrates and Antigone, Jack Carter does not submit to death, but instead, in a moment of carelessness while trying to punish his brother's murderer, he is fatally wounded by the latter with a knife. Jack wants to stay alive till the very end, but he is always willing to sacrifice himself if necessary. His death ultimately contributes to the revelation of the truth behind Frank's death, thus forcing the legal authorities to prosecute the murderer. His violent death is not entirely pointless; it is a message for the living. The names Frank and Jack Carter are indelibly etched into the historical memory of their home town. It would be incorrect to reduce our understanding of the crime novel to the mere platitude that whoever sows violence will reap violence. The fundamental statement is that whoever defends his personal, familial happiness without compromise has no place in the ruling culture, within which life is good. Death is not only a natural limitation of life but also a sanction of the ruling culture, which regulates death as the limit.

References and Further reading:

Crime novels and other texts by crime writers
Chandler, Raymond: *Selected Letters of Raymond Chandler*, edited by Frank MacShane, New York 1987
Chandler, Raymond: *The Long Goodbye*, New York 1988
Chandler, Raymond: *The Big Sleep*, New York 1992
Christie, Agatha: *And Then There Were None*, London 2007 (first edition: *Ten Little Niggers*, London 1939)
Christie, Agatha: *An Autobiography*. London 1977

Davis, Mildred: *They Buried a Man*, New York 1955

Lewis, Ted: *Jack's Return Home*, London 1985

Marlowe, Dan J.: *The Name of the Game is Death*, New York 1993

Literature about crime fiction and death

Agatha Christie Lesebuch, 8th edition. Bern/Munich 1998 (no author)

Bacon, Francis: *The Essays or Counsels, Civil and Moral*, Oxford 1999

Barthes, Roland: 'Der Wirklichkeitseffekt', in: Barthes: *Das Rauschen der Sprache*, Frankfurt am Main 2006, 164–172 (French edition: Barthes, Roland: 'L'effet de réel', Communications, vol. 11 (March 1968), 84–89)

Benjamin, Walter: *Charles Baudelaire*, Frankfurt am Main 1974

Butler, Judith: *Politics and Kinship. Antigone for the Present*, 2001

Compart, Martin: 'Noir Star: Die schwarze Welt des Ted Lewis', in: Ted Lewis: *Jack rechnet ab*, Strange 2002, 207–218

Esser, Andrea: 'Der Status des menschlichen Leichnams', in: *Deutsche Zeitschrift für Philosophie* 1/2008, 52–54

Euchner, Walter: *Egoismus und Gemeinwohl. Studien zur Geschichte der bürgerlichen Philosophie*, Frankfurt am Main 1973

Gehring, Petra: *Theorien des Todes zur Einführung*, Hamburg 2010

Gripenberg, Monika: *Agatha Christie*, Reinbek bei Hamburg 1994

Gumbrecht, Hans Ulrich: *Stimmungen lesen. Über eine verdeckte Wirklichkeit der Literatur*, Munich 2011

Hegel, Georg Wilhelm Friedrich: *Phänomenologie des Geistes*, Werke 3, 9th edition. Frankfurt am Main 2005

Heidegger, Martin: *Sein und Zeit*, 7th edition. Tübingen 1953

Jameson, Fredric: 'On Raymond Chandler', in: Glenn W. Most/William W. Stowe (eds.): *The Poetics of Murder. Detective Fiction and Literary Theory*, San Diego/New York/London 1983, 122–148

Jameson, Fredric: 'The Synoptic Chandler', in: Joan Copjec (ed.): *Shades of Noir*, London 1993, 33–56

Jankélévitch, Vladimir: *Der Tod*, Frankfurt am Main 2005

Kant, Immanuel: 'Der Streit der Fakultäten', in: Kant: *Schriften zur Anthropologie, Geschichtsphilosophie, Politik und Pädagogik 1*, Werkausgabe Vol. XI, edited by Wilhelm Weischedel, 11th edition. Frankfurt am Main 1996, 261–393

Knight, Stephen: "A Hard Cheerfulness': An Introduction to Raymond Chandler', in: Brian Docherty (ed.): *American Crime Fiction. Studies in the Genre*, Houndmills/London 1988, 71–87

Kojève, Alexandre: 'Zusammenfassender Kommentar zu den ersten sechs Kapiteln der "Phänomenologie des Geistes"', in: Hans Friedrich Fulda/Dieter Henrich (eds.): *Materialien zu Hegels ,Phänomenologie des Geistes'*, Frankfurt am Main 1973, 133–188

Kühl, Kristian: *Die Bedeutung der Rechtsphilosophie für das Strafrecht*, Baden-Baden 2001

Löwith, Karl: 'Heidegger: Problem and Background of Existentialism', in: Löwith: *Sämtliche Schriften 8. Heidegger – Denker in dürftiger Zeit*, Stuttgart 1984, 102–123

MacShane, Frank: *The Life of Raymond Chandler*, Harmondsworth 1979

Montaigne: *Essais*, edited by Ralph-Rainer Wuthenow, Frankfurt am Main 1976

Morgan, Janet: *Agatha Christie. A Biography*, London 1985

Osborne, Charles: *The Life and Crimes of Agatha Christie*, London 2000

Platon: 'Phaidon', in: Platon.: *Sämtliche Werke 3*, Hamburg 1959, 7–66

Porter, Dennis: 'The Private Eye', in: Martin Priestman (ed.): *The Cambridge Companion to Crime Fiction*, 4th edition. Cambridge/New York u. a. 2009, 95–113

Rother, Wolfgang: *Verbrechen, Folter, Todesstrafe*, Basel 2010

Sartre, Jean-Paul: *No Exit and Three Other Plays*, New York 1989

Scherer, Georg: 'Philosophie des Todes und moderne Rationalität', in: Hans Helmut Jansen (ed.): *Der Tod in Dichtung, Philosophie und Kunst*, 2nd edition. Darmstadt 1989, 505–521

Seel, Martin: *Ästhetik des Erscheinens*, Frankfurt am Main 2003

Tugendhat, Ernst: *Vorlesungen über Ethik*, 4th edition. Frankfurt am Main 1997

Tugendhat, Ernst: 'Über den Tod', in: Tugendhat: *Aufsätze 1992–2000*, Frankfurt am Main 2001, 67–90

Tugendhat, Ernst: 'Unsere Angst vor dem Tod', in: Tugendhat: *Anthropologie statt Metaphysik*, Munich 2007, 159–175

Wittwer, Héctor: *Philosophie des Todes*, Stuttgart 2009

York, R. A.: *Agatha Christie: Power and Illusion*, Basingstoke 2007

10

The Consolation of Crime Fiction is Stronger than the Consolation of Philosophy

Consolation of Philosophy, or Philosophiae Consolationis libri V in the original Latin, is the title of Boethius' classic philosophical text from 524 AD. These writings begin with a crime story in which Boethius finds himself in a prison cell. He is wrongly accused of high treason and sentenced to be executed. An unknown woman of high standing and with penetrating eyes comes to visit him. She is willing to help him under the condition that he openly tells the truth: 'If you want a doctor's help, you must uncover your wound.' Who is this mysterious stranger? Is she a lawyer, a detective, a witness for the defence or an agent of some secret power come to prove his innocence and save him from death? No, she is the philosophy he met in his youth and no longer recognises. Once the visitor's name is revealed it becomes clear that the narrative will no longer progress like a crime story. Instead, the story serves to present philosophical thoughts that console the prisoner.

Philosophical consolation
What does consolation in philosophy consist of? Boethius laments the injustice that has been done to him, the suffering and the misfortune that he has encountered. Fate has turned against him. Philosophy points out that he ought to know that fate is fickle and that he had been blessed with much fortune and a variety of goods. As a philosophically educated man he ought to know that all earthly goods such as wealth, fame, beauty, health and more are imperfect and transient and therefore invalid. Such goods do not live up to their promise, do not make one happy or indicate the path to great fortune. For this reason, it is wrong to set one's heart on them and mourn their loss. Boethius still has his friends, his most precious possessions. An adverse situation is of greater use to man than a favourable one because the former educates you while the latter merely

175

deceives. As one who has been dispossessed of all his worldly goods, he can now focus on the search for true and perfect good fortune. God is the highest, most perfect and indestructible fortune. If a person wants to be truly happy, he must find his fortune within his own soul, find God and be a part of this divine bliss that philosophy provides. God is the beginning and the end of all things. He directs all things with His benevolence.

But if the Almighty guides the world with His benevolence, how does evil come into the world? Boethius was particularly interested in this question because it was the deeds of evil people that caused his misfortune. The Almighty is all-knowing and thus knows evil and every criminal deed down to the smallest detail. If God can foresee evil, why does He let it happen? The only possible reason is that man is able to decide between good and evil of his own free will. As a result, we are left with the fundamental philosophical problem that has been passed down through the ages: how are divine providence (*providentia*), human fate (*fatum*) and free will connected to one another? Only events that are the result of a chain of causes and effects are foreseeable. If a person chooses evil of his own free will, even God cannot foresee or guide it. The consequence of this would be that He is not all-knowing or almighty. Boethius solves the problem by positioning God's wisdom outside the human experience of time and the chronological sequence of events. God is eternal and therefore not subject to time. For this reason, He always knows everything. He also punishes those who are evil even if their worldly lives treat them well. Man's most important possession is his immortal soul, which experiences its greatest bliss in God. This is the good person's reward, which is only given fully after death. Philosophy guides us towards this divine reward by showing us the decrepitude of worldly possessions. In this sense, philosophy really does mean to learn to die, for its duty is only fulfilled after death by completely and utterly giving in to God. By steering us along this path, guiding our soul and supporting it, philosophy gives us consolation.

Boethius' argumentation resembles neo-platonic ideas influenced by Christian doctrine such as the teachings of Augustine, whom he greatly admired. In view of the fact that Boethius was a member of the Catholic Church, his shift towards platonic philosophy instead of Catholicism in later years, facing the prospect of death, is remarkable. The misfortune he encountered while doing his duty in the highest public office in

Theoderic's kingdom is connected with his philosophical opinions. He followed the platonic idea that philosophers like him, while not rulers of a state, should at the very least advise the king and exert influential political authority. He observed the philosophical principles of truthfulness and conscientiousness which led to his doom, because of the rampant political intrigues in which he refused to take part. Boethius was right in assuming that philosophy was being accused and persecuted along with him. In his last hour, philosophy is his only consolation.

The question remains, however, whether the consolation that philosophy provides to the condemned Boethius is a general gift that is available in principle to all. The consolation relies on assumptions that are questionable and which cannot be proved reliably by Boethius' arguments. At the centre lies the idea of a benevolent and almighty God to whom the immortal soul returns to find true bliss. If a person does not share this notion, all arguments collapse. Even though Boethius gives various reasons for his opinion, they are not entirely compelling. For instance, he assumes that God, the perfect good, must exist because of man's idea that – based on the imperfection of known worldly possessions and contrasting ideas of perfection – there must be a perfect good. A thought or an idea, even if it is widely spread, does not guarantee that the idea is true. The ideal of perfection may simply be the wish of man, which sadly cannot be fulfilled in reality. It is certainly possible that the universe is driven by random coincidences instead of the reasonable guidance of a perfectly benevolent higher being, as Boethius believes. The imperfection and perishability of worldly possessions such as health, enjoyment of life, beauty, wealth and more do not necessarily make them any less desirable. On the contrary, some people will appreciate them even more because of their impermanence, as long as they are able to enjoy them. The change from loss to renunciation that underlies Boethius' philosophy and is praised as the path from compulsion to freedom by his admirers may be understandable due to his tragic situation. Psychologically, his philosophy may be interpreted as a compensatory illusion.

Alexandre Jollien points out that Boethius' theory runs the risk of justifying pointless suffering; more precisely, the kind of suffering that is inflicted wrongfully upon people. It would certainly be presumptuous to wish to live according to one's own law, one's individual arbitrariness. Nonetheless, this does not mean that we surrender powerlessly to a fate that supposedly obeys divine rules. If people have the freedom to create reasonable laws for their community, they should also have the right to use them, observe them and prevent or punish injustice as long as they live by these laws. This is irrespective of whether someone believes in God or not. A belief in God does not imply a resigned acceptance of the injustice we suffer at the hands of others. If it did, every individual's bad deeds would be God's will, which contradicts the idea of a benevolent God. Admittedly, Boethius' arguments are more complex than that. However, it is not necessary to trace all implications of the consolation of his philosophy in order to demonstrate its weaknesses.

Another plea against his philosophy results from what he did in reality at the time when he composed his writings on consolation. It is likely that writing steadied him spiritually and kept his fears at bay. This is supported by his taking on a more active role in order to deal with his situation, similar to a child who, as Freud observed, plays the 'gone-there' game when its mother is away. But there is more that speaks for the consolation Boethius found while writing. The text is not a strict, academic – in other words, dry – philosophical treatise. Instead, it is the telling of a story, Boethius' personal story, which also expresses his misfortune. The story is enriched with dialogues between the visitor Philosophy and the prisoner, which are interspersed with occasional verses and songs. As a result, Boethius found consolation not only in philosophy, but also in the muse of poetry. It is a performative contradiction: at the beginning of the narrative Philosophy refers to the muses as harlots and chases them away since they would only increase Boethius' pain and suffering. In reality, they were always there, as his writings prove. His book also secured him a worldly outcome that philosophy criticises: his fame as philosopher and his continuation as a part of cultural memory, the end of which is unforeseeable.

A book by a contemporary writer ties in with Boethius' own text: Alain de Botton's *The Consolations of Philosophy* (2000) derives different types of consolation from the ideas of six famous philosophers. Socrates' philosophy, for instance, is supposed to offer consolation to the unpopular, Epicurus consoles those lacking money, Seneca's philosophy consoles the frustrated, Montaigne offers consolation for imperfection, Schopenhauer consoles the broken hearted and, finally, Nietzsche's philosophy offers consolation in times of trouble. In some respects, de Botton's book resembles some aspects of Boethius' work and subjects itself to similar objections. Even though they are two different philosophers, they share the opinion that we must distance ourselves from worldly good so that we may not suffer their loss (for instance through a death sentence, as in the cases of Seneca and Socrates) too greatly and be devastated to the very depths of our soul. Such an approach to life need not be connected with self-imposed poverty and abstinence. But an individual should not entirely give in to the enjoyment of life or depend on the worldly possessions that the majority of people value. Similarly, Schopenhauer sees the essence of philosophical wisdom in our attempt to avoid pain rather than seeking pleasure. Montaigne and Nietzsche, in comparison, partly diverge from the notion that we should distance ourselves from the majority and their desired possessions. Nietzsche appreciates suffering and pain because coming to terms with them yields the noblest results in life. The reader wonders: what is consolation if the individual is unable to come to terms with his suffering productively? What if the individual is unwilling to give up worldly pleasures and possessions? Wherein, then, lies the consolation of philosophy? Montaigne leans more towards the enjoyment of life. He develops a relativising sceptical attitude towards the ruling ideals and opinions of his contemporaries by comparing different cultures and ways of life. De Botton's examples, such as the advantages and disadvantages of particular ovens, have little or nothing to do with today's philosophy. His book provides a critical view of everyday problems that can be solved or mitigated by the wisdom we attain in life. In part, De Botton's book sounds more like a self-help guide. It contains illustrations as well as narrative passages depicting the lives of individual philosophers and events in the author's or fictional characters' lives. The stories demonstrate how a particular philosophy offers consolation to the author and his contemporaries. Implicitly, he asks whether specific philosophical teachings are able to console a person who is in a situation that differs from that of the book's author or other philosophers. The advice given in the book is only partly the result of philosophical arguments. For the most part, the advice is based on the life experiences of the author and the philosophers mentioned. De Botton's writings contain no stringent philosophical argumentation, but a mixture of stories, philosophical teachings, the interpretation of images and recommendations. In short, what we are dealing with is not actually the consolation *of* philosophy, but the consolation provided by experience of life, reading experience and Alain de Botton's advice based on philosophical teachings.

Umberto Eco's newspaper article 'The Consolation of Philosophy' published in *Corriere della sera* in 1975 is another text by a contemporary writer. The article deals with the reform of philosophy lessons in higher education. Eco defends philosophy classes with a portrayal of the history of philosophy because in his opinion, all debates in philosophy relate to present-day problems. For this reason, it is not enough for students in the humanities to read crime novels as though they were Parmenides. Instead, Parmenides should be read as though he were a crime novel. Eco demonstrates what he means by using not the writings of the philosopher Parmenides, but those of his pupil Zeno. Zeno taught the immobility of being and claimed that motion cannot be proved. According to him, the flying arrow cannot move forward in the motionless space it takes up. Despite his teachings of motionlessness, Zeno accepted death in order to change the movement of history, the world of appearance. He led a conspiracy against the tyrant Nearchus, but was caught and tortured. Before his death he cunningly named all the tyrant's friends as his fellow conspirators so as to completely isolate him. According to Eco, Zeno demonstrates that language can create a *possible* world by this act. Such a world 'is', so much so that it can change aspects of the real world by making the tyrant believe his friends to be enemies, thereby isolating him. Moreover, with his superficially false claim Zeno actually strengthens a fact that is indeed true, namely that tyranny works with the help of suspicion and betrayal. Zeno's lie collides with the tyranny's hidden truth and destroys it. Eco sees Zeno's actions as an example that proves that the history of philosophy can be understood and taught as a chronicle of current events.

If we compare Eco's text with those of Boethius and de Botton, we notice that he, too, does not offer a series of philosophical arguments to come to a conclusion regarding the consolation of philosophy. Instead, he *tells* us about Zeno's life to illustrate the use and consolation of philosophy. Interestingly, some philosophical arguments and theorems are portrayed as potentially contradictory and absurd. Thus it is less philosophy as such that consoles the reader, but rather primarily a story about philosophy and philosophers.

To conclude the subject, we shall turn to a well-known text by Bertrand Russell that has no need of a narrative: 'The Value of Philosophy'. Philosophy's aim is enlightenment; the kind of enlightenment that takes place when someone critically examines the reasons for our convictions, opinions and prejudices. According to Russell, however, philosophy has not been very successful in its quest to find definitive answers to its questions. Nonetheless, this should not stop anyone from working on these questions to hold the world's speculative interest, which would otherwise most likely wither if we relied solely on indisputable knowledge. Philosophy's value particularly depends on the uncertainty it brings with it rather than a clearly defined standard of knowledge. Those who have never pondered a philosophical question live as if in a prison of common prejudices, opinions and convictions. Even if philosophy is unable to give definitive correct answers to posed questions, it opens up possibilities that broaden our view and free us from the tyranny of the familiar. The highest value of philosophy lies in the fact that it frees us from narrow-minded personal purposes when we open our eyes to greater things. The wider view of philosophical contemplation does not split the world in two – friends and enemies, good and evil etc. Rather, it impartially encompasses the whole. The other that lies beyond our will to assert ourselves comes into view and the contemplative mind opens up to the infinity of the world we observe. When we philosophise, we are turned into something greater by the greatness of the world. We become a citizen of the world and are no longer inhabitants of an enclosed town that is at war with the world. In another text, Russell claims that a philosophical investigation begins with something quite common and familiar and ends with something entirely incredible and outrageous.

To view matters from a greater distance that goes beyond the stubborn ordinary interests and opinions will console those who are burdened by everyday difficulties and worries. Nonetheless, philosophical questions that yield no answer may also lead to intense uncertainty, which may be worrying or even upsetting. In such a case, philosophy is the opposite of support and consolation for the soul. In my experience, the consolation of philosophy lies not in specific assumptions such as the soul's immortality or concepts of a successful life, but in a notional and linguistic aspect: complex argumentation and its precise and objective prose animate our intellect and offer consolation in and of itself because they demonstrate that our reasoning is sound and useful. Interestingly, such philosophical representation shares this type of consolation with the argumentation and prose of other disciplines such as history and literary theory. To sum up, we have discovered that philosophy can offer consolation, but it depends on the circumstances, content and forms of teaching and how every individual reader reacts to them. All in all, it is a rather weak kind of consolation that crime fiction may be able to top.

Furthermore, there are particular phenomena in reality that contradict our conceptual understanding, such as what we perceive in the context of injury and death. If the philosophical discourse passed down through the years attempts to grasp and reflect such a reality, this can only be possible by deflecting, according to Cavell. Therefore, philosophy appears to know of no other possibility to 'deal with' an injured body than as a fact. The result is a soul that cannot be 'saved' by philosophical arguments when it is exposed to this painful reality. In contrast, literature is capable of expressing such resistant reality and helps body and soul in distress to express themselves. According to Cora Diamond, philosophy can only accept a reality as resistant and traumatising as this without deflection by becoming literature. Her claim supports the idea that, as a rule, literature rather than philosophy offers greater consolation for the tormented soul.

b) *The consolation of crime fiction*

At the beginning of his book *Murder Must Advertise*, H. R. F. Keating asks, 'Is there anything, when life gets a little much, as comforting as a detective story?' The problem with providing a balanced view of the consolation of philosophy and crime fiction is that, apparently, there is no representative empirical data relating to this topic. Of course there will always be people who enjoy philosophy, but have no interest in crime fiction and vice versa. The question of consolation is easily answered in such isolated cases. In fact, we would need a *general or average empirical evaluation* of consolation to answer this question comparatively. Unfortunately, this cannot be offered in the scope of this book. It must suffice to establish the likelihood of consolation based on considerations on principle, observing the specific characteristics of both genres.

A crime story is, as the name indicates, a story. Therefore, it is no argumentative or defining text, but rather a narrative. What are the arguments for the consolation listeners and readers find in the telling of a story? And what arguments support the assumption that particularly a crime story, in all its variety, is suitable for offering consolation?

A famous crime writer whose name I have forgotten once said that what appeals to readers of crime stories is that at least one or two problems are solved in the story, while the reader's own serious problems in real life often remain unsolved. This is mostly true of the classic detective story, in which the murderer is caught and punished, innocent suspects are exonerated, rational explanations are found for mysterious incidents, and loose ends are tied up to reveal the central theme. The legal and moral order that was disturbed by the crime is re-established. The detective's observation skills and superior intellect used to solve the case suggest to the reader, who identifies with him, that he, too, is capable of managing his life with the same observation skills and a keen mind, no matter how difficult life may seem. Like the detective who is forced to react to criminal acts, the reader has a rather passive reacting role in the course of events which increases his or her identification with the protagonist, since both successfully engage their intellectual capacities. The detective uses them to solve the case while the reader requires them to follow the story's events, clues and explanations. Therefore, the detective story acts differently from the philosophical exploration that Russell represents. The story begins with something incredible and shocking, a mysterious murder or some other terrible crime, and it ends with the solving of the case, thus bringing the deed back to the familiar and ordinary. Since the reader shifts from unsettling uncertainty to comforting certainty, from suspense to solution, the detective story is more likely to offer emotional support in times of disquiet and sorrow than philosophy. Crime fiction does not view man as a reed that is easily snapped by the slightest breeze (Blaise Pascal). It proves in a number of stories that man is a 'tough bitch' and cannot be broken that easily. Even if the story ends in a catastrophe, the victim is found dead, the murderer escapes, and the detective fails, there is always one comforting maxim: it is better to have a terrible ending than to have terror with no end.

Not all, but at least some problems are also solved in crime fiction genres such as the spy or psycho-thriller, which make the same promise for the reader. Like the detective story, they display the same arrangement of suspense that is geared towards surprising the reader with plot twists again and again, so that he is kept wondering how the story will go on. Someone following a crime story develops assumptions and understands the succession of events as a significant whole in time. The events are not random unconnected incidents; they are part of an arranged order that satisfies the reader's longing for orientation and repetition of the course of events in memory. Beginning, ending and transitions in a process can be experienced. The events, random as they may appear, attain meaning in the story. They show the reader how people are able or unable to react to unexpected events. The hero's successful search develops and frees him because to escape the 'labyrinth' of crime means to emerge changed into another. The reader identifies with the hero's transformation.

The suspense of the crime story distracts the reader from his own worries and complaints even if the story presents the protagonist's daily life realistically and refuses to romanticise it. However, to distract the reader does not equal deceiving him. It is possible for a reader to get so engrossed in the fictional world that the way he perceives his own environment suffers. This, however, is an exception, since most readers of crime fiction are able to cope with life. The realistic representation is supported by a ground rule for the narration of crime stories which differentiates it from some other genres. I am not referring to the fair play rule between writer and reader in the classic whodunit, according to which the reader must be able to follow and logically process the clues and events in the story in the same way the detective does without being deceived by the author's tricks and concealment. No, there is a far more essential rule: everything that happens, as extraordinary and unlikely as it may be, must conform to the laws of nature and be explained rationally with the help of scientific findings and, if possible, the conclusions of social studies. There is something immensely comforting in the knowledge that everything happens for logical reasons and there is nothing supernatural or spooky about it, despite the terror a serial killer spreads. Anything that can be represented rationally can also be explained rationally and is therefore controllable. This is the unspoken fundamental promise of every crime story. In this respect, the crime story stands in the tradition of the Enlightenment. All knots, even the Gordian knot, can be undone because we tie it ourselves, says Bernhard Schlink. This is especially the case when a crime writer's knot is tied in such a way that it can be undone in the end. The pleasure of reading crime fiction stems from two impulses that, according to John Rawls, do not accept compromise: the search for truth and the longing for justice. Both are powered by the voice of the intellect, as Freud called it, which may be soft but does not rest until it has been heard. The fiction of a crime story has real effects by teaching us to see our world and our actions from a new point of view presented through literary means. As a result, fiction changes the way we act in our new, changed world.

The most important consolation crime fiction offers, however, is caused by mechanisms that are primarily unconscious. Reading crime stories about horrific deeds, culprits and innocents is meant to free the reader of any feelings of guilt. Most people feel guilt, some for good reason, others for no apparent cause, unconsciously or consciously. These feelings can develop in the world of business, where large profits are made more often than not from unfair dealings. Someone who purchases a particularly low-priced product often feels guilty, because they know the people involved in its production and sale only earn low wages. A person who eats meat and fish is guilty of the suffering animals endure. Someone who flies to a holiday destination is guilty of contributing to climate change. There are many more examples like these which are not criminal, but can still cause suppressed feelings of guilt. They develop as early as childhood, when we experience that desire is fundamentally amoral. It does not matter if we give in to a desire that violates our laws or morals and thus become guilty. Only the desire that accepts no limits, and which everyone has, is 'sinful' and causes feelings of guilt. Of course, there are also people who burden themselves with real guilt by their criminal deeds. In an interview, the German crime writer Ingrid Noll rightly said that the appeal or the construction of most crime stories stems from the fact that we all have skeletons in our closet. Nobody is entirely innocent. It means also that anyone is a potential culprit, be it the protagonist in a crime story or the reader in real life. When asked what skeletons were in her own closet, she said, 'I'll be damned if I tell you.'

How come crime stories tend to free us of feelings of guilt, at least temporarily, as W. H. Auden claims, instead of reinforcing them? On the surface, the plot is an important factor. A person who first appears to be innocent is revealed to be the guilty murderer, while someone we first suspected is in fact proved innocent. If the reader – who tends not to be a killer – identifies with the innocent suspect instead of the murderer, he will feel validated in his innocence once the true murderer is revealed and the suspects are exonerated. It does not matter whether these suspects were dishonest in their actions or statements, which might have made them look guilty in the first place, since they did not commit that particular crime, just as a person going on holiday may well be guilty of destroying our climate, but has not committed a murder. Compared to murder, his guilt is merely a drop in the ocean, even if his actions contribute to a worsening or even the destruction of many people's living conditions. The charged murderer, however, is used as a scapegoat onto whom everyone's guilt is placed so that they can be free of it.

Underneath the surface, removing these feelings of guilt is far more complicated. First, let us look at the role of narration in the life of the individual. From an early age onwards, we are accustomed to and requested to talk about our lives and what we experience. Parents want to know what happened in kindergarten and at school; friends want to know what our holiday was like etc. From the start, we as individuals are subjected to the social fear of losing other people's love and respect, so narratives about ourselves, our actions, intentions and thoughts are indeed used to justify ourselves. The justifying character of our narratives may not always be particularly obvious, though. By telling others about ourselves we show them who we are. It is more obvious to others than it is to ourselves. According to Adriana Cavarero, the narrative of our own lives is part of the development of the self in the social exchange with others. Narration is also useful for an individual to explain his actions – especially any erratic behaviour – and explain believably his intention to better himself. Therefore, narration is often related to guilt and feelings of guilt, from which the narrator expects to free himself.

So, how does this relate to someone who is not telling a story about himself, but who is reading or listening to a crime story? Someone else, the crime story's narrator, speaks about the (fictional) life of individual protagonists. In the background there is an observing entity that demands justification, such as federal law that comes down on crime, a local community whose trust has been shattered by murder or another similar entity. This would explain why, according to Rex Stout, everyone likes crime stories apart from anarchists. Radical anarchists assume that everyone is guilty, but they reject the government or other authorities which require them to justify themselves. The classic crime story, as the term whodunit indicates, is a narrative about *who* someone is, whether someone is the sought-after murderer or an accessory, witness, avenger, or victim of a crime. The point is to not be fooled by 'what someone is', i.e. their social status as doctor, teacher, minister, midwife, taxi driver etc. Who someone really is and what he did or will do and for what reasons is meant to be shown in a manner similar to how we narrate aspects of our lives. By narrating a story about the guilt of a person before the imagined authority that demands justification, the reader himself is not required to provide a narrative that illuminates his own guilt and justifies his actions. The crime story's narrator does so on the reader's behalf in a somewhat magical ritual that is meant to unburden him. In a way, this ritual resembles a voodoo ritual in which a doll is pierced by pins, thereby freeing a person from the burden of killing someone himself.

If the comparison seems nonsensical and far-fetched, we should be aware of the quasi-magical daily rituals that are scientifically analysed under the term 'interpassivity' (Robert Pfaller). Here are some examples: A lecturer wants to fully prepare himself for his seminar and copies a large number of texts in the library for this purpose. From the beginning, it is clear that he will never have the time to even read most of the material. His potential feelings of guilt for not being properly prepared, however, are appeased by the fact that he has copied all important texts so that the copier has, in a way, read all the texts on his behalf. A media expert wants to know about the content of all important TV shows. For this reason, he records several hours of TV shows every day. He will never have the chance to watch even the majority of shows, but he consoles himself with the fact that he has everything on tape and that the video recorder has seen all shows in his stead. And now, as a final example, a man loves watching sitcoms on television. As we know, they are constructed in such a way that an imaginary audience laughs after every gag as if it were a live performance, similar to the staging of a play. The supposed audience's laughter saves the viewer's laughter and he is not required to understand every gag precisely. The virtual audience is enjoying itself and laughs on his behalf. The thing about such magical everyday rituals is that the person in question would never believe that the copier has read all the texts, the video recorder has seen all the shows or that a real audience laughed at the gags. The illusion of vicarious relief exists even though the person in question knows better. This means that not only the reader's actions, but also the illusion itself is delegated. Others are under the illusion. Yet, the magical everyday ritual brings an important additional effect to the fore, namely the impish pleasure in having (partly) divested ourselves of the demands of reading, seeing and laughing, despite having successfully foregone the daily grind. Above all, we have eluded the illusion underlying it.

However, unburdening oneself of feelings of guilt and other hardships is never complete and final. Even the pleasure we take in the knowledge that we have tricked the demands of our everyday lives is temporary. For this reason, it is necessary to watch sitcoms or read crime stories again and again. Consolation must be renewed after a certain period. Even though the consolation of crime fiction is usually stronger than the consolation of philosophy for reasons mentioned earlier, this does not mean that it is the strongest consolation we can find in life. When we have everyday worries, a helpful chat amongst friends can console us much more effectively than crime fiction and philosophy put together. Moreover, a chat amongst friends about crime fiction *and* philosophy must surely be one of the most wonderful experiences life can offer us. My hope is that this book will encourage you to try it yourself.

References and Further reading:

Crime fiction and literature about crime fiction
Alewyn, Richard: 'Anatomie des Detektivromans', in: Jochen Vogt (ed.): *Der Kriminalroman II: Zur Theorie und Geschichte einer Gattung*, Munich 1971, 372–404
Auden, Wystan Hugh: 'The Guilty Vicarage: Notes on the Detective Story, by an Addict', in: Auden: *The Dyer's Hand and Other Essays*, London 1962, 146–158
Eco, Umberto: *Postscript to 'The Name of the Rose'*, New York 1984
Keating, H. R. F.: *Murder Must Appetize*, New York/London 1981
Marsch, Edgar: *Die Kriminalerzählung: Theorie – Geschichte – Analyse*, 2nd edition. Munich 1983
Nusser, Peter: *Der Kriminalroman*, 4th edition. Stuttgart/Weimar 2009
Schlink, Bernhard: *Die gordische Schleife*, Zurich 1988
Todorov, Tzvetan: *Einführung in die fantastische Literatur*, Munich 1972
Waldmann, Günter: 'Kriminalroman – Antikriminalroman', in: Jochen Vogt (ed.): *Der Kriminalroman I: Zur Theorie und Geschichte einer Gattung*, Munich 1971, 206–227

Philosophical and psychoanalytical literature as well as literary theory
Baltes, Matthias: 'Boethius Staatsmann und Philosoph', in: Michael Erler/Andreas Graeser (eds.): *Philosophen des Altertums. Vom Hellenismus bis zur Spätantike*, Darmstadt 2000, 208–224
Boethius: *Trost der Philosophie*, Stuttgart 1971 (English edition: *The Consolation of Philosophy*, Oxford/New York 2001)
Cavarero, Adriana: *Relating Narratives: Storytelling and Selfhood*, London/New York 2000
De Botton, Alain: *The Consolations of Philosophy*, London 2000

Diamond, Cora: 'The Difficulty of Reality and the Difficulty of Philosophy', in: Alice Crary/Sanford Shieh (eds.): *Reading Cavell*, London/New York 2006, 98–118

Eco, Umberto: 'Vom Trost der Philosophie', in: Eco: *Im Labyrinth der Vernunft. Texte über Kunst und Zeichen*, 3rd edition. Leipzig 1995, 371–375

Freud, Sigmund: 'Jenseits des Lustprinzips', in: Freud: *Gesammelte Werke XIII*, Frankfurt am Main 1960, 1–69 (English edition: Beyond the Pleasure Principle, http://www.bartleby.com/276/)

Freud, Sigmund: 'Die Zukunft einer Illusion', in: Freud: *Massenpsychologie und Ich-Analyse. Die Zukunft einer Illusion*, Frankfurt am Main 1984, 83–135

Graeser, Andreas: *Interpretationen Hauptwerke der Philosophie Antike*, Stuttgart 2004

Hampe, Michael: *Die Macht des Zufalls. Vom Umgang mit dem Risiko*, Berlin 2006

Jollien, Alexandre: *Liebe Philosophie, kannst Du mir helfen ? Briefe an Boethius, Schopenhauer und den Tod*, Munich 2009

Klingner, Friedrich: *Einführung*, in: *Boethius: Trost der Philosophie*, Stuttgart 1971, 5–39

Lyotard, Jean-François: *Das postmoderne Wissen: Ein Bericht*, Graz/Vienna 1986 (English edition: *The Postmodern Condition: A Report On Knowledge*, Manchester 1984)

Mattern, Jens: *Paul Ricœur zur Einführung*, Hamburg 1996

Pascal, Blaise: *Gedanken. Eine Auswahl*, Stuttgart 1987 (English title: *Pensées*)

Pfaller, Robert: *Die Illusionen der anderen. Über das Lustprinzip in der Kultur*, Frankfurt am Main 2002

Raatzsch, Richard: *Philosophiephilosophie*, Stuttgart 2000

Rawls, John: *A Theory of Justice*, Cambridge MA 1971

Ricœur, Paul: 'Narrative Funktion und menschliche Zeiterfahrung', in: Volker Bohn (ed.): *Romantik. Literatur und Philosophie*, Frankfurt am Main 1987, 45–79

Rorty, Richard: *Philosophy as Cultural Politics. Philosophical Papers, Vol. 4*, Cambridge 2007

Russell, Bertrand: *The Problems of Philosophy*, London 1912

Spade, Paul Vincent: 'Die mittelalterliche Philosophie', in: Anthony Kenny (ed.): *Illustrierte Geschichte der westlichen Philosophie*, Frankfurt/Main;

New York 1995, 69–120 (original title: *The Oxford Illustrated History of Western Philosophy*, Oxford 1994)

Trabant, Jürgen: 'coltura – mondo civile – scienza nuova. Oder: Was für eine Kultur-Wissenschaft ist Vicos Neue Wissenschaft?', in: *Zeitschrift für Kulturphilosophie* 2010/2, 179–193

Žižek, Slavoj: *Liebe Dein Symptom wie Dich selbst! Jacques Lacans Psychoanalyse und die Medien*, Berlin 1991

Žižek, Slavoj: *Looking Awry: An Introduction to Jacques Lacan through Popular Culture*, Cambridge (Mass.)/London 1991

Index

191